Two Worlds Are Ours

An Introduction to Christian Mysticism

John Macquarrie

*Two worlds are ours; 'tis only sin
Forbids us to descry
The mystic heaven and earth within,
Plain as the sea and sky.*

John Keble

Fortress Press
Minneapolis

TWO WORLDS ARE OURS
An Introduction to Christian Mysticism

First Fortress Press edition 2005

Cover image: Sunset Long Lake MN © Christopher C. Faust. Used by permission.

ISBN 0-8006-3710-0

The paper used in this publication meets the minimum require-ments of American National Standard for Information Sciences — Permanence of Paper for Printed Library Materials, ANSI Z329.48-1984.

Manufactured in the U.S.A.

09   08   07   06   05   1   2   3   4   5   6   7   8   9   10

Contents

Preface   vii

1 What is Mysticism?   1

2 Biblical Roots of Christian Mysticism:
   Old Testament, Moses   35

3 Biblical Roots of Christian Mysticism:
   New Testament, Paul   48

4 Greek Input, Platonism: Clement of Alexandria,
   Origen   62

5 Greek Input, Neo-Platonism: Gregory of Nyssa,
   Augustine of Hippo, Dionysius the Areopagite   75

6 The Dark Ages: Maximus Confessor,
   John of Damascus, John Scotus Eriugena   97

7 The Early Middle Ages: Symeon the
   New Theologian, Bernard of Clairvaux,
   Richard of St Victor   113

8 The High Middle Ages: Bonaventure,
   Meister Eckhart   128

9 Women Mystics: Julian of Norwich,
   Catherine of Siena, Catherine of Genoa   144

Contents

10 Some Spanish Mystics: Ignatius Loyola,
    Teresa of Avila, John of the Cross   162

11 Post-Reformation Mystics: Jakob Böhme,
    Blaise Pascal, George Fox, William Law   178

12 Eighteenth Century: Jonathan Edwards,
    John Woolman   199

13 Nineteenth Century: John Keble,
    Søren Kierkegaard, Charles de Foucauld   215

14 Twentieth Cenbury: Henri Bergson, Rudolf Otto,
    Pierre Teilhard de Chardin, Jacques Maritain,
    Thomas Merton   234

15 Concluding Remarks   261

    Notes   267

    Index   283

Preface

For the past year or thereabouts I have been in very good company, reading and pondering the writings of Christian mystics, men and women who have made closeness to God and faithfulness to him the chief goal in their lives. They took their Christian faith much more seriously than most of us do, and I found that sharing their experiences did me a lot of good, both in challenging my complacency and in giving me a deeper appreciation for what Christianity should mean to us. So I want to share it with as many people as possible, and that is why I have written this book.

I do not claim to be a mystic, and I have not hesitated to criticize some of their ideas. But on the whole they have brought great benefit to the Church and I think they can still do so. Here then is an introduction, from biblical times down to the present, expounding their teachings mainly in their own words.

I express thanks to various people who have helped me, chiefly by lending me or obtaining for me material which was difficult to come by: Dr John Morgan, President of the Graduate Theological Foundation, for the *Journal* of John Woolman; the librarians of Pusey House for access to the Tracts of John Keble and the writings of Charles de Foucauld; to the Librarian of the Theology Faculty Library of Oxford University for putting me on the track of writings of George Fox; and the Librarian of All Saints Convent, Oxford, for material relating to Thomas Merton. I have again been greatly helped by my wife Jenny in preparing the material for the publishers. I am also indebted to the many authors and publishers who have published, translated or interpreted the writings of the mystics discussed in the following pages.

John Macquarrie
Oxford, January 2004

1

What is Mysticism?

Mysticism – the very word invites our attention. The human being seems to be curious by nature, and finding that there are many mysteries in the world, has an inward drive to set about unravelling them, or throwing light on them, whatever metaphor we may choose to use. So perhaps we have to begin by asking, 'What is mystery?', for that would seem to be an idea already assumed when we talk about mysticism. According to *Webster's Third New International Dictionary*, 'mystery', in the most general sense, refers to 'something that has not been or cannot be explained, that is unknown to all or concealed from some and therefore exciting curiosity or wonder, or that is incomprehensible or uncomprehended'. In this broad sense, there are mysteries in the phenomena of nature, and the scientists wrestle with them and often do find explanations that take us at least some distance in understanding these phenomena. There are many other mysteries, whether or not they deserve the name. One of the most popular branches of modern literature is devoted to the fictitious detectives who solve the mysteries of crime and bring the criminals to justice. But before *Webster's Dictionary* mentions the broad general scope of 'mystery', it has located the word in the discourse where it originated, namely, religion. The dictionary has already defined 'mystery' in a narrower, more technical sense, as 'a religious truth revealed by God that man cannot know by reason alone and that once it has been revealed cannot be completely understood'.

The suggestion in this definition, especially in the last four words, 'cannot be completely understood', seems to be that a mystery has a depth of meaning which we can never fully exhaust. A mystery is certainly not completely unintelligible, otherwise we could say nothing about it. But whatever we say, there is always more to be said and more that remains unsaid. Gabriel Marcel familiarized us with the distinction between problems and mysteries. Problems, he held, are limited, can be considered objectively, and can in many cases be solved by a demonstrable explanation. Mysteries, in Marcel's language, cannot be encountered as objective entities. Any understanding of them is possible only to the extent that we are ourselves involved in these mysteries. Examples are freedom, evil, love, selfhood and (in Marcel's thought, the basic mystery) being, which many theologians have equated (or nearly equated) with God.[1] Mysteries cannot be investigated by the methods that are appropriate in the natural sciences. Rather, they call for deep meditation or contemplation on some of our human experiences. Such contemplation is what we find among the mystics, but whether it can lead to knowledge, which, though different from the knowledge gained through the sciences, can nevertheless also be reckoned as knowledge, is one of the major problems with which one is confronted in any study of mysticism, and we shall be returning to it.

Meanwhile, the relation between mystery and problem may be explored a little further. Perhaps Marcel went too far in his distinction between mysteries and problems. I am inclined to believe that the distinction between mysteries and problems cannot always be maintained. I have said that what distinguishes a mystery is its unfathomable depth, the point that any alleged explanation falls short of completeness and leaves more to be said (or left unsaid). By a process of reductionism, a scientist limits the problems, and reaches explanations which solve them. But it is usually the case that every explanation brings with it new problems, so here too more has to be said, and further explorations carried out. This is especially the case when the scientist treats of such truly enigmatic concepts as space, time, matter, energy, evolution and many others. Inevitably, a point is reached at which thought has to become more speculative and where science merges into metaphysics. These ultimate problems, which do not appear to admit of any final solution, cannot be ignored, for the concepts implied in them are already assumed in some form in the limited problems which have already been carefully isolated in the reductionist attempt to assure that they will be manageable. Problems cannot be finally isolated from their contexts, and there is something to be said for the (impossible) allegedly Hegelian claim that one cannot understand anything short of understanding everything.

Another point worth noting is that science is a human activity and that human beings are inevitably involved in the pursuit of science. In its application as technology, it has become probably the major factor in shaping human life. It can hardly claim to be a purely objective study, concerned only with what is 'out there'. Science and its application is giving human life its form, often for good, but sometimes for ill. Surely this means that, as an important human activity, science must be concerned not only with logic but with ethics as well. And ethics – the meaning of good and evil, the choice of goals for human development in both its individual and its social aspects – cannot escape from mystery in the sense we have been considering.

We did note that in a narrower sense of the term, the word 'mystery' has religious connotations. In particular, the term 'mysteries' was used to designate certain cults which flourished in ancient Greece and in other parts of the classical world, alongside the official religions. These cults were supposed to bring light to their devotees about some of the mysteries of human life and death, and in their secret rituals would re-enact the story of some mythical or legendary figure; for instance, the story of a dying and rising hero. At the beginning of the twentieth century, some scholars believed that the model of the mystery religions had been a main influence in the rise of Christianity, or even believed that Christianity itself could be numbered among the mystery religions.

But the attempts to associate Christianity with the ancient mystery cults have almost completely fallen out of favour. In the words of Walter Burkert, perhaps the greatest living authority on Greek religion, 'Mysteries were too fragile to serve as religions on their own ... Ancient mystery-cults did not form communities, in the sense of Judaism and Christianity. Even Reizenstein had to acknowledge that the concept of church (*ecclesia*) has no equivalent in pagan religion.'[2]

However, even if the influence of the ancient mysteries on Christianity was not great, the Greek word *mysterion* passed into the Christian vocabulary, and came to be applied to the Christian sacraments, in which the acts performed and the words used have to be understood in a deeper sense than appears on the surface. These sacraments have therefore the same structure as mystery, and since the sacraments have a central place in catholic Christianity, this suggests that mysticism, if indeed it does lead to some understanding of the mysteries of God and human existence, has, in spite of its own distinctive features, a continuity with all religious experience, and that conversely what we may call 'ordinary' religious experience has a mystical element which, in some cases, develops into a full-blown mysticism.

I have mentioned the attractiveness of mysticism for human beings who have a natural curiosity that impels them to probe the unknown. But not everyone would agree. In 1917 the philosopher Bertrand Russell published a collection of essays entitled *Mysticism and Logic* in which he expounded a frankly materialistic and atheistic view of the world. He asked whether there are two ways of knowing the world or knowing about the world – the scientific way and the mystical way. He claims that there is only one – the scientific way, which bases itself on logically constructed inquiry, while mysticism, according to Russell, is no more than an emotional attitude, with no cognitive significance. 'Insight,' he declares, 'untested and unsupported, is an insufficient guarantee of truth.'[3] I think I would agree that an untested and unsupported opinion based on emotion is not a guarantee of truth, but I do not think that the description fits mysticism, as we shall see. Just one minor point for the moment: the cognitive claims of mysticism are in fact claims that have been tested and supported by a very large number of people, so while, as I have already said, mystical knowledge is not objective by scientific norms, it is at least intersubjective and not just the opinion of a few individuals. It is of some significance also that mysticism is not confined to the Christian or any other single religious tradition, but is found to some extent in all the religions, both Eastern and Western.

Russell rather grudgingly acknowledged that mysticism (he used the term in a fairly loose sense) does have some merits in the area of human behaviour, but I think that he could make even a minor concession only by implicitly admitting that mysticism is more than emotion. Russell himself, to do him justice, had strong moral convictions, and even went to prison for his defence of pacifism and his objections to atomic warfare. Surely something intellectual, something cognitive, call it 'insight' or 'judgement' or 'discernment' or what you will, was at work here, though doubtless with emotional accompaniments. However, I firmly believe with Russell that religious belief needs whatever rational support it can get, and cannot rest on even a wide swath of unsupported assertion. But the question can be left for the moment.

So I have frankly to say that I approach mysticism with a somewhat divided mind. I have acknowledged already that I am attracted to mysticism, but I am not myself a mystic. As an undergraduate, I read and was much impressed by one of the many books of the Japanese writer, Daisetz Suzuki, who did much to popularize a version of Buddhist mysticism in the English-speaking countries. I was able to go along with him until I came to a place where he challenged his readers to lay aside logic and to throw themselves into the mystical frame of mind. I found myself like a would-be swimmer who stands on the bank but is too timid to take the plunge into the deep water. That has remained my attitude, as will become apparent in the rest of this book. But the attraction is still strong, and with it my respect for the mystics and their form of religion.

But, you may say, can anyone study mysticism or venture to write about it if he or she has not taken the plunge and known at first hand what it means to be immersed in the mystical experience? A former Princeton Professor of Philosophy, W. T. Stace, wrote an excellent study entitled *Mysticism and Philosophy,* and near the beginning of the book he cites a story which he attributes to the prophet Muhammad. He claimed that Muhammad compared a scholar who writes about mysticism though not himself a mystic to a donkey carrying a load of books. We do not suppose for a moment that the donkey has any understanding of the matters treated in the books, and it is being suggested that the non-mystic's relation to the writings of the mystics is no different from that of the donkey's to the books.[4] Perhaps there is some point in the story. But Stace himself did not let it deter him from writing his book. I should think myself that if one is interested in and sympathetic to the mystics, then one may be able to advance some way into their understanding of things, as Stace himself and William James and many other writers have done, and as I intend to do.

Now it is time for us to consider more carefully just what the distinguishing characteristics of mysticism are. There are many forms of mysticism, and it occurs in the context of many religions. Even if we confine ourselves to Christian mysticism, we meet with quite a wide spread of varieties. I am going to mention ten characteristics which keep occurring among the mystics, though I freely admit that one might choose a larger or smaller number.

Directness

The mystic claims to have a direct relation to God. In much religious experience, there is some mediation between God and the human worshipper. In Christianity the Bible provides such mediation, and the average Christian would probably say he or she knows God through the Bible. The Christian would also say that on an even more fundamental level, Jesus of Nazareth is the mediator between divine and human. In most of the great world religions, there is some personal mediator who has taught about God and has provided the basis on which the religion has been developed. The founders of these religions – Buddha, Confucius, Moses, Muhammad and others – have provided bases on which the several religions have built up their beliefs and worship and behaviour.

It would seem therefore that these personal 'mediators'[5] must themselves have had some direct experience of Deity, and have then passed it on to others. Some of them, at least, did claim to have had 'revelations', visionary or locutionary experiences in which they were in direct relationship to God. In the Hebrew and Christian traditions, there is some ambiguity in the idea of a direct vision or other direct experience of God. One view seems to have been that no human being could see God without being destroyed by the sight. So when Moses asks of God, 'Show me your glory, I pray', he gets the answer, 'You cannot see my face; for no one shall see me and live' (Ex. 33.18 and 20). But that was not taken to mean that God is invisible, for although Moses may not see God's face, he is permitted to see his back (Ex. 18.23). But in another passage, Moses and Aaron, accompanied by the elders of Israel, did see God: 'and God did not lay his hand on the chief men of the people of Israel; also they beheld God, and they ate and drank' (Ex. 24.9–11). Another example is connected with the encounter which Jacob had with a supernatural being (an angel or even God?) at the ford of Jabbok. They wrestle with one another, and after the struggle the disabled Jacob, now renamed Israel, says, 'I have seen God face to face, and yet my life is preserved' (Gen. 32.30). Isaiah too 'saw the Lord' in his celebrated vision in the temple (Isa. 6.1). Perhaps more common than visions were locutions, in which prophets might receive their call, or teachings to pass to the people as the word of God. Here again there was some direct experience of God on the part of the prophet, who in his turn mediated the word to the people. A well-known example of a locution was the experience of Samuel in the shrine at Shiloh when he heard God calling him by name. Whatever the initial experience may have been, a continuing relationship followed, with Samuel directly in touch with the Lord and then mediating the message to the people of Israel: 'And all Israel from Dan to Beer-sheba knew that Samuel was a trustworthy prophet of the LORD. The LORD continued to appear at Shiloh, for the LORD revealed himself to Samuel at Shiloh by the word of the LORD. And the word of Samuel came to all Israel' (1 Sam. 3.20–4.1).

In the New Testament, especially in John's Gospel, Jesus

Christ is closer to God the Father than was any Hebrew seer or any angel, a closeness that was developed and given definite form with the rise of incarnational and trinitarian doctrines. Consider the Johannine verses: 'No one has ever seen God. It is God the only Son, who is close to the Father's heart, who has made him known' (John 1.18). Thus, although Jesus Christ is the mediator between divine and human, as the second person of the Trinity he is himself a divine person, so in a sense a relation to God through Jesus could be regarded as a direct or mystical relation. So the argument that there can be no such thing as Christian mysticism because the Christian relationship is mediated through Christ, cannot stand. Christian mysticism is normally a Christ-mysticism, though some Christian mystics, such as Meister Eckart, may have sought a direct relation to God that bypasses the persons of the Trinity. This is a point to be examined later, in a discussion of the mysticism of Paul (see below, p. 50).

Cognition

The mystical experience has a cognitive aspect and brings an understanding. In saying this, I am going against Bertrand Russell's view that mysticism is purely a matter of the emotions. But many philosophers would go against Russell in this question. William James, for instance, writes of the 'noetic' character of mysticism, and the word 'noetic', from the Greek *noesis*, meaning intellectual 'comprehension' or even simple 'perception', makes a cognitive claim. He writes:

> Although so similar to states of feeling, mystical states seem to those who experience them to be also states of knowledge. They are states of insight into depths of truth unplumbed by the discursive intellect. They are illumina-

tions, revelations, full of significance and importance, all inarticulate though they remain; and as a rule they carry with them a curious sense of authority for aftertime.[6]

I would add that emotions or feelings ordinarily and apart from mystical experiences carry with them something like perception or direct awareness. Fear, for example, implies awareness of a threatening environment. To give another example, anxiety or *angst*, as analyzed by Kierkegaard[7] and others, is a feeling which forcefully makes us aware of human finitude. The mystic's claim to understanding can be neither dismissed nor accepted on the basis of mere assertion. But it can be defended by argument.

I would also point out that there are different kinds of knowledge. When I talk of knowing a person, that knowledge is different from knowledge of a fact. Some languages, though not English, use different verbs to distinguish these two kinds of knowing; but they both qualify as knowledge. Clearly, the mystic's claim to have knowledge of God is closer to knowing a person than to knowing a fact. Yet the two kinds of knowledge are not entirely separable. To know a person is also to know something about that person; for instance, that he or she really exists. And the distinction does not only apply where one of the instances is a person. What does it mean, for example, to have knowledge of a country? It might be factual knowledge – area, population, industries, expectation of life and so on – or it might be the kind of knowledge that could be gained only by walking its hills and forests, chatting to the people, even just breathing its air. The mystic's knowledge of God is not of the kind that can be tabulated in reference books or recorded by scientific investigation, but of the kind that is gained through the experience of living, and I think this is borne out by the constant use by the mystics themselves of words denoting intellectual operations such as discernment, judgement, evaluation. Also, most mystics stress the interrelatedness of knowledge of God and self-knowledge, to such an extent that sometimes it is hard to say where the knowledge of the one leaves off and the other begins. Even someone who wished to deny any knowledge of God to the mystic could hardly deny that mystical insight does yield self-knowledge.

Ecstasy or Rapture

This is a third characteristic of the mystic experience, though it should not be exaggerated, and the wisest mystics are eager to play down the importance of ecstasy and other paranormal experiences. Mystical experience, however, is not something that remains at a constant level. It has its 'highs' and also its 'lows'. As the word 'ecstasy' implies, at such a moment the mystic seems to be taken out of himself or herself, as if the soul were lifted out of the body, if one may use such a way of speaking. These are moments of joy and of a sense of union with God or with all reality, though paradoxically there may also be intense pain. These times of ecstasy seem to be of fairly short duration, though as the senses are apparently sometimes suspended in ecstasy, one cannot rely on the mystic's estimate of the length of time for which the experience lasted. We hear them mentioning 'half an hour' or even 'a whole day', but perhaps we can say only that these intense moments are of relatively short duration. The lows, on the other hand, are characterized by what the mystic calls 'dryness', times when the soul is imprisoned in bodily existence and the drabness of everyday life.

I have mentioned that some of the great mystics tend to play down the moments of rapture, and they do so partly for ethical reasons. There must be a temptation to aim at achieving the joy of ecstasy, thereby perverting mysticism from a high spirituality into a form of pleasure-seeking. Some critics of mysticism do in fact level the accusation that it diverts the religious believer from the moral obligations of faith and from the demands of service to the neighbour, to a selfish enjoyment of union with God. I do not think that the best mystics succumb to this temptation, but they are well aware of it as a danger which remains a threat even to those who have advanced far along the mystic way.

This is the point at which we may glance at the relation of mysticism to the taking of certain drugs. Mysticism might appeal to some persons not as a way to God or to spiritual growth, but rather as a way of escape from the harsh realities of life into new and exhilarating areas of consciousness. In Mexico, for instance, there has for long been an association between some forms of religion and the taking of the drug psilocin derived from a mushroom and inducing an expanded consciousness. On a more sophisticated level the relations between drugs and mysticism were explored by the writer Aldous Huxley. Perhaps the serious problem of drug addiction in the Western world today is in part due to the quest for a surrogate for religious experience. Eric Blakeborough, who devoted many years to combating the evils of drug addiction in the London area, saw the turning to drugs as related to the decline of religious faith, and sadly noted that 'hippies try to gatecrash heaven with a quick fix of drugs'.[8] Eighty years earlier, William James was already aware of the problem and expressed himself with admirable human sympathy for those who turn to alcohol and drugs as an escape:

The sway of alcohol over mankind is unquestionably due to its powers to stimulate the mystical faculties of human nature, usually crushed to earth by the cold facts and dry criticisms of the sober hour. Drunkenness brings its votary from the chill periphery of things to the radiant core. It makes him for the moment one with truth. To the poor and the unlettered it stands in place of symphony concerts and of literature.[9]

Alcohol and other ecstasy-producing drugs bring in the end depression and misery, and it is interesting to note that several of the mystics claim that the genuineness of an ecstatic experience becomes clear only in its consequences.

Near the beginning of this section on ecstasy, I mentioned 'other paranormal phenomena' and I had in mind principally visions and locutions. The best mystics do not encourage the desire for such experiences involving the senses. They place a higher value on what they sometimes call 'intellectual visions', apparently purely spiritual and imageless revelations (some of these will be mentioned in due course). As far as locutions are concerned, I think they could be explained in a number of ways on different occasions. Sometimes, perhaps, a clap of thunder as at Paul's conversion, might be interpreted as a word from God, sometimes an actual human voice using words which happen coincidentally (or providentially) to respond to someone's spiritual questioning as at Augustine's conversion experience, is so interpreted; or perhaps it is simply that a powerful moral or spiritual constraint, first felt inwardly without any clear expression in words, becomes in the course of reflection clothed in an explicit discourse, a possible example being the exchange between God and Moses at the burning bush. But here we seem to reach the limits of useful speculation.[10]

Apophaticism or Negative Theology

The mystics themselves have recognized the limits of language and the difficulties of trying to communicate their experiences to persons who have not fully shared them. Not only mystics, but theologians and other students of religion recognize that if God is infinite, he is far beyond the reach of our thinking and language. Paul Tillich, for example, thought that we can literally say about God only that he is Being itself, and anything beyond that is, in his terminology, 'symbolic'.[11] But although Tillich gave a fresh impetus to God-talk, he was simply repeating ideas that go back to early patristic times. Thus Clement of Alexandria held that 'God is above both space and time and name and conception', but that by a process of abstraction 'we may reach somehow to the conception of the Almighty, knowing not what he is but what he is not'.[12] Dionysius the (so-called) Areopagite went much further along the road which Tillich was to follow, and developed the idea not only of an apophatic or negative theology which denies the literal application of such concepts as even love and goodness to God, but reinstates these concepts within a cataphatic theology, in which they would be understood in a symbolic or analogical sense.

It must be confessed that it is very frustrating for the ordinary non-mystical person to read in the writings of some mystic that he or she has had, in a time of ecstasy, a vision of God in which the whole mystery of the Trinity had become clear, and then to be told in the next sentence that he or she had forgotten or could no longer describe the content of that vision as soon as the moment of ecstasy had passed. No one is likely to deny that the infinite God must, to a great extent, be ineffable. Yet it is a fact, at the same time, that we cannot help talking about God, and even the mystics have much to say about him. Perhaps their favourite symbol for God is light. 'God is light and in him there is no darkness at all' (1 John 1.5). There was light at the creation, light at the bush where Moses received his revelation, light at the birth of Christ, light at the conversion of Paul, light whenever God was at work. Some would say that it was an inner light, intellectually perceived rather than sensibly; others with a love for paradox would say that this inner light so far transcends ordinary physical light that it is blinding and a kind of darkness. So darkness for the mystic is not simply a negative idea, for it symbolizes the unknowableness of God, and in the pilgrimage into God the soul is embarked on a journey into an ever-expanding awareness of God. It seems that the end of the pilgrimage will not be a static vision in which one can rest. Gregory of Nyssa, who interpreted the life of Moses as a spiritual pilgrimage, declared that 'the perfect life is that in which no boundary sets a limit to progress in perfection',[13] and he gives his reason for this judgement; namely, that if God is infinite, there can be no end to the exploration of God. In later chapters of this book we shall find many examples of the ways in which the mystics have found symbols and analogies to explain, as far as is possible, what they have discovered of the mystery of God.

We must note, however, that there are some mystics of an austere turn of mind who try to dispense with any language relating to the world of sense. Such was Meister Eckhart (see below, pp. 140 ff.) who sought to penetrate beyond even the Trinity to a region where all distinctions vanish. Here we come close to a pure apophaticism. It reminds me of a form of Buddhist mysticism, associated with the shrine called the Boro Budur in Java, where the pilgrims ascend a hill at the base of which are images of the Buddha. Further up, the images are screened from view. At the top, there is only the empty sky. Surely this pushes the negative theology to its limit.

Self-knowledge or Inwardness

In the section of this introductory chapter in which I wrote about the cognitive element in mysticism, I mentioned that it included knowledge of the self as well as the claim to knowledge of God. In some mystical writers self-knowledge is given a very prominent place. When mysticism is mentioned, we are perhaps most likely to think of Nature mysticism, as found in Wordsworth and other Romantic poets who were conscious of a divine presence in the world around them, something that was perhaps easier to experience in times before the development of industry and urbanization had so largely transformed the surface of the planet. But perhaps the most typical mystics are those who have retreated into the depths of their own minds and there, in isolation from everything visible and material, have found God. John Keble, a younger contemporary of Wordsworth, wrote in one of his hymns:

> Two worlds are ours: 'tis only sin
> > Forbids us to descry
> The mystic heaven and earth within,
> > Plain as the sea and sky.

It was not indeed the case that Keble rejected the belief that God is revealed in Nature, but a Christian believes that God is to be found more directly and less ambiguously in inward experience.

A good example is Augustine of Hippo, who was very

influential among later mystics. In his *Confessions*, he tells us of his quest for God, which is at the same time God's quest for him and also his own self-discovery:

> I entered into my inward self, thou leading me on; and I was able to do it because thou wert become my helper. And I entered, and with the eye of my soul saw above the same eye of my soul, above my mind, the unchangeable light. Not this common light, which all flesh may look upon, nor as it were a greater one of the same kind . . . but very different. It was above me, not as heaven is above earth, but it was above because it made me, and I was below because I was made by it.[14]

These words could, of course, have just as well been spoken by a pagan philosopher, and Augustine had in fact been influenced by the neo-Platonism of Plotinus. But he goes on to say, 'And I sought a way of acquiring strength sufficient to enjoy thee; but I found it not until I embraced that mediator between God and man, the man Christ Jesus.'[15]

Not everyone agrees that Augustine is to be counted a mystic, but the passages quoted show that he had strong mystical tendencies, shared with many other men and women who certainly would be counted as mystics. They all speak of retreating deeply into their own souls, and finding God there. From a theological point of view, this language has a certain plausibility. According to the biblical doctrine of creation, God made the first human couple 'in his own image and likeness' and it is said also that he breathed into the man's nostrils the 'breath of life'. So if we ask how God can be encountered in the depth of the human spirit, the answer seems to be that God is already there. The human person is at least potentially the bearer of the divine image and has the possibility of growing more and more into the divine likeness;

or, following the other creation story, the human being has received the divine breath (the same Hebrew word denotes both 'breath' and 'spirit'). Some mystics (Berdyaev, for instance) have spoken of a divine 'spark' in the human being, though theologians tend to frown on this language as verging on pantheism. Certainly, Christianity allows for an affinity between God and man, as well as the difference that lies between Creator and creature.

Let us suppose then that deep in a human being God can be found, as Augustine found him. What does it mean for a human person to go into the very depth of his or her own soul? Are we not already within ourselves, so how can we enter into ourselves or descend more deeply? The question is raised by mystics themselves. The answer can only be that for most of the time we are not in ourselves, or, to express the matter differently, we are not really ourselves, we are alienated from ourselves. 'Sin' is the word which denotes this alienation. If we were fully and truly human beings, we would be in the likeness of God, and he would be manifest not only in the core of the human being but in all of human life. 'Recollection' is a word used by many mystics, and in its profoundest sense it refers to a kind of reassembling the fragments of our humanity around the God-given core. Or we may think of that core as itself a kind of magnet holding the fragments in unity. It is perhaps identical with conscience when that abused word is given its full value. Or perhaps we should think of recollection as analogous to memory. In recollection, the mystic through an introspective delving into his or her own being traces that being back to its origin, and finds that origin is God. Here we may see a parallel between some Christian mystics and some of the Gnostics who claimed to 'remember' their true origin in God or some spiritual reality.

So for the mystic knowledge of God is correlated with knowledge of the self. God is not only a cosmic power but, in words from the Koran, closer than my jugular vein. We dwell in him and he dwells in us. We are now quite frankly skating on thin ice. There is a danger, as we have already noted, of pantheism, and even of confusing God and ourselves. There is also a danger of retreating so far into ourselves that we lose contact with and responsibility for the world. Both of these dangers must be considered before we can conclude this introductory chapter.

The Doctrine of God

We have noted how, in the experience of many mystics, self-knowledge and the knowledge of God are intertwined. But if someone finds God in the very depths of his or her own soul, and in a moment of ecstasy experiences a union with God so close that, in an imagery which has been widely used by some Christian mystics, it is understood as a mystical marriage between God and the soul, has not the difference between God and the creature been reduced almost to vanishing point? Is there a danger here that the mystic confuses finite human being with divine being? The wisest mystics tell us that even in the union with God there still remains the danger of a falling away from him. The deadly sin of pride still haunts the most saintly man or woman. In the modern world, there is prevalent, especially in the Western world, a form of Nietz-schean humanism in which the human being has usurped the power of God and claims to be the superman (*Übermensch*) who seeks and believes he can attain to domination over the world. This is a kind of distortion of the mystical quest for unity with the divine. It is a danger that goes with mysticism, and sometimes the language of individual mystics indicates that the danger is very real.

The great Christian mystics avoid the danger of falling into an atheistic or near-atheistic humanism, but their claim to union with God and even to a mystical marriage with God or with Christ understood as the divine Son and a person of the Trinity, does raise questions about how these mystics understood the doctrine of creation. Their notion of a kind of reciprocity between God and human believers, he in us and we in him, is, I think, a great spiritual insight, but it can obscure the priority of God. Augustine, we have seen, attempted to avoid this by insisting that the light of God, which he has found in the depth of his being, is 'above' him, precisely in the sense that God 'made him' (see above, p. 17). In the New Testament itself, Paul also is careful to insist on the priority of God in Christ, even while acknowledging some kind of mutual indwelling: '[Christ] is the image of the invisible God, the firstborn of all creation; for in him all things in heaven and on earth were created, things visible and invisible . . . He himself is before all things, and in him all things hold together.' [See above on recollection, p. 18.] He is the head of the body, the church; he is the beginning, the firstborn from the dead, so that he might come to have first place in everything. For in him all the fullness of God was pleased to dwell, and through him God was pleased to reconcile to himself all things, whether on earth or in heaven, by making peace through the blood of his cross' (Col. 1.15–20). And a little further on, Paul, like Augustine, stresses that the mediation of Christ is required, beyond the speculations of philosophy or natural theology: 'See to it that no one takes you captive through philosophy and empty deceit, according to human tradition, according to the elemental spirits of the universe, and not according to Christ. For in him the whole fullness of deity dwells bodily' (Col. 2.8–9). There are, of course, several points here that would call for discussion if Paul's teaching were to be restated in a modern terminology. For example, we might want to question whether the 'fullness' of the infinite God could 'dwell bodily' in the finite human being Jesus of Nazareth, and I have suggested elsewhere that 'fullness' could be taken here to mean 'essence'.[16] I believe, however, that along lines opened up by Paul, Augustine and some of the later mystics, the mystical quest for union with God does not necessarily lead us into pantheism. It may very well, however, demand some form of panentheism or, as I prefer to say, 'dialectical theism', which can never be free from some element of paradox. It implies an understanding of God which attributes to him both total transcendence and total immanence.

But even if some progress has been made in the foregoing paragraph, I think that the shadow of pantheism is still haunting the mystics' doctrine of God, and demands further discussion. It is significant that Evelyn Underhill, in her outstanding book on mysticism,[17] frequently talks of 'the Absolute' rather than of God, and when we remember that this book was first published in 1911 when the philosophies of Bradley, Bosanquet and other writers in the Anglo-Hegelian tradition were still in the ascendant, it reinforces the belief that the mystical understanding of God was closer to some kind of 'higher pantheism' than to traditional theism. This was unquestionably the case with F. H. Bradley, who abandoned the panlogical philosophy of Hegel and held that the Absolute is suprarational, and that God is therefore less than the ultimate Reality.[18] This would suggest that there is a God beyond God, a Reality beyond the God of theism. Some of the mystics believed this, or came close to it, Meister Eckhart being an example. Such an idea is not easily incorporated into Christian theology, though it has resurfaced in the theology of Paul Tillich.

A related problem concerns the personal character of God. It is true that in Christian belief God is not a person, but three persons in one, and therefore one might say he (it? she?

they?) is suprapersonal. Perhaps it need not be embarrassing for Christian theology to say that God is suprapersonal, and perhaps it even has the advantage of opening dialogue with those Eastern religions in which God is impersonal or the religion even appears atheistic. To say God is suprapersonal would seem to claim that God includes yet transcends person-hood, just as a human being includes but transcends animal-ity. It may even be the case, as some philosophers have argued, that personhood implies finitude. But obviously in talking about God or in prayer and worship, we cannot do other than use personal language. We just do not have either the vocabulary or the logic for any literal description of God or any exact way of speaking of his activity. The very fact that we fall into paradoxes and glitches in our God-talk is evidence of this lack, and the reticence of the mystics in their apophatic mood is a warning against being too confident or too familiar in speaking of God.

One other point about a possible lapse into pantheism should be mentioned. Does 'union' with God mean that either in this life or in some possible life beyond death, the human person is absorbed into the Deity, or does it continue to exist in some distinct way, in 'communion' with God rather than complete union? I think the mystics remain ambiguous on this point. Some seem to believe in a distinctness of the finite person even after death, and this probably accords with Christian orthodoxy. But those who use the imagery of raindrops falling into a lake or a river running into the sea seem to have slipped into something like pantheism.

Individualism

'The flight of the alone to the Alone' is a phrase often used as a description of mysticism (see below, p. 80). There is indeed some justification for it. Just as the mystic withdraws from the pleasures and distractions of the world, so he or she may withdraw from human society with all its entanglements and temptations, and perhaps live as a hermit or an anchorite, concentrating the whole being on the quest for God or communion with God when he is found. And several of the characteristics of mysticism described in the foregoing pages reinforce the impression of a solitary existence, though of course a solitude that is enlightened and enriched by the greatest of all possible companionships, the friendship of God himself. If one enjoys that friendship, what more is there to desire?

This is a point where mysticism is open to critical questioning, though I think we should be aware that the mystics themselves know the dangers and are constantly self-critical. The criticism is that mysticism can become a kind of spiritual hedonism. One reads of the spiritual marriage, of the joys of ecstasy, of consolations, perhaps also of visions that expand our consciousness and add new dimensions to life. For some people, probably never more than a tiny minority, the mystical way pursued in solitude is an ideal which offers for those persons the most satisfying life. But a purely spiritual life or a life given over entirely or almost entirely to contemplation cannot be the human ideal. It might be an angelic ideal, if indeed angels are purely spiritual beings, but a human being is a being-in-the-world, not only spiritual but physical as well, and so constituted that the spiritual and physical are in constant interaction and affect one another. Thus, as Catherine of Siena, following the Epistle to the Hebrews, points out, an angel could not be the saviour of mankind but only another human being (see below, p. 156).

The mystic, at least for as long as he or she lives on earth, has a measure of responsibility for the earth and for other human beings. The wise mystic does not see a rivalry between the sisters Mary and Martha, representing the contemplative and practical lives respectively. Though in the Gospel Mary is said to have chosen the better part (Lk. 10.42), both are demanded in the fully committed Christian. Thought and prayer are needed to discern what is demanded of the Christian, but they remain sterile if they never issue in the obedient act of service to the neighbour. On the other hand, the Christian activist does little good if his or her mind has not been prepared by appropriate meditation. It has been said that nothing is more frightening than ignorance in action. Catherine of Siena, mentioned above, has sometimes been herself called a 'social mystic', because from time to time she came out of her convent to involve herself in ecclesiastical and political affairs. Human beings are essentially social beings, and although mystics have sometimes collided with the ecclesiastical authorities in matters of doctrine, most mystics have acknowledged the need for the Church.

Passivity

Some years ago, I was asked to write a piece on prayer. I had to ask myself what lies at the heart of prayer. What kind of behaviour is prayer? I tried to answer my own question by testing the idea that prayer is thinking. But there are many kinds of thinking. The first distinction I made was to say that prayer is passionate thinking; not a cold, detached thinking about some problem, but a thinking infused with passion and longing. Certainly this would be true of mystical prayer. But concerning the prayer of the mystics, I think one would also want to say that it is passive as well as passionate thinking. What do I mean by that?

In everyday life, most of our thinking is active rather than passive. It is investigative thinking, an active probing into the tasks and problems that confront us. Part of our endowment from God is intelligence, the capacity to understand events and their connection with each other. This investigative thinking reaches its highest level in science, where we seek to probe the mysteries of Nature. But here we have to recall Marcel's distinction between problems and mysteries (see above, p. 2) and recognize that the approach of the scientist to the physical world or the methods of the detective investigating a crime are ways of thinking very different from the thinking of the mystic. The thinking of the scientist and of the detective is active and even aggressive and is aimed at mastering some situation. The thinking of the mystic, meditation and prayer, is passive and submissive and aims not at mastery but at letting oneself be mastered, immersed in a power and wisdom transcending one's own. This kind of experience can be known apart from specifically religious or mystical engagement in prayer. In landscapes of great natural beauty, for instance, one may simply stand still and 'take it in', as we say. The same receptivity is present when we are listening to great music. And even though these experiences are not specifically religious, they are perhaps near to religion, for there is in them a sense of awe, a sense of being encountered by a Reality that transcends what we encounter in the region of the everyday. But even in what we call the 'everyday' or the 'commonplace', such a sense may come to us. The mere fact that we exist, if we think about it, is awesome. Tillich talked about the shock of non-being, the realization that one will cease to exist.[19] I think myself that more primordial than the shock of non-being is the shock of being. As I once heard Austin Farrer say, in a typically Oxonian way, 'It seems terribly odd that we exist.'

We did not choose to exist, we simply find ourselves caught up into existence or, as some have chosen to express it, thrown into existence, though the second expression perhaps too much suggests a chance happening, like the throw of a dice. We human beings are caught up or thrown not only into existence but into thinking. We know that we exist and we have to think about it, for existence is open and only partially formed. As we have seen, our everyday existence is given shape by an active thinking by which we solve or try to solve the problems that arise in practical living. But we have seen also that there is a passive thinking, passive in the sense that we let our thinking be formed by opening our minds to forces which impinge upon us – appreciations of beauty, feelings of thankfulness, the love given us by friends.

There is a famous sentence in the fragmentary writings of Parmenides (early fifth century BCE) which is usually translated, 'Being and thinking are the same'.[20] If this translation is correct, there is still a further difficulty in understanding what it means. One possibility is that we are caught up not only into being and not only into thinking but into the thinking of being, by which I mean not so much thinking objectively *about* being as rather the universal Being's thinking in us. The human being has often been called a 'microcosmos', a miniature universe, and so he or she is, for we include in our mode of existence the full range of being from the purely physical through the organic and animal to the spiritual and mental, and we know, not conceptually or explicitly, that there are areas of being beyond our existence, that in our being we have transcended and are transcending towards higher levels of being which we call 'God' and who (for we use personal pronouns in this connection, as the best language available to us) remains largely unknowable and ineffable. I say 'largely' but not 'wholly', for if God were 'wholly other', as some theologians have said, we could not even have a name for him or any idea of him. As well as the otherness, there is an affinity between God and humans, and our human characteristic of self-transcendence is the pointer to this dimly conceived God. Indeed, one might say that it is the basic fact that we *exist* that is our strongest evidence for the reality of God and our right to speak of a *knowledge* of God. It has often been said that in the truest form of prayer, it is not we who pray but the Spirit of God praying in us. To put it another way, we are caught up into God's own longing for the final completion and perfection of the cosmos – heaven, paradise, nirvana or whatever it may be called. This is not another fallible argument for the existence of God, but an insight given in and with the gift of existence. It is the cosmos coming to thought in us at its growing edge. Perhaps this is what the 'ontological' argument of Anselm was driving at.

The Holistic View

At this point I may add one further characteristic of many mystics, what I shall call the holistic view of things. By that I mean, trying to see or understand things in their wholeness and interconnectedness. The world is not just a collection of facts, each self-contained and unaffected by other facts. This would be the case if there were such things as 'atomic facts', as both Russell and the early Wittgenstein believed. The word 'atomic' is used here in its basic sense of 'indivisible'. I think that in recent decades we have been swinging towards the idea common among the mystics that at least in some minute degree every entity exerts an influence on every other entity, and is itself influenced by every other entity. We are talking here about something that is probably insusceptible of any proof, though equally of any disproof. It is a vision which some men and women have in certain moments of experience when they become conscious of the unity of all things, themselves included. Heidegger, for instance, in a description of the mood of *Angst*, tells us that the divisions or distinctions among things disappear, and one is left with a feeling of totality or perhaps of nothingness, it is not quite clear which.[21] It is somehow as if everything collapsed into one, or successive moments were united in a flash of understanding. One is reminded of Kant's famous saying that the starry heavens above and the moral law within combine to produce a sense of awe before the mystery of existence.

In some ways, this holistic view of the mystic is at the opposite extreme from the analytic view of the scientist. Scientists believe that problems need to be limited if they are to be manageable and soluble, so they select only limited aspects of human experience and then limited areas within this or that aspect, for their investigations. This reduction is admirable for the purposes of science, and we can object to it only if it is claimed that there is nothing else. The mystic, on the other hand, tries to see everything in the context of everything else. The scientist certainly achieves a degree of clarity denied to the mystic, who lapses into vagueness or even silence. But when we come to the really big questions of human life, it may be the bigger but vaguer speculations of the mystic that point us in the direction of a fuller and richer existence.

Those mystics, such as Plotinus, who carry the notion of the unity of all things to its extremes, find the ultimate Reality in what they simply call the One, and of which everything else is an emanation. It is difficult to identify the One with the God of Christian belief, for the One includes the mystics themselves, and if they are in God, then the notion of a meeting or encounter with God is hard to describe. Again, one seems to have reached the borders of pantheism. God, the cosmos and the finite self are all inextricably linked together.

In any case, I think that the foregoing remarks do help us

towards an understanding of the nature of mysticism. The mystic seeks union with God, and in this quest surrenders himself or herself so that in prayer the thinking of Being enters into the mind of the one who prays.[22] The mystic knows God, not as the result of a logical argument (that would be the wrong tool) or of an encounter with a supernatural Other, but as something given in the very fact of human existence.

Prayer

The mention of prayer in the last paragraph brings with it the demand that by way of a tenth distinguishing mark of mysticism, something should be said about prayer. Of course, prayer has in one way or another been assumed in all our earlier discussions of what constitutes mysticism. Like all Christians, the mystic engages in that communication between the human soul and God which we call prayer. Indeed, the mystic and the ordinary believer who would not think of himself or herself as a mystic share many of the same prayers. They share the Lord's Prayer, that model for all Christian prayer, a model which already illustrates the complex nature of prayer, as including thinking and passion, reflection and willing, asking and receiving, and whatever else enters into prayer. They likewise share liturgical prayer or common prayer, which brings all Christians together in a united community and lies at the heart of the Christian religion. But common prayer shades off into the various forms of private prayer, and private prayer is very much diversified.

We must not allow ourselves to be drawn into a general consideration of prayer, which is too vast a subject to be treated here, and which would distract us from our special concern with mysticism. Our business is to ask about the special characteristics of mystical prayer that mark it off from other kinds of prayer.

I think it can be said that all prayer involves asking and desiring. In its simplest beginnings, prayer was no doubt self-centred, and whatever gods or powers were recognized were asked to supply material goods or perhaps health or some other tangible advantage. Eventually such prayers are seen to be morally and intellectually unworthy, and they are discarded. It is morally unworthy to pray for material advantages which we could obtain by hard work, and intellectually unworthy to pray for events that would violate the laws of the physical universe.

It may take a long time to grow out of prayers that are prompted by mere selfishness, laziness or ignorance, and, as I have said, such prayers are eventually discarded, both in the higher religions and in the lives of individuals. But all prayer is not discarded, and perhaps one now prays for forgiveness of sins or to become a better person. Perhaps too one prays more for other people than for oneself, especially for those in sickness or in bereavement or in other kinds of difficulty. Even prayers that one had thought had been discarded suddenly come back almost instinctively in emergencies. When I was a chaplain in the British Army many years ago, men would often say to me that there are no atheists under fire. That may be true, and it is even more likely to be true that when a loved one is very ill and in danger of death, people who rarely think of God and are perhaps sceptical about prayer in any form find themselves involuntarily interceding for the sick person. No one can explain convincingly whether or how such prayer can be effective, but even the sceptic knows and submits to the urge to pray.

The mystic too knows the prayer of asking. He or she may pray for purgation from sin, for illumination in the truth, for the vision of God and even union with God. Desire and will are there in the prayers of the mystic, but desire that has been purified, and will that has been redirected to spiritual ends. But a more subtle change takes place in the prayer of the mystic. If prayer is indeed a kind of communication between human beings and God, there must be on the part of the person who prays a listening or receiving as well as an asking and desiring. All this is, of course, a matter of degree, and even at what we may call the ordinary levels of prayer as practised by the ordinary believer, listening and receiving are not absent. In the mystic, however, they tend to become dominant features of prayer. The prayer is a kind of opening of the self so that the Spirit of God may pray in us and our wills may become attuned to the divine will.

Meditation is an example of the receptive kind of prayer. One may read the story of Jesus's life in the New Testament, and from that learn about the resources of our own human nature and be strengthened to make advances in Christian character (see the *Exercises* of Ignatius Loyola, below, pp. 166–7). Imagination has its place in this kind of meditation, as we try to think ourselves into the situation described and become, in a sense, participants. Ignatius himself had read the lives of the saints, and then found himself wanting to do what St Francis had done or what St Dominic had done. Another good example is supplied by *The Christian Year* of John Keble, where the various seasons and festivals are interpreted by his imaginative poetic gifts so as to catch the reader up into the spirit of these moments.

But many mystics wish to go beyond even meditation. The highest kind of prayer, they tell us, is contemplation. The distinction between meditation and contemplation is not always clear; for instance, in Ignatius Loyola, the terms seem interchangeable. Generally speaking, meditation has a clearly definable content, such as an episode from the Gospels or a festival of the Christian year. Contemplation dwells rather on some single idea. The so-called 'Jesus Prayer' of the monks of Mount Athos is a fairly simple illustration of a contemplative prayer, in which the name of Jesus or some brief formula containing his name is repeated over and over again. This is not just 'vain repetition' (Mt. 6.7) but helps to concentrate the mind on the name of Jesus and the vast range of connotations which that name calls up. Thus meditation involves discursive thinking in which the mind moves from one aspect to another of the narrative or argument or whatever the content may be, while in contemplation, one grasps some larger truth in its wholeness. For instance, Teresa of Avila claims to have visualized the soul as a castle containing many rooms before she traced the spiritual journey through these rooms (see below, p. 169). Another example would be the difference between participating in the eucharist and following it through its different moments, and then, after the action is over, praying before the reserved sacrament, which sums up in itself the whole of the preceding movement. To give a material illustration, one can play a recording of a symphony occupying perhaps forty minutes, but the entire symphony is also there simultaneously in the disc containing the recording.

It may be the case that what is known in a moment in contemplation has been gradually accumulated and put together in many earlier thoughts or experiences, but the fact that it often seems to come suddenly has led some mystics, including Teresa, to claim that it is infused by God. This would be another distinction between contemplation and meditation, for meditation requires the thinking (admittedly passive) of the meditator and therefore has an element of synergism. I would myself doubt whether even in contemplation there is simply an infused idea, and would believe that there must be some human contribution even here. Theoretically, there are three possibilities in the relations of God and the human soul. These are human activity, divine activity, and a relation to which God and the finite soul both contribute. I believe that in fact there is always to some degree this double relationship of synergism or co-working.

The content of contemplation is usually much more indefinite than the content of meditation. Some mystics seem to aim at a contemplative state in which all images have been transcended. We did take note of this possibility in our discussion of apophaticism (see above, pp. 14–15). But what would contemplation mean if one were to come to that point? Would it be simply a blank state of mind, and if so, that would hardly commend itself to those of us who have not had the experience. That experience is surely something more than blankness.

The notion of contemplation may be further clarified if we turn for a moment to a philosopher, Iris Murdoch. Though, in our secularized society, she wrote of 'The Good', understood in a quasi-Platonist sense, rather than of God, her remarks seem to me very relevant to understanding what mystical contemplation is about. She writes:

> I think there is a place both inside and outside religion for a sort of contemplation of the Good, not just by dedicated experts but by ordinary people; an attention which is not just a planning of particular good actions, but an attempt to look right away from self toward a distant transcendent perfection, a source of uncontaminated energy, a source of new and quite undreamt-of virtue.[23]

She acknowledges that 'a genuine mysteriousness attaches to the idea of goodness and the Good'.[24] But we are not reduced to just a blank state of mind. Rather, we have a space which can be occupied by 'scattered intimations' of the Good. She does not use words like 'passivity' and 'infusedness', but they seem to me not inappropriate to what she is indicating. She does, however, fasten on love as 'the unmistakable sign that we are spiritual creatures, attracted by excellence and made for the Good'. At this point it seems to me that her thoughts are very close to those of the Christian mystic, or, more generally, to Christianity as such. At this point too it seems to me that contemplation of the Good combines with meditation on the life of Jesus Christ.

Another word which may be used for the higher exercise of prayer is 'adoration'.[25] Etymologically, the word suggests 'praying toward', a kind of reaching out towards God which is also a kind of going out of oneself; yet this reaching out is not brought about simply by our own volition, we are drawn out by the divine Other. We get an idea of what this means when we think of how this word 'adoration' is used sometimes in our human relationships. We may say that the lover adores the beloved. Such adoration is close to what the mystic calls 'contemplation', and since it may be silent but is never just a blank, we can understand that contemplation likewise is not a blank state of mind, even if it is wordless.

No doubt much more could be said in answer to the question, 'What is mysticism?' But let us not forget the story of the donkey which I quoted near the beginning of this chapter. Perhaps we have learned so far nothing or very little. At any rate, the donkey has now carried his load of books across the stage and taken his exit. In the remaining chapters, we shall be hearing the experiences and claims of the mystics themselves, expressed, so far as they can express them, in their own words; and, apart from a few hee-haws by way of comment, the donkey will be silent.

2

Biblical Roots of Christian Mysticism:

Old Testament, Moses

Can we find the roots of Christian mysticism in the Bible? Perhaps we can, but we should understand that the question is a controversial one. Some people contrast mystical religion with prophetic religion, and hold that the latter is much more typical of the Bible, especially the Old Testament, but the New Testament also. Mystical religion, as we have seen in the first chapter of this book, is largely concerned with the quest for God, with prayer and spiritual development, with the inner life of men and women, usually considered as individual units. Prophetic religion, on the other hand, though it also looks to God, stresses the moral demands of God, the need for action in the world, and the significance of religion for society. I believe that there is no ultimate opposition between these two interpretations of religion. Both mystical and prophetic religion may claim justification from the Bible, and perhaps ideally the Christian should be responsive to both of them. But perhaps that is asking too much, and in practice we find that in individuals and in communities one of the alternatives is emphasized more than the other. But it is important that neither side in the controversy should write off the other, as if of no value.

We have already seen that mystics themselves condemn the distortion of the mystical way into a selfish spiritual hedonism or into an attempt to escape the responsibilities of living in the world and in human society. Equally, one must criticize the extravagances of those activists who in recent years have advocated a 'religionless' Christianity in which prayer and spirituality would be reduced to the barest minimum if they survived at all, and Christianity would become no more than another political or social movement. Already the inadequacy of a secular Christianity has become clear, but of course it is neither more nor less to be blamed than an individualist pietism that ignores worldly realities.

I shall try to show that Christian mysticism can legitimately claim to have roots in the Bible, though in its developed forms it owes much also to Greek classical sources. Christianity in its early centuries was sometimes regarded as a kind of 'third nation', synthesizing elements from both the Hebrew and Greek traditions. The justification of biblical roots will consist in studies of Moses from the Old Testament and Paul from the New. Neither of them would usually be described as a mystic, but both had strong mystical tendencies, and I have already claimed that an element of mysticism seems to enter into all religious experience.

The figure of Moses is so distant in time, probably thirteenth century BCE, that one can no longer have any clear and reliable details of his life. What has come down in the tradition is so deeply covered over with legend that it is hard to know what we can believe with any confidence. I think it may be asserted with reasonable certainty that Moses did exist, and that his personality imprinted itself on the Hebrew people so deeply that a trustworthy picture of the man can still be constructed from the Hebrew scriptures, and some of the events of his life can still be discerned amid the mass of legendary material. In placing him in the thirteenth century BCE, I am following the mainstream tradition. I am aware that this fairly early date has been challenged, mainly because

Egyptian historical records do not mention any revolt or disaffection of Hebrew slaves at this time. But I think this is a very weak objection. Egypt, like most ancient civilizations, owed much of its success to the fact that it had enslaved people from other ethnic groups. Revolts must have been quite common, and while for the Israelite the departure of the tribes from Egypt was the major event in their early history, it may have seemed of very little moment to the Egyptians, as they probably had plenty of other slaves.

On the other hand, the traditional dating gets support from the fact that Exodus mentions that the slaves built cities for the Egyptians, probably in the reign of Rameses II, who succeeded to the throne in 1290 BCE. Also significant is the fact that in the preceding century there had lived the pharaoh Akhnaton, credited with having been a monotheist, and this may have had some influence on Moses. It is indeed not inconceivable that Moses was himself an Egyptian who came to espouse the cause of the Hebrews, for the suffix 'Moses' formed a component of many Egyptian names, corresponding to the Scottish prefix, Mac, 'son of'.[1] He was regarded by the Midianites as an Egyptian when he lived in exile among them (Ex. 2.18–19). The Book of Exodus has a romantic story that Moses was born to Hebrew parents, but was adopted and brought up by an Egyptian princess; but this story may simply have been a device to claim him as a genuine Hebrew, for it would have been unthinkable for the writer to admit that the national hero was an Egyptian!

The trouble in trying to get a clear view of Moses is partly due to his being such an overwhelming character in the origins of the people of Israel that they tended to ascribe almost everything in their tradition to him. He was esteemed the greatest of the prophets, he was the national hero who had delivered the people from slavery in Egypt, he was the lawgiver who had received the Ten Commandments from

God on Mount Sinai, he was a miracle-worker who had brought plagues on Egypt and had divided the Red Sea, he was a magician who had a magic wand by which he could work wonders greater than the Egyptian magicians could perform. If he had mystical tendencies, they would be obscured by the more sensational powers that were attributed to him.

But a closer scrutiny reveals that he seems to have possessed quite a deep mystical capacity. Though he is called a prophet, it is important to note that when this term is applied to Moses, it does not carry the connotations that it was to have in later times, in the time of the so-called 'classical' prophets of Israel whose teachings have been preserved in written form in the Hebrew scriptures, such as Amos, Hosea, Isaiah, Micah, Jeremiah, Ezekiel and others. We base on them our idea of prophetic religion, which I briefly characterized above. When Moses is called a prophet, the term is used in a vaguer and more ambiguous sense. The word 'prophet' translates the Hebrew word *nabi,* and the first meaning given for this word in the standard Old Testament lexicon[2] is 'spokesman'. A prophet is a spokesman for God, not primarily foretelling future events, but commenting on public events, both in domestic affairs and international politics, and making judgements about them according to what he believed to be God's will. In this sense, I suppose Reinhold Niebuhr could have been called a prophet, and this function was much like that of the classical prophets of Israel. But the word 'prophet' is used in the Old Testament of earlier figures whose activity was more private and inward – persons who had ecstatic experiences which they then expressed so far as they could in words.

In what is almost a throw-away verse, the text of Exodus tells us that when Moses felt himself called by God to take the leadership among the Hebrews, he tried to excuse himself, pleading that he was not eloquent or equipped to be a public spokesman. Is this perhaps a genuine reminiscence that has survived in the tradition about Moses, in spite of all the legendary overloadings of that tradition? It does suggest an introverted nature, and we have seen that this is common among mystics.

In any case, it seems to me that perhaps the most important and formative event in the life of Moses, and the event which was the foundation for his future significance as the central figure in the history of Israel, was his encounter with God at the burning bush, a theophany which has all the marks of a genuine mystical experience.

In trying to assesss that experience, we have to begin by considering Moses' mood at the time when it came to him. Whatever may have been the cause, he was filled with a desire to liberate the Hebrews from their enslavement, and he committed an act which forced him to flee from Egypt. One day, he had seen an Egyptian mistreating a Hebrew slave, and had intervened on behalf of the slave. There must have been a scuffle, and in the course of it Moses killed the Egyptian. He hid the body in the sand, but the news leaked out that he had done the deed. Before any action could be taken against him, he had slipped out of Egypt and found refuge in Midian, a region across the Gulf of Aqaba.

There Moses settled, apparently for quite a few years. He married the daughter of the priest of Midian and was given the job of looking after his father-in-law's flocks. It was the ideal job for anyone with a mystical temperament. Surrounded by semi-desert spaces and with vast skies above, he had plenty of time for thought and meditation. There was probably a considerable measure of *Angst* in his mind, even perhaps a feeling of guilt. He had taken up the cause of the Hebrew slaves, but if any news reached him from Egypt, it was that the condition of the Hebrews was worse than ever.

'The Israelites groaned under their slavery, and cried out' (Ex. 2.23). Moses must have wondered if he had damaged rather than helped their cause by his rash act in killing the Egyptian. There must have been conflicting thoughts in his mind.

Then one day came his mystical experience, and the conflicts were resolved, at least for the time being. He was pasturing his flocks near Mount Horeb, better known nowadays as Mount Sinai. His eye was caught by a bright light, apparently coming from a bush. In the words of the Exodus text, 'the bush was blazing, yet it was not consumed'. We may suppose that it stood out in that rather drab landscape, perhaps a solitary bush, catching and reflecting the rays of the sun. As Moses approached the bush, he felt a sense of the holiness of the place, and removed his shoes. Here he had his encounter with God, or, as the text of Exodus says, with the angel or messenger of God. He feels himself addressed directly by name: 'Moses, Moses', for his mind is already attuned by his thought to a readiness for this experience.

'Moses says, "Here I am", and the caller identifies himself, "I am the God of your father, the God of Abraham, the God of Isaac, and the God of Jacob." And Moses hid his face, for he was afraid to look at God' (Ex. 3.6). Moses is then told that this God of the Hebrews has heard the cry of his people, and will send him to bring the people out of Egypt. Moses then asks, 'If I come to the people of Israel and say to them, "The God of your ancestors has sent me to you", and they ask me, "What is his name?" what shall I say to them?' God said to Moses, 'I AM WHO I AM ... I AM has sent me to you' (Ex. 3.13–14). This is the climax of the event. God has revealed his name and made himself known as the ultimate Reality, he who really is.

Of course, I am not suggesting that such a phrase as 'ultimate Reality' occurred to Moses' mind. He was not a philosopher raising metaphysical questions, but a human being wrestling with moral and spiritual problems. It is true that a new name had been revealed of the God who had been worshipped by Moses' ancestors. It may also be true that the new name, spelt in Hebrew by four consonants transliterated as YHWH in the Latin alphabet and probably pronounced Yahweh, is connected with the Hebrew verb meaning 'to be', but Moses presumably was unaware of such details. It is quite likely that in his mystical experience, all that was accessible to the sense was the glowing light from the bush, for light seems to be a universal symbol of the divine for mystical mentalities. The heart of Moses' experience was inward, and probably, to begin with, wordless. Only after long and deep reflection did Moses, or his interpreters or those who composed the text of Exodus, find words that brought to expression the content of an experience which was at first ineffable. Only long after that did philosophical thinkers such as Philo, Maimonides, Aquinas, Hegel and many others tease out the meaning of the 'I am who I am'. Could we say, however, that although Moses would not have put it in this way, it was an insight that had arisen out of the depth of his own being? If it was a veridical experience, then indeed it was an encounter with God, with the Source of being which gives existence to all finite beings, and at the same time it was a new self-knowledge on the part of Moses, an understanding that he was called in his being to become a spokesman or prophet of the Lord. It was both an irruption of the divine into the being of Moses and at the same time a resolution of his inner conflicts, a moment of recollection, in the sense previously explained (see above, p. 18).

The story goes on to tell how Moses did go back to Egypt and brought his people out. To do this, the story-teller has to represent Moses as a magician. He performs tricks with his magic wand, changing it at will into a serpent or back again into a staff. More seriously, he afflicts Egypt with plagues. The

Nile is turned to blood, life is made intolerable by invading swarms of gnats and flies and frogs, and finally by the deaths of the eldest sons in Egyptian families. Most of these plagues of Egypt are explicable as natural disasters that from time to time occur in the Nile valley, and in fact have been given natural explanations by modern commentators.

The explanations are on the whole credible and adequate, though some are rather weak; for example, the suggestion that the Nile being turned to blood comes simply from the red reflection of the setting sun on its waters. The most difficult to explain is the death of the young Egyptian men. It is true that epidemics were common enough in the ancient world, but how could a disease, whether spread by air-borne or water-borne or insect-borne agents, have affected the Egyptians without also killing off the Hebrews? If I were to venture a speculation, I would suggest that it may have been a sexually transmitted disease, perhaps an early form of AIDS (Acquired Immunity Deficiency Syndrome) that has been so destructive of human life in our own time. Although Egyptians and Hebrews would be intermingling every day as they went about their duties, there was almost certainly a social segregation or *apartheid* between the slaves and the slave-owners. Sexual relations between members of the two groups would be rare and were possibly illegal. A parallel situation exists in South Africa today, where AIDS is widespread in the black population, while the white population is relatively free of the disease.

In any case, whether or not one can give a satisfactory explanation of the plagues, or indeed whether all of these plagues actually occurred, there is no doubt that both the Egyptians and the Hebrews would believe that these disasters were being sent by God or the gods, and the Egyptians may well have been persuaded that the offended God of the Hebrews was responsible for their woes, and that it would be for the country's benefit if it rid itself of these troublesome Semites. But there was much wavering before it was decided to let the Hebrews go, and they were hardly gone when the Egyptians had second thoughts: 'What have we done, letting Israel leave our service?' (Ex. 14.5). There followed the well-known dramatic events of the exodus from Egypt, Israel's crossing of an arm of the Red Sea and the disasters that befell the Egyptians as they attempted to pursue them. All these events can be given a natural explanation, and may have happened rather differently from what is described in Exodus. But we need not linger over these matters, since our concern is to examine the mystical element in the character of Moses.

So we pass on to the next stage in his career, the pilgrimage eastward as the Israelites sought to return to the land of Canaan in which, as they believed, their ancestors had settled several generations earlier. The chief event in this period that throws some light on Moses was the giving and receiving of the law of God, summarized in the famous Ten Commandments.

In the careers of many of the mystics, there is an initial experience of the divine, an encounter which comes as a revelation, and in some cases is a conversion experience. Ecstatic experiences of this kind are usually of brief duration, but their effects are lasting, and one of these effects is the desire to renew the experience, to enter again into a meeting with God. We can see this taking place in the career of Moses. Even in its account of the event at the burning bush, the writer or editors of Exodus have inserted into God's words to Moses a promise: 'When you have brought the people out of Egypt, you shall worship God on this mountain' (Ex. 3.12). This reflects the significance that Mount Sinai or Horeb had acquired in the mind of Moses. It was a holy place, the place where God had encountered him and let himself be known. Moses must have had the desire to go back to that place and to renew his relation with the Lord. (The name that had been revealed, Yahweh, was considered so sacred that it was not to be pronounced, and for it was substituted the title 'Lord'.)

So when Moses led his band of Israelites out of Egypt, they did not attempt to proceed by the direct road towards the land of their ancestors, Canaan or Palestine as it came to be called. They took a detour, and it brought them to the holy mountain of Sinai, destined to become a holy place not only for Moses but for all Israel and eventually for Christians.

The people camp in front of the mountain. According to the narrative in Exodus, Moses prepares the people for a solemn act of consecration to the Lord, a covenant with the God who had delivered them from slavery. They were to become his people and he was to be their God. Moses, as the mediator between God and the people, first ascends the mountain on his own, in response to what he hears as a word from the Lord: 'I am going to come to you in a dense cloud, in order that the people may hear when I speak with you and so trust you ever after' (Ex. 19.9). It is interesting to note that in this passage it is not said that God will appear in light, as on the former occasion, but in a dense cloud. This is perhaps an early example of the later mystical idea that the light of God is so dazzling that finite minds experience it as darkness as they are drawn into the mystery of the unknown God who is nonetheless making himself known. Moses comes back down from the mountain and commands the people to prepare themselves for some great event that will happen on the third day.

On the third day there is lightning and thunder, symbolizing the presence of God and the voice of God, a meaning which they had not only for mystics but for people generally in the ancient world. The people, we are told, trembled at the violence of the storm which seems to have been accompanied by an earthquake. 'Moses would speak and God would answer him in thunder' (v. 19). So we are told in the Exodus account, which no doubt has been much dramatized and made to conform to what in those days was considered proper to a divine revelation. Perhaps this account of the events was dramatized in the course of a liturgical re-enactment.

The continuation of the story in Exodus has become somewhat confused.[3] Moses goes back into the mountain, now accompanied by some of the chief men of Israel. He receives the Ten Commandments, a kind of basic summary of the moral law. This was a time when many other nations in the Near East were drawing up codes of law, which they too attributed to God, whatever his name might be for each nation. The Ten Commandments do not constitute a law code, but provide a basis for one, and in fact are followed by one in the present text of Exodus. From what has already been said about the knowledge of God and its relation to self-knowledge among the mystics, we may believe that the Ten Commandments were indeed a divine revelation to Moses, but a revelation mediated through his own conscience, his inward awareness of his being as derived from God. In the words of Cardinal Newman, 'conscience is the aboriginal vicar of God'.[4]

Although in this chapter I have been making the case for considering Moses as a Hebrew mystic, the story about the giving of the law on Mount Sinai makes it clear that his mysticism could not possibly be considered something only inward or individualistic. The inward encounter with God was indeed the core and source of this man's religion, but it is succeeded by a public revelation, and it expressed itself in a life of service to the nation (which showed him scant gratitude in his lifetime), and cemented the connection between prayer and practical service, a connection which has continued to mark the best types of mysticism in the Jewish and Christian traditions.

We need not linger over the remainder of Moses' history as it is told in the Old Testament. He continued to lead the people towards their promised land, but they constantly rebelled against him, and even when he was on the mountain receiving the Commandments, some of them were busy fashioning the golden calf and proclaiming it to be their god in place of the Lord who had brought them out of Egypt.

The example of the life of Moses shows us, I believe, that a mystical form of existence is not foreign to biblical religion. One may hesitate to describe Moses as a mystic *tout court*, but it can hardly be questioned that he had strong mystical tendencies, and one could point to similar tendencies in some of the later prophets. Actually, it was a book of the Old Testament that became a favourite with many of the Christian mystics. I am referring to *The Song of Songs*. It is very likely that the poems of which the book is made up were celebrations of sexual love, but they would never have been included in the canon of Hebrew scriptures if they had not already been given a mystical significance, signifying no doubt the love affair not so much of God and the individual soul as between God and his people Israel. The use of erotic imagery became quite common among the medieval mystics and was used with considerable frankness.

Moses, of course, antedates such developments by a very long time. But quite fittingly, this mystic or quasi-mystic ended his life in mystery. He did not himself enter the promised land but was permitted to view it from a mountain on the east bank of the Jordan River. Into these Transjordanian Mountains he took a journey one day, but never came back. For the last time, he had heard the voice of the Lord addressing him, and the words in which Moses interpreted the divine communication were these: ' "This is the land of which I swore to Abraham, to Isaac, and to Jacob, saying, 'I will give it to your descendants'; I have let you [Moses] see it with your eyes, but you shall not cross over there." Then Moses, the servant of the LORD, died there in the land of Moab, at the LORD's command. He was buried in a valley in the land of Moab, opposite Bethpeor, but no one knows his burial place to this day' (Deut. 34.4–6). The Hebrew seems to imply that it was the Lord himself who buried Moses. In the New Testament, we read in the Epistle of Jude (v. 9) that it was not actually the Lord but the archangel Michael deputing for God who buried the body. Needless to say, there has been much speculation about this mysterious end of Moses' life. Sigmund Freud, taking up a suggestion by an Old Testament scholar that Moses had finally been murdered by the rebellious Israelites, used this story to illustrate his theory of the Oedipus complex. Moses was the father of the people and therefore the object both of their admiration and of their envy. But this opinion is no better founded than another one found in a Jewish apocryphal document of the first century CE and entitled *The Ascension of Moses*. According to this document, Moses was assumed into heaven at the end of his life, and at the end of the age, all the people of Israel will follow him there. That would certainly be a fitting conclusion for this great spiritual leader.

Biblical Roots of Christian Mysticism:

New Testament, Paul

When we move from the Hebrew scriptures to the New Testament, we find that as far as the question of mysticism is concerned, there was to a large extent a continuity of the traditional attitudes. Jesus himself grew up in a devout Jewish family, and was a practising Jew throughout his lifetime, circumcised in infancy and celebrating the Passover just a day before his death. Although he criticized some of the distortions of his times, especially hypocrisy and excessive legalism, he was loyal to the tradition, and this is nowhere more obvious than in the matter of spirituality, where, like the prophets of the Old Testament, he devoted himself both to prayer and to good works. It is unlikely that he ever foresaw a separation between his own disciples and the Judaism which both he and they embraced. According to Matthew, he said himself of his mission that he was 'sent only to the lost sheep of the house of Israel' (Mt. 15.24). But as time went on, it became clear that his life and teaching had significance beyond the boundaries of any one people. From about 40 CE his followers were being called 'Christians' (Acts 11.26), relations between them and the Jewish leaders were deteriorating, and gradually they became two distinct religions, often in the course of history divided by bitter rivalry.

During the process of separation, changes did take place

which affected spirituality, and led to forms of mysticism which could no longer be fitted into the pattern which we have seen exhibited in the mysticism or quasi-mysticism of Moses and the prophets of Israel. The most important of these changes was connected with the person of Jesus himself. Within the limits of Jewish religion, he might well have come to be esteemed as a prophet and might possibly have superseded Moses as the greatest of the prophets. Moses had in fact promised that 'The LORD your God will raise up for you a prophet like me from among your own people;[1] you shall heed such a prophet' (Deut. 18.15). These words of Moses were presumably in the minds of those Jews who are mentioned in John's Gospel as saying of Jesus, 'This is indeed the prophet who is to come into the world' (Jn 6.14). These Jews were a small minority in the nation, and the majority rejected Jesus as the expected prophet promised by Moses. In the meantime, however, the Christians had themselves widened the gap that was opening between them and the Jews by claiming that Jesus was more than a prophet in the succession from Moses. He was more even than a Messiah. He was, at quite an early stage in Christian thinking, a divine as well as a human being, a Son of God, to use the common phrase, even the only Son. The strict monotheism of Jewish faith did not allow for any other divine person alongside the Lord (Yahweh) and Christians had to spend two or three hundred years thinking out the doctrine of the Trinity. This doctrine, they believed, allowed them to remain monotheists while acknowledging the divinity of the Son and of the Holy Spirit alongside that of the Father. Now that there are happier relations between Jews and Christians than there were at many times in the past, probably a great many Jews would gladly accept Jesus as an outstanding or even *the* outstanding prophet in the great line of Jewish prophets, but that would no longer bridge the gap between the two religions.

The recognition by Christians of Jesus as a divine being and the second person of the Trinity does introduce a new element which differentiates Christian from Jewish spirituality. Although there is a sense in which Jesus is mediator between humans and God the Father, he is also believed to be so closely related to the Father that to know Jesus as the Christ is to know God. I mentioned 'directness' as the first of the characteristics by which I tried to delineate mysticism, and the fact that Christianity posits Jesus Christ as the mediator might seem to rule out the possibility of a Christian mysticism (see above, p. 9). But if Christ is God – and presumably he is as a person of the Trinity – then to know Christ is to know God, and the relation would be a direct one. On the other hand, did Moses perceive God directly? We remember that the Hebrew scriptures are very chary about the notion of 'seeing' God (see above, pp. 7–8). Moses sees a light, which can be regarded as a symbol of God or 'angel' of God. It is indeed said that Moses and the elders of Israel 'saw the God of Israel. Under his feet there was something like a pavement of sapphire stone, like the very heaven for clearness' (Ex. 24.10). It is added that God 'did not lay his hand on the chief men of the house of Israel; also they beheld God, and they ate and drank' (v. 11). This additional verse suggests that it was by a special favour that these men were permitted to see God without being harmed, and in any case the earthly imagery of what they saw indicates that it was not properly a direct seeing of God, but a symbolic vision representing God. One may compare with the verse from Exodus a verse from John's Gospel in which Jesus says, 'Whoever has seen me has seen the Father' (Jn 14.9). But the finite Jesus is not identical with the infinite Father, though a Christian may believe that the divine essence – pure love? – may be visible in a finite human person. So I do not think that the status of Jesus Christ as simultaneously mediator of the Father and yet coequal person of the Trinity rules out the claim of the Christian mystic to a direct relation to God.

I now intend to take up these problems of a Christian mysticism with its roots in the New Testament by considering Paul the Apostle and asking whether he can rightly be regarded as perhaps the first great Christian mystic; or, if not a mystic, at least a Christian with very strong mystical tendencies.

I have been careful to qualify my description of Paul as a mystic (as I did also in the case of Moses) by adding that, if not a mystic, at least he had very strong mystical tendencies. I find that if one does venture to say that Paul was a mystic, the reaction is usually, 'Surely not!' I agree that mysticism is probably not the *defining* characteristic of Paul's religion, for he was very much an activist. But his activism, I would say, arose from a source that can truly be called mystical: namely, his being 'in Christ', to use his own frequently repeated phrase.

The New Testament scholar who has been possibly the best-known advocate for seeing Paul as a mystic was the German, Adolf Deissmann (1866–1937), and the book in which he stated his case most clearly was *Paul: A Study in Social and Religious History*.[2] Deissmann's book met with considerable criticism, but I think that in the main he gives a very fair picture of the Apostle. Deissmann makes a distinction between 'acting' and 'reacting' mysticism, the former being a mysticism in which the initiative comes from the mystic who seeks to ascend to God, while the latter is a mysticism in which the initiative comes from God, drawing the mystic to himself. Deissmann further distinguished between a mysticism which ends in the union or absorption of the mystic into God, and the mysticism which reaches its goal in a communion of the mystic with God and with fellow-believers. Paul, he maintains, is a mystic of the reacting and communal type. I think that these distinctions answer the criticisms that some theologians have urged against Deissmann's classification of Paul with the mystics. I think also Deissmann's emphasis on communion meets the criticism of John Knox that Paul's phrase 'in Christ' can be taken as meaning 'in the Church', rather than as signifying a mystical relation of the individual to Jesus Christ. I should say myself that the 'in Christ' has both of these meanings, though sometimes one, sometimes the other, is more prominent. But the phrase will be examined more closely later on.

Paul, also called Saul in the earlier part of his life, is much nearer to us in time than Moses, and in addition we have about a dozen letters or epistles from the man himself, revealing quite a lot about him. We cannot give exact dates for Paul's life, but there are allusions which allow us to fix a frame within which his life took place. Thus, when he was present at the martyrdom of Stephen, he is said to have been a *neanias*, a 'young man', and in Jewish usage, the word was applied to someone not yet thirty years old (Acts 7.58); when he wrote his letter to the escaped slave Philemon, he refers to himself as a *presbytes*, an 'old man', a term which was applied in the usage of that time to men over fifty (Philemon v. 9). The death of Stephen took place probably about 35 CE and Paul wrote his letter to Philemon about the year 62, near the end of his career. So Paul was not yet thirty in the year 35, but was over fifty in the year 62, and therefore the frame of reference for Paul's life seems to stretch from about 5 CE at the earliest to a date after 62. These indirect evidences point to a date well into the first decade of the Christian era for his birth, and his death is believed to have occurred at Rome in the persecution of the Christians by Nero, say in 64.

Paul was a member of the Jewish race, and had been born to a family living in the diaspora, in the city of Tarsus. Like many other cities in the Hellenistic world, Tarsus had its

Jewish community with their synagogue, and Paul grew up with a strong, even fanatical, attachment to the faith of his fathers. To quote his own words, he was 'a member of the people of Israel, of the tribe of Benjamin, a Hebrew born of Hebrews; as to the law, a Pharisee' (Phil. 3.5). At some point he moved from Tarsus to Jerusalem, where he was educated by a famous Jewish rabbi, Gamaliel, in the twenties of the first century. His education was 'according to our ancestral law' (Acts 22.3). In the following decade of the thirties, he was caught up in the increasingly bitter conflict between Christians and Jews. Again in his own words, 'I was violently persecuting the church of God and was trying to destroy it. I advanced in Judaism beyond many among my people of the same age, for I was far more zealous for the traditions of my ancestors' (Gal. 1.13–14). We have noted already that he was present at the lynching of Stephen, and it is recorded that he approved of the mob's action in killing him (Acts 8.1).

The killing of Stephen was the beginning of a general persecution of Christians. Their homes were being ransacked and they themselves were being thrown into prison, though by what authority is not clear. Saul, as he is still called in the text of Acts, took a leading part in this. He planned to extend the persecution to the city of Damascus, and set out for that city. But now comes a dramatic reversal in his attitude to the Christians. It is called a conversion, though it was not a conversion from Judaism to Christianity, since these two forms of faith had not yet become separate religions, and Paul no doubt then and probably for the rest of his life still thought of himself as a good Jew. But his conversion was nevertheless an important moment in hastening the final rupture between Church and synagogue.

It is well known that however sudden a conversion may seem, it has generally been preparing in the mind of the person converted. Just as Moses had been troubled by an inner conflict before his experience at the bush, so Paul, in spite of his fanatical assurance, must have been having doubts about where he was going. Perhaps the death of Stephen or his own struggle with the law had had a profound effect on him, or in a more general way he was beginning to see that the way of Jesus Christ was not a denial of the faith of Israel but a fulfilment. When we examine Paul's conversion, I think we cannot escape the conclusion that it falls within the category of mystical experience.

Most mystics had some deep experience at the beginning of their careers, and what followed in their lives was given its character by the initial experience. Leading to Paul's conversion was first the *Angst* in his own mind, the self-doubt that led him to question his own conduct. But what was needed next was, so to speak, a trigger. That trigger could be supplied by some apparently chance event, a natural event not envisaged by the person to whom it happened, yet seeming to him or her to be a direct answer to the self-questioning that had arisen. For Moses, the burning bush was such a trigger; for Augustine, a voice from a neighbouring garden. What was it in Paul's case? There has been a lot of speculation, much of it unconvincing. One common explanation is that Paul had an epileptic seizure. This explanation is based partly on the fact that he fell to the ground, partly on his own statement that he suffered from some physical condition which he calls only a 'thorn in the flesh', given to him to keep him from becoming too elated (2 Cor. 12.7). But I do not think that epilepsy throws any light on his experience. He must have had recurring attacks of that affliction, if indeed he had it at all, and he would hardly regard such an attack as a divine revelation. The most plausible explanation I have come across[3] is that as Paul and his companions were getting near to Damascus, they ran into a storm of lightning and thunder, quite common in that part of the world, and Paul was struck by lightning. This would fit in well with the description of the incident in Acts – Paul's being thrown to the ground and seeing a great light which blinded him. The fact that his sight returned after a few days is further evidence that lightning may have been the cause of his blindness. We have to remember too that for people in those days, lightning and thunder were not understood as natural events. They came from God, from Zeus or Yahweh or however God might be named. The lightning is the symbol of the divine presence in the event, the thunder is the voice of God, expressing displeasure at Paul's course of action.

Like Moses at the bush, Paul interprets the divine voice in human words. He is addressed, 'Saul, Saul, why do you persecute me?' Paul asks, 'Who are you, Lord?' The voice replies, 'I am Jesus, whom you are persecuting' (Acts 9.4–5). As he takes in his dramatic experience, Paul's whole attitude to Christ and the Christians changes. He is led into Damascus and is kindly received by the followers of Jesus in that city. His sight returns and he is baptized and begins to preach the gospel of Jesus Christ with as much fervour as he had previously shown in opposing it. Before long he had become a trusted leader among the Christians and had embarked on a missionary career which resulted in the founding or strengthening of churches in many cities of the eastern Mediterranean region.

An interesting point to note at this stage is the close resemblance in structure between the initial experiences of Moses and Paul, a structure which we shall find again with variations in later mystics. I have hinted at some of these resemblances already, but it may be useful to bring them together in a summary. There are, I think, six moments that can be distinguished.

1 There is a mood of questioning which is also a searching – I have used Kierkegaard's word, *Angst*, to describe this state of mind.

2 There occurs an objective event in the physical world, seeing a burning bush (Moses) or being caught in an electric storm (Paul) which triggers a mental or spiritual event.

3 The spiritual event can be described only by a metaphor. It is as if the person's inward being is illuminated by an inward light which is taken to be nothing less than the touching of that person by a divine being.

4 The person feels himself to be directly addressed, 'Moses, Moses!' or 'Saul, Saul!'

5 At the next stage in the experience, there is the beginning perhaps of a transition from the experience itself to the first reflections on the experience. Moses and Paul both ask, 'Who or what is addressing me?' The experience is clothing itself in interpretative words. Who can be addressing them, except the being who has been preoccupying their thoughts for days or months or even years? For Moses, the God of Abraham, Isaac and Jacob, whose name is now revealed as 'I am who I am'; for Paul, the radical rabbi from Nazareth, Jesus, whose name he now has to confess as Christ and Son of God.

6 Further reflection leads to a sense of vocation to a particular mission. Moses is called to the liberation of the Hebrews, Paul to the preaching of the Christian gospel, especially to the Gentiles.

These first mystical experiences of Moses and Paul were probably followed by others. If we are to judge from the experience of later mystics, the encounter with God is repeated throughout the mystic's career, and likewise the self-dedication of the mystic to whatever mission he has come to recognize as his vocation.

So we saw how Moses, having escaped from Egypt, was drawn back to Mount Sinai, where once again in the lightning and thunder he had a new encounter with God and received the Ten Commandments. Paul likewise had further encounters with Christ, and sometimes the language which he uses to describe his experience is very close to the mystical idiom. The following example, taken from his Second Letter to the Corinthians (12.2–4) is the most striking, and I quote his own words in full:

> I know a man in Christ who fourteen years ago was caught up to the third heaven – whether in the body or out of the body I do not know; God knows. And I know that such a man – whether in the body or out of the body I do not know; God knows – was caught up into Paradise and heard things that are not to be told, that no mortal is permitted to repeat.

The 'man' to whom Paul refers is Paul himself, and this practice of referring to oneself in the third person is quite common among mystics. Perhaps it arises from their experience of ecstasy, for ecstasy or *ekstasis* is simply the Greek way of expressing the idea of 'standing out of oneself', of being able to look at oneself from outside, as it were. In some degree, every human being has this potentiality. The Latin word corresponding to *ekstasis* is *existentia* or existence. For a human being, to exist is also to know that he or she exists, and therefore to have the capacity for self-direction and self-criticism. This is a mystery at the heart of personal existence. What does it mean to say, 'I am angry with myself' or 'I am ashamed of myself'? Who is the 'I' that seems to be distinct from the 'myself'?

What did Paul mean when he said he did not know whether he was in the body or out of the body? Obviously he was trying to express what it means to be in a mystical ecstasy, yet the fact that in ordinary language we can talk about ourselves or even feel an emotion of anger, let us say, towards ourselves, shows both the complexity of any human being and also that mysticism seems to be a possibility for any human being, though only a few develop that possibility. We could say, I believe, that ecstasy is an exaggerated form of existence. As to the talk of being out of the body, we find it difficult nowadays to think of a soul distinct from the body, for certainly our mental life is dependent on bodily functions to a high degree. Yet we hear from time to time of near-death experiences, where someone who has been clinically dead for a length of time nevertheless reports an experience from that time, and interestingly the report often includes seeing a light. Even the atheistic philosopher, Alfred Ayer, seems to have had a near-death experience of this sort. The relation between body and soul is still far from being understood.

Paul also mentions being in the 'third heaven'. This again is mystical language. Just as many mystics have distinguished stages on the way towards union with God, so those who have had visions of heaven have believed that there are, so to speak, levels of heaven. Some have visualized a seven-storey building, others have been satisfied with three. Paul probably believed in three storeys, for in late Jewish belief, the third heaven was the highest of all. But Paul does not tell us much about it. His mystical experience was ineffable – no mortal is permitted to repeat what had been revealed in the experience. Here we see in Paul a possible influence of the Greek mystery-cults. Brought up in the Hellenistic city of Tarsus and fluent in Greek both as a speaker and writer, he must have known something of these cults.

The description by Paul in 2 Corinthians of his 'vision'

seems to me a sufficient rebuttal of those who dismiss out of hand the idea that he was a mystic. Mysticism almost certainly entered into his character. It is perhaps also worth mentioning that the vision to which Paul refers is not the vision that he had on the way to Damascus, though that first vision had the mystical quality of directness (Gal. 1.15–17). This follows from a chronology of Paul's life and letters. Let us suppose that his conversion took place within a year of the death of Stephen: that would place it in 36 CE. 2 Corinthians, in the opinion of many New Testament experts, is a composite document made up of several fragments of letters that Paul had addressed to Corinth in the fifties. The story of the vision we have been considering is in a fragment probably written about 57, so fourteen years earlier would take us to 43, that is to say, seven years after Paul's conversion. Moreover, Paul's account of his vision makes it clear that it was one of many.

Further evidence of Paul's mysticism, if any is required, can be gained from considering what he himself says about his relation to Jesus Christ. In one place, he makes the declaration, 'to me, living is Christ' (Phil. 1.21). His whole life was, so to speak, immersed in Christ. A constantly recurring phrase in his letters is 'in Christ'. When Paul speaks of Christ in this way, he is not thinking of the historical Jesus, of whom he does not say very much,[4] but of the crucified and risen Christ as a present reality in his life and consciousness, Christ in his spiritual being, scarcely distinguishable in Paul from the Holy Spirit. And Christ is also one with the Father, 'God was in Christ' (2 Cor. 5.19) or he can also say, 'For us there is one God, the Father ... and one Lord, Jesus Christ' (1 Cor. 8.6). Thus, although the full working out of trinitarian doctrine came after Paul's time, the essentials of that doctrine had already taken form in his thinking. We may note also that although Paul speaks very much of his being in Christ, he can change the phrase around and talk of Christ's being in him, most strikingly in the verse where he says, 'I have been crucified with Christ; and it is no longer I who live, but it is Christ who lives in me' (Gal. 2.19–20). This is the mutual indwelling so characteristic of the mystical relation and also the goal of the Church's regular worship, as expressed in the eucharistic prayer 'that we may evermore dwell in him and he in us'. Unlike bodies, spirits may, so to speak, interpenetrate one another, something of which we can derive an idea in close friendships or in marriage.

Two points emerge in the foregoing defence of Paul's mysticism. His close identification of Jesus Christ with both the Father and the Holy Spirit, a close communion which is not simply absorption, justifies us in saying that Paul's mysticism, although it may rightly be called a Christ-mysticism, is at the same time a direct relation to God, understood in trinitarian terms. The second point is that the mention of the eucharist draws attention to the social rather than individualist character of Paul's mysticism. When we noted John Knox's claim that to be 'in Christ' may mean to be in the Church, the question was raised whether this view was in conflict with the belief that the phrase 'in Christ' denotes a mystical relation. I said then that both points of view can be true (see above, p. 52). The Church is not only a historical association existing objectively in the world, it is also a spiritual reality which is described in the Anglican eucharistic liturgy as the 'mystical body' of Christ. Paul thinks of all Christians as 'in Christ' in the mystical body and therefore in relationship with one another.

It is interesting, though not of vital importance, to speculate whether elements of Greek mysticism are beginning to combine with the Hebrew influences in the thought of Paul. Certainly, in the experience which he describes in 2 Corinthians 12, he uses the language of ecstasy and stresses the ineffability of whatever was disclosed to him in his vision (see above, p. 57). But his teaching that it is not permissible to make known what he had seen and/or heard comes not so much from mysticism as from the mystery-cults. In the New Testament the mystery of the divine working is open to all Christians, not just to a favoured élite.

Paul's interpretation of the two basic Christian sacraments, which were called in Greek *mysteria*, have mystical overtones which facilitate a move away from a purely Hebrew spirituality towards a more definitely mystical understanding of their meaning, but it would be going too far to say that any major Greek influence was at work here. Of baptism, he wrote, 'Do you not know that all of us who have been baptized into Christ Jesus were baptized into his death? Therefore we have been buried with him by baptism into death, so that, just as Christ was raised from the dead by the glory of the Father, so we too might walk in newness of life' (Rom. 6.3–4). Through baptism the Christians are incorporated into the mystical body of Christ, and united with his Spirit. Paul's teaching about the eucharist expresses the same complex relationships. 'The bread that we break, is it not a sharing in the body of Christ? Because there is one bread, we who are many are one body, for we all partake of the one bread' (1 Cor. 10.16–17). Paul's knowledge of the Greek world may have had some effect on his understanding of these matters, but I think in the main such an understanding arises out of the mystical tendencies in his own experience as it had been shaped at his conversion and in subsequent ecstatic moments.

But as the history of the Church continued, Greek elements became increasingly combined with the original Hebrew material, and in the mature Christian mysticism which reached its full stature in the patristic and medieval periods, Greek influences, especially neo-Platonism, became increasingly important, as we shall see in the chapters which follow.

4

Greek Input, Platonism:

Clement of Alexandria, Origen

We have noted that the Christian Church was sometimes regarded in the ancient world as a 'third nation', somewhere between Jews and pagans. I have been arguing that Christian mysticism can be traced back to Jewish roots, but in its developed form it owes much to Greek influences, and these appeared quite early. The Jews, scattered as they were across the Roman Empire, had already been subject to a measure of Hellenization, and though they resisted attempts to introduce elements of pagan religion into Judaism, some educated Jews, especially in the diaspora, were acquainted with Greek philosophy and found it helpful in interpreting their own religion.

This may seem surprising, for early Greek philosophy had a rational and scientific bias, and was critical of the mythologies and stories of the gods which filled the writings of the poets. Quite typical of these early philosophers was Anaxagoras (500–428 BCE), who is credited with having discovered the true cause of eclipses. He was expelled from Athens about the year 450, having been charged with impiety, because he had said that the sun is not a god but a great mass of white-hot rock, as big as the Peloponnesian peninsula of southern Greece. Many other philosophers were materialists, atheists or sophists, generally sceptical about the claims of religion, at least as these were expressed in the current mythology.

But a major change of direction took place in Greek philosophy in the fifth century BCE. This change was effected largely by the teaching of Socrates (470–399 BCE). In the early part of his career, Socrates had followed the prevailing fashion and had studied the natural sciences, but quite soon he shifted his attention to human and especially moral problems. He was not himself a mystic, though he did claim that sometimes he was guided by an inner voice, and it was in response to what he believed to be a commission conveyed through the oracle of Delphi from the god Apollo (whom he sometimes called simply 'God') that he embarked on his main philosophical mission. This was his attempt to persuade the citizens of Athens to concern themselves less with the pursuit of money and status, and to devote themselves rather to the cultivation of the soul; that is to say, to the moral and spiritual aspects of human life. One might say that this counsel of Socrates was very close to a saying of Jesus from more than 400 years later: 'What will it profit them to gain the whole world and forfeit their life?' (Mk 8.36). Such teaching is not likely to be popular among those engaged in commerce, and Socrates finished up like Jesus by being condemned to death for upsetting the established ways of his fellow citizens. By diverting the course of Greek philosophy from Nature to human affairs, Socrates did make it more relevant to the concerns of mystics and theologians.

The trend continued and intensified after Socrates with Plato (428–347 BCE), the greatest of all the Greek philosophers. Since Socrates wrote nothing himself and we know of his teachings mainly through the dialogues of Plato, it is hard to know where the philosophy of Socrates ends and that of Plato begins, and no doubt there was an overlap. We can certainly say that Plato, like Socrates, stressed the importance of the soul, the inward invisible life of the human person. From a Platonist point of view, a human being is primarily defined by the soul, with the body understood as an instrument of the soul or even sometimes as a hindrance to the soul's development. Such a point of view encourages not only mysticism but all forms of spirituality. For Plato, the everyday world of time and space, of bodies and motion, is not the real world or has only a secondary degree of reality. Beyond it is an ideal world, the world of forms, perceived by the mind rather than by the senses. The things of space and time come into being and pass out of being, but the forms are eternal. The soul too seems to have been considered eternal, having pre-existed the birth of the person whose soul it is, and then continuing to exist after the death of that person's body.

The forms, also called ideas, constitute a hierarchy, and at its head is the Form of the Good. This form is for Plato the ultimate reality, and he seems to say that the Good is not only superior to all the other forms but has actually brought them into existence. So we read:

> In the case of science and of truth, it is right to regard both of them as resembling Good, but wrong to regard either of them as identical with Good. The objects of knowledge not only derive from the Good the gift of being known, but are further endowed by it with a real and essential existence; though the Good, far from being identical with real existence, goes beyond being (*epikeinas tes ousias*) in dignity and power.[1]

The passage quoted is admittedly obscure, but seems to make the Form of the Good the ultimate creative Power in the universe. Is the Form of the Good then God? Probably not, for Plato does not appear to think of the Good as having any of the personal characteristics that we normally attribute to God; or, at any rate, to the God of the Bible. We have already seen, however, that the personality or personhood of God is not clear in some of the Christian mystics and even in orthodox trinitarian theology.

Plato himself, like Socrates, should not be called a mystic in an unqualified way, but he was not without mystical tendencies, and shows them most clearly in the dialogue called the *Symposium*. The setting is a banquet, at which some of the participants make speeches in praise of Eros, the god of love. One of the speakers is Socrates, presumably here a spokesman for Plato's own thoughts. Socrates sets forth a progression or ascent in the love of beauty. We proceed from the beauty of one individual form to the beauty of many forms; from concrete manifestations of beauty to the universal beauty exemplified in the many forms; and finally we come to the Form of the Beautiful, to Beauty itself.[2]

Three comments may be made here. First, although in this dialogue the talk is of the Form of the Beautiful, I do not think that this is intended to be something different from the Form of the Good. In Greek, *agathos*, 'good', has very similar connotations to *kalos*, 'beautiful'; and the Greeks had actually a compound word, *kalokagathia*, 'nobility', the combination of beauty and goodness. Second, there is a logical problem here. The Forms of the Good and the Beautiful embrace all the good and beautiful people and things that manifest these qualities by participating in the forms, but are the forms themselves good or beautiful? If so, are we in danger of getting into an infinite regress, in which we predicate forms of forms of forms? I suppose it might be argued that the form concentrates or sums up in itself the good or the beautiful, but it is certainly not clear just what the ontological status of such a form is. I think, however, we are not talking here about God, though possibly about a substitute for God. The ancients were aware of this problem but, so far as I know, had no clear solution for it. Third, the final step in the ascent to the Beautiful itself is said to be different from those that have gone before. It is a vision or intuition. Does this imply that philosophy finally reaches its goal in some mystical ecstatic experience? Many philosophers would be appalled at the very idea (but see below on Plotinus, p. 76).

The Platonist philosophy, teaching that the deepest realities lie beyond the world of sense, that the ascent to these realities is not a purely intellectual exercise but is motivated by passionate love (*eros*) and is drawn upwards by the pull of the Good and the Beautiful, a journey which seems to end in an ecstatic leap at the final step, all this seems to have the marks of mysticism, and characterizes a philosophy which could serve as the basis of a religion hospitable to mystical forms of spirituality. Burkert remarks, 'What mystery priests had sought to make credible in ritual thus becomes the certainty of the highest rationality.'[3]

Burkert uses the expression 'philosophical religion' to designate the new possibilities that were taking the place among many educated Greeks of the discredited mythology of the traditional religion and also of the sceptical philosophies which had already usurped the rule of mythology in the minds of thoughtful students of natural science, of whom I cited Anaxagoras as an illustration. Although I have laid stress on the achievements of Socrates and Plato in this change of direction in Greek philosophy, 'philosophical religion' included elements from Stoicism, Aristotle and other sources. It presented a new and much more acceptable face of pagan culture to Jews and Christians than the traditional Hellenistic religions had done. Both Jews and Christians were implacably opposed to polytheism and to what they regarded as the idolatry accompanying it. But the religious elements in Greek philosophy were of a kind which might be incorporated into the Judeo–Christian stream of faith.

Philo of Alexandria (20 BCE–50 CE), a Jewish thinker of the diaspora, is the best known of those Jewish scholars who brought some of the Greek ideas into relation with the teaching of the Hebrew scriptures. Although he was roughly contemporary with both Jesus and Paul, it was only later that his influence began to be apparent among Christian writers. There has been endless discussion about whether he was known to the author of John's Gospel, and this remains doubtful; but it is probable that his work was known to and used by Justin and the Alexandrian theologians, Clement and Origen. Philo himself tried to tone down the anthropomorphic presentations of God in the Hebrew Bible by allegorical interpretations which help to remove any mythological flavour from the narratives, but possibly his most lasting achievement was his use of the Logos or Word concept. In Greek the noun transliterated as Logos had been used to mean not only 'word' but also 'reason', even in the wide sense of the reason which was supposed to govern the universe. In the Old Testament, the Word of God is a central idea; God spoke his Word at the creation, he sent his Word to the prophets, so it did not demand any revolutionary change to think of the Word as a kind of intermediary between God and the creatures, and even to hypostatize the Word. As I have said above, it is not certain whether Philo's influence is to be seen in the prologue to John's Gospel, where it is declared the Word became flesh, and the Word is equated with Jesus Christ. An example of the use of the concept by Philo himself is his claim that it was the Word which spoke to Moses at the bush. It may be worth recalling, however, that already in the Hebrew text of Exodus it is the angel of the Lord who appears in the bush to Moses (Ex. 3.2).

Justin Martyr (100–165 CE) was a Christian apologist writing about the middle of the second century. He had been born in Palestine and was a pagan philosopher until his conversion to Christianity. He continued to wear the dress of a philosopher after his conversion and opened a Christian school in Rome, where he maintained that Christianity is the true philosophy. But this did not prevent him from being hospitable to the philosophies which he had taught in his earlier days. He went so far as to say that some of the Greek philosophers (he mentioned Socrates and Heraclitus) had been 'Christians before Christ', because 'they lived according to the Word'.[4] Whether or not he learned it from Philo, he was deeply attracted by this concept of the Word or Logos, and believed that all human beings have a share in it. Jesus Christ was the Word incarnate, and accessible to the human race, a 'second God', though this expression is to be understood in a subordinationist, not a polytheistic sense. God the Father is an ineffable mystery, who does not appear on earth but communicates through his Word. 'The ineffable Father of all neither comes to any place, nor walks nor sleeps nor rises, but always remains in his place, acutely seeing and hearing, not with eyes or ears but with a power beyond description.'[5] There does not seem to be much room for an inappropriate anthropomorphism in this conception of God. But I am not saying that Justin himself was an early Christian mystic: I have cited him merely to show that by the middle of the second century, Greek influences which became important for the mystics had already deeply penetrated Christian thought.

Clement of Alexandria (150–215 CE) is believed to have been born in Athens, but moved to Alexandria and became head of the Christian school there about the year 190. We have already had occasion to note his approval of negative theology – we can say what God is not, but not what he is (see above, p. 14). Like Justin, he thought of the Father as virtually unknowable, and accepted both an allegorical interpretation of the Bible and the Logos theology.

His own principal writings comprise three works[6] which acquired a significance for understanding the structure of the mystical path to union with God – 'deification' as it was called by Clement and other Christian writers of his time. The first of the three works is the *Protrepticus* ('Exhortation'), so called from its opening words, 'An exhortation to abandon the impious mysteries of idolatry for adoration of the divine Word and God the Father'. This first work, though it is appreciative of Plato, is mainly negative. It treats of the errors and immoralities of paganism, and exhorts its readers to turn from them to the truths of Christianity. The second work is the *Paedogogus* ('Tutor'), and if we ask 'Who is the Tutor?', Clement answers, 'He is called Jesus. The Word, then, who leads the children to salvation is appropriately called the Tutor or Instructor.' The bulk of the work is taken up with a highly detailed instruction of how the Christian should conduct his moral and social life, even in such ordinary everyday activities as washing and dressing. The third work is called the *Stromata*, also written *Stromateis* ('Miscellanies'), a plural noun meaning something like a patchwork quilt. Clement himself explains the term as 'these notes of ours of varied character, patched together, passing constantly from one thing to another'. This uneven collection extends to over 600 pages in the English translation. It is believed that Clement had the intention of writing a more systematic conclusion to his trilogy, but never got around to it. In addition to the Bible, Clement draws heavily on Philo, the Stoics and Plato in his description of the perfect Christian life. He stresses moral excellence alongside intellectual penetration. Critics have claimed that he relies as much on Greek philosophy as on the Bible, a charge which was later urged against that other great Alexandrian theologian, Origen. He does seem to set as much value on the Stoic virtue of *apatheia* ('equanimity') as he does on love or charity. The Christian who achieves perfection or, as it might be better expressed, maturity in his faith, is called a 'gnostic', though this word was also applied to adherents of sects that were either non-Christian or heretical from a

Christian point of view. So at this period in Christian history, there was a strong tendency which nowadays most people would think unfortunate, to think of a kind of two-tier Christianity, the true initiates and those still at the learning stage.

Clement was forced to flee from Alexandria during the persecution of the Church in 202. He withdrew to Cappadocia, and died there about 215.

The version of Platonism usually called 'Middle Platonism', which we have met in Justin and Clement, continued to exercise a strong influence in Alexandrian Christianity, and is very evident in the man who became not only the greatest of the Alexandrian theologians, but one of the outstanding figures of the whole patristic period. This was Origen (185–254 CE). He was probably a native of Alexandria and had been brought up as a Christian. The young Origen was zealous in his Christian faith, even to the point of seeking martyrdom in the persecution that had driven Clement out of Alexandria, and in which Origen's own father was killed. At some point, Origen studied philosophy, possibly under a distinguished teacher of those days, Ammonius Saccas, whom we shall meet again at a later time when he was tutor of Plotinus. At some time after Clement had left Alexandria, the bishop invited Origen to become head of the Christian school.

This was a time when many educated pagans were turning away from the old religion and embracing a philosophical faith which looked to such teachers as Socrates and Plato. Origen followed the example of Clement in seeking to reach the educated classes, and in believing that to use the idiom of Platonism was the most hopeful way of establishing a channel of communication with them. Much of Platonism Origen believed to be acceptable and compatible with Christianity. Such, for instance, was the Platonist idea of God as an incorporeal Being beyond space and time, not contained in

the created order but containing it, and so in a sense immanent within it while at the same time transcending it. The
Word or Logos is distinct but not separate from the Father, a
second God not in a numerical but in a subordinationist
sense: for instance, one should not pray to the Word or Son,
but only to the Father through the Son. The finite rational
beings are created by the Father, but, as in Plato, they have
existed from the beginning. For some reason not explained,
the rational souls have fallen away from the Father, with the
lone exception of Jesus Christ. In him the Word is incarnate,
and through him the souls are on pilgrimage back to the
Father from whom they came. It is not clear just how the
souls are helped on their pilgrimage by the incarnation of the
Word. The suggestion seems to be that just as the souls were
free to fall away, so they are free to return to God. Even in
their fallen condition, the souls retain their freedom. Such a
view would have been regarded as Pelagian by later orthodoxy.
It does seem to take too optimistic a view of human willpower
in the face of temptation. On the other hand, if it is claimed
that the human race has completely lost its freedom of choice,
the alternative to Origen's view would seem to be an oppres-
sive doctrine of original sin with an accompanying fatalistic
creed of predestination, such as we find in Augustine and
later in Calvin. Origen was right to defend the belief that
freedom is an inalienable part of the human constitution, but
wrong in not recognizing the necessity for the assistance of
divine grace and of searching for a compromise in some form
of synergism. But while he may have passed over some of the
problems too quickly, Origen was surely right in holding to
the hope that all the souls that God has created will eventually
reach their goal in a universal salvation, the doctrine known
as apocatastasis. That final goal is understood not just as
restoration, the reinstatement of the *status quo*, but as a new
relationship from which there can be no falling away.

Some of the concessions made to Platonism by Origen, such as the pre-existence of finite eternal souls, their power to ascend to the Father by their own efforts, the universality of salvation, roused opposition to his teaching even in his own lifetime, and the attacks against his teaching continued sporadically until his views were condemned at the Fifth General Council (Constantinople II) in 553.

We may think that Origen was unfairly condemned, and that a more sympathetic reading of him is possible and desirable. If we turn from his theological to his spiritual writings, we may get a more balanced picture. It is true that in his treatise on prayer he states the view mentioned above, that prayer should be directed only to the Father, who is God in himself, and not to the Son, who is begotten of the Father. Most of the Church's prayers are in fact directed to the Father through the Son, but the Church has not read into this practice the doctrine that the Son is subordinate to the Father. I think the very fact that Origen attaches importance to prayer calls in question the accusation that he believes that the human soul ascends to God by its own unaided volition. There is an acknowledged synergism here.

This synergism, based on mutual love, becomes clearer if we consider another spiritual work of Origen, his *Commentary on the Song of Songs*. Like some other mystics, Origen saw in this Old Testament scripture an allegory of the love between God and the human race, including both human beings in their solidarity and in their individuality. He begins his commentary as follows:

> This book (*Solomon's Song*) seems to me an epithalamium, that is, a wedding song, written by Solomon in the form of a play, which he recited in the character of a bride who was being married and who burned with a heavenly love for her bridegroom, who is the Word of God. [Possibly it

is unnecessary to interject at this point that in the language of the mystics, the human soul, whether it be that of a man or a woman, is always treated as feminine; the soul is the bride, the bridegroom is God or Christ.] For whether she is the soul made after his image, or the Church, she has fallen deeply in love with him.[7]

Origen is well aware that using erotic language about the love between the divine and the human is a dangerous procedure, which can easily be trivialized or even perverted in a way which drags down the love of God (the expression to be understood as both objective and subjective genitive) to unworthy levels. He gave it as his opinion that only mature Christians (gnostics, in the sense in which Clement used the word, see above, pp. 69–70), should be allowed to read the *Song of Songs*. On the other hand, there is nothing in our earthly experience so deep or so instructive about what is meant by 'mutual indwelling' as the marriage relation between a man and a woman. The Bible itself talks of them becoming 'one flesh' (Gen. 2.24 and Mk 10.8). Perhaps, however, Origen was going a little too far when he comments on *Song* 5.8 which he takes to mean that the soul is wounded by a dart or arrow, an allusion to the mythological figure of Eros (Cupid) in classical pagan lore, who inspired love in people by shooting them with his dart.[8] It is quite possible that it was this passage in Origen which inspired Bernini to create his famous sculpture in which a decidedly impish Eros, masquerading as an angel, is piercing the body of Teresa of Avila with the arrow of divine love (see below, p. 172). Origen certainly roused the wrath of the Swedish theologian Anders Nygren, who accused him of mixing pagan *eros* (desirous love) with Christian *agape* (disinterested love), and more generally of exalting Platonism at the expense of Christianity.[9] I think that Origen in his writing clearly distinguishes the different forms of love, and on the more general question, I find Nygren's exclusiveness less attractive than the tolerance of Origen, who writes elsewhere: 'We are careful not to raise objections to any good teachings, even if their authors are outside the faith.'[10]

Around the year 230 Origen fell out with the bishop in Alexandria, and removed to Caesarea in Palestine. There he founded a Christian school, where he continued his teaching and writing. In the persecution of the Church which took place in the year 250, he was roughly handled, and died in 254.

Origen has continued to have his admirers in the Church and they can point to his work in biblical studies, both in textual criticism (the *Hexapla*) and in hermeneutics (his continuation and extension of the allegorical method of interpretation which he took over from Clement). One would mention also such a work as his *Contra Celsum*, in which he vigorously defended Christian teaching against pagan criticism. His own claim was, 'I wish to be a man of the Church, not the founder of heresy.'[11]

Origen was definitely more of a mystic or – better expressed – had stronger mystical tendencies than either Justin or Clement. But following his advice about profiting from any good teaching, even if it comes from a non-Christian source, let us move on to Plotinus, whose so-called neo-Platonism was to become an all-pervading influence in Christian mysticism and to continue as such for centuries.

5

Greek Input, Neo-Platonism:

Gregory of Nyssa, Augustine of Hippo, Dionysius the Areopagite

We have seen how, in the thought of the great Alexandrian theologians, Clement and Origen, the influence of Plato on Christian theology and spirituality had been very considerable. But although there were complaints about this from those Christians who wanted to hold strictly to the Bible and resist the encroachment of non-Christian influences, Clement and Origen were themselves men of the Bible, and a reasonable judgement might be that they had not gone too far in their incorporation of Hellenistic ideas, especially if this made easier the communication of Christian teaching to the pagan world. But from the third century onward, a new wave of Hellenistic philosophy came sweeping into the Church and brought deeper changes in Christian spirituality: changes which were more controversial than those introduced by Clement and Origen. This new wave is known as neo-Platonism, though, as we shall see, it was much more than a revision of the teachings of Plato himself. Its effects were so profound and long lasting that we must spend a little time in examining its teaching before we consider its impact on Christian mysticism.

The founder of this new philosophy was Plotinus (205–270

CE), a thinker probably worthy to be ranked alongside Plato and Aristotle in the history of classical philosophy. He was about twenty years younger than Origen, and scholars have speculated that they may both have been students of Ammonius Saccas, though clearly at different times, But while Origen became a Christian theologian, Plotinus stayed with philosophy, and never mentions Christianity, though he could hardly have been unaware of it. He was a philosopher who was also a mystic, and one for whom the philosophical quest reaches its goal in an ecstatic experience. According to his biographer, Porphyry, Plotinus had this ecstatic experience four times in his career. But Plotinus himself does not mention this, which suggests that like other great mystics, he did not wish to overrate the high moments in the mystic life.

He was born in the city of Lycopolis in Egypt. He seems to have been one of those persons who mature only later in life, for he is said to have studied at length for eleven years under Ammonius Saccas and then travelled in the East before opening a school in Rome. He was over fifty when he began to write, but from then his ideas flowed freely. After his death in 270, his biographer and former student, Porphyry, collected his writings and published them in six books, each one containing nine treatises. The complete work is known as the *Enneads* ('groups of nine').

Although the philosophy created by Plotinus is called neo-Platonism, it is much more than a recycling of Plato's ideas: it draws on the whole legacy of Greek thought and, in the words of the leading expert on Plotinus, A. H. Armstrong, he was 'an original genius of the first rank'.[1]

Plotinus envisages a hierarchy of being, of which the head and centre is the One. It might be called the Absolute in other philosophies. Plotinus thinks of the One as not just numerical unity, but as an all-embracing unity, in which everything is related to everything else. Everything affects everything else, and in turn is affected by everything else. But just as the One is not simply numerically one, so it is not simply the unity of all things. Plotinus is not a pantheist, though he has been so regarded by some critics. The One is not only the unity of all things, but also the author of all things, not in the sense of a Creator external to his creation, but in the sense that all that exists has emanated from the One and therefore in some way has received from the One something of his or its own substance. I have argued that there is not a hard and fast distinction between creation and emanation, and pointed out that in the second account of creation in the Book of Genesis, God breathes his own breath into the body of the man. Some Christian mystics have held that there is a 'spark' of the divine in the human soul. Such language has been discouraged as tending towards pantheism, yet how could there be any affinity between God and man were there not something of the divine being in the human constitution? All Christians accept that there is in the human being something of the image of God, even if it is acknowledged that the image has been sadly marred by sin. Most mystics, it seems to me, have been right in trying to hold together the two opposing characteristics of transcendence and immanence in God. In some respects he is 'wholly other', the Infinite as opposed to the finite; in other respects, he is, to use again words quoted earlier from the Koran, closer than one's jugular vein. If one is tempted to call Plotinus a pantheist, others have taken his words about the unknowableness of the One to mean a being so distant that he or she or it could have no significance for human life.

We may be inclined to say that in Plotinus' thought, the One is ultimate Being, but he tells us that unity is prior to being. He points out that the objects which we know in the world already appear to us as unities, and argues that 'if unity is necessary to the substantial existence of all that is, unity must precede being and be its author'.[2] Plotinus was a dialectical thinker and here he is concerned to do justice to the facts of unity and multiplicity in the world, which would be unintelligible if it were either an undifferentiated unity or a sheer multiplicity of unrelated particulars.

In putting the One at the very heart of reality, is not Plotinus moving towards the biblical idea of God? One of the major affirmations of the Hebrew scriptures is: 'Hear, O Israel! The LORD is our God, the LORD alone' (Deut. 6.4). But the 'one God' of the Bible is one in a numerical sense, as against the polytheism of the pagans. In any case, the nameless One of Plotinus could not be identified with the personal, even anthropomorphic God of the Hebrew scriptures.

Plotinus himself states clearly that the One is not God. But this does not mean that there is no God in his scheme of things. The One, we must remember, is the Source from which comes a whole series of emanations. Plotinus is not a monist, if that means positing an eternal unchangeable Absolute, alongside which everything else is unreal or illusory. The emanations from the One are real, including matter itself, though their reality is of a lower order than that of the One.

The two highest emanations, called respectively Mind (*Nous*) and Soul (*Psyche*) are divine, and together with the One constitute a Triad, which is God in Plotinus' philosophy. Immediately this mention of a Triad invites comparison with the Christian doctrine of the Trinity or the triune God, the God who is one in three and three in one. Plotinus does not suggest that the members of his Triad are related so closely as the persons of the Christian Trinity, but it is clear that comparisons can be made. The One, as the Source from whom the Mind and the Soul emanate, could, if we leave aside for the moment the impersonal language, be equated with the Father, who begets the Son and from whom the Spirit proceeds. The Mind certainly invites comparison with the Son, understood as the Logos. The Soul likewise has a resemblance to the Holy Spirit, understood as a pervasive immanent presence. There is no question here of a borrowing, either by Plotinus from Christianity, which he never mentions, or by Christians from Plotinus. I have claimed elsewhere[3] that the doctrine of a triune God or at least of a threefold God belongs to natural rather than to revealed theology, and it is a simple fact that it is found not only in Christianity and in neo-Platonism, but in other religious or philosophical ideas of God as well.

In this connection, it may be of interest to mention that although Plotinus does not mention Christianity, he does make a comparison between the One and the supreme gods of the Greek pantheon. In classical times, the supreme God was Zeus, equated with the World-soul; but according to the mythology, this had not always been the case. Before Zeus, Kronos had ruled the universe in an age of gold, and this was the age of Mind, of the realm of ideas before they fell into time and space and matter. Before Kronos, the supreme ruler was Ouranos. Now *ouranos* is the Greek word for 'sky', so Ouranos is the archetypal One, the nameless undifferentiated ineffable Source, symbolized by the open and infinite sky.[4] So here, we are touching again on an idea which we met quite early in our discussion of mysticism. I remarked then that it pushes the idea of ineffability to its utmost limit, and perhaps mysticism to its limit also. This idea is found in a few (presumably unorthodox) Christian mystics, and in Buddhism (see above, pp. 15–16).

Something more needs to be said about the two great emanations, Mind and Soul. We could say that with the emanation of Mind, the treasures that lay buried in a formless undifferentiated state in the One are brought out into the light of intelligible forms. The unity has not been destroyed, but it is now the unity of an ordered cosmos. This is not yet the sensible or material cosmos, but a cosmos perceived intellectually in a manner analogous to the way in which our senses perceive the material world. Soul is inferior to Mind which grasps everything intuitively and simultaneously, whereas Soul proceeds discursively from one thing to another. Soul seems to be immanent in everything, though in plants and animals it would be better called simply 'life'. Whether soul is present even in dead matter is doubtful. Such matter is far down on the scale of reality, and the great gap between matter and the higher emanations is another reason for denying that Plotinus could be called a pantheist.

Why, it might be asked, would the One send out these emanations? Two reasons are given by Plotinus. The first is that 'the One must not be solely the solitary, for if it were, reality would remain buried and formless, since in the One there is no differentiation of forms'.[5] The One would remain dark and totally unknown if it did not go out of itself. This reason is important, since it seems to contradict Plotinus' own phrase about 'the flight of the alone to the Alone'[6] (see above, p. 22). Ironically, these are about the only words from Plotinus' extensive writings that one ever hears quoted. Yet here he is, telling us that the One must not remain alone. The second reason is related to the first. 'Seeking nothing, possessing nothing, lacking nothing, the One is perfect, and, in our metaphor, has overflowed, and its exuberance has produced the new. This product has turned again to its begetter and been filled and become its contemplator.'[7] In other words, even if one is speaking only metaphorically, one must say that the One is generous and giving towards the beings it has brought forth.

So where is the human being in this complex metaphysic? Like everything else, he or she has come forth from the One, and the highest aim must be to return to the One. This he must do by rising above the lure of the material and sensible to the region of Mind, and finally, by a mystical leap, to union with the One. We have already noted that Plotinus himself accomplished this leap four times.

By our standards, ideas spread slowly in the centuries before the advent of printed books. The writings of Plotinus, probably composed in the two decades from 250 to 270 CE, do not begin to show their influence in Christian mysticism until about a century later, though once that influence began, it became very extensive. After all, here was a philosopher not only sympathetic to the mystic quest, but apparently a mystic himself!

Gregory of Nyssa (330–395 CE) was one of the earliest Christian mystics to show fairly definite signs of the influence of Plotinian philosophy.[8] However, he is best regarded as an intermediate figure between middle Platonism and neo-Platonism. Thus, as was mentioned in the last chapter, his teaching remains close to that of Origen.

In 371, he was consecrated Bishop of Nyssa, though he was driven out of the diocese by the Arians in 376, returning two years later. He became a widely respected figure in the Church, taking part in its councils. We should remember too that Gregory is the first mystic considered in this book who lived after Constantine had established Christianity as the official religion of the Roman Empire, so that there was now no persecution and there were many new converts to Christianity. These new converts included people with a knowledge of classical religion and philosophy, but with probably only a vague understanding of Judaism and Christianity. Gregory was seeking to speak to this new swath of Church members as well as to those who had a longer history of membership, and this situation demanded that he should use the language and concepts of Hellenistic culture. He died about 395.

The work which best shows his mystical side is his *Life of Moses*. More than twenty years ago, I attended a seminar devoted to the study of this work guided by three eminent

Oxford scholars of the time, and I still remember the impression it made on me. To write a life of Moses was nothing new in Gregory's time. Others, including both Philo and Origen, had written such lives before him. Moses was, in those days, a fascinating figure and was regarded as the paragon of virtue. But a *Life of Moses* was understood in a way different from how we would understand it today. We would expect of a history of Moses, to be told when he was born and what conditions were like in his time, and then be told about the achievements that make his life worth studying. In a very minor way, this is what was attempted in Chapter 2 of this book. We began by placing Moses in the thirteenth century BCE, then giving a very tentative account of his career, carefully filtering out the legendary elements in the tradition, and paying special attention to what we can still know or at least surmise about those events in his life which might show him as a mystic. That would not be at all the way in which Gregory and others of his time would understand a *Life of Moses*.

Actually, Gregory wrote two lives of Moses. The first part of his work is a history (*historia*) of Moses; that is to say, a narrative of the objective events of his life. It corresponds roughly to the account of Moses given in Chapter 2 of this book, except that since Gregory lived long before the age of science, he accepts the whole account in the Old Testament as veridical, making no attempt to cut out the legendary embellishments. The second part of the work is a contemplation (*theoria*) in which Gregory attempts to go behind the literal sense of the biblical story to the allegorical or mystical meanings, which for him constitute the value of the story. Every episode and every person or item mentioned in the episodes is given a spiritual meaning. This style of exegesis is mystical in a double sense – it reaches beyond the obvious meaning of the words to find a hidden, spiritual meaning, and what is required for this task is contemplation (*theoria*). For instance, the Egyptian princess who takes Moses into her household represents pagan philosophy, assumed to have been taught to Moses in his early life. Such philosophy, Gregory tells us, is barren.[9] Yet, like Justin and Origen, Gregory remains ambiguous about pagan philosophy. It can sometimes be helpful in the quest for the right way of life, but sometimes misleading. So, for example, it teaches that the soul is immortal (correct) but teaches also that the soul migrates from one body to another (incorrect).[10]

When Moses kills the Egyptian, that is his victory over idolatry. When he flees to Midian and takes up the work of shepherding there, that is his adoption of the solitary contemplative life. Gregory tells us that Moses' quiet peaceful occupation was the prelude to his mystical encounter at the bush, but I would rather believe my own account in Chapter 2 that Moses was assailed by doubt and self-questioning, though in either case this can be only speculation. Incidentally, in my account of Moses, I placed most of the emphasis on his experience at the burning bush. Gregory does indeed recognize the importance of that experience, but he places more weight on Moses' return to Sinai after the liberation of the people from Egypt. Perhaps he thinks that Moses needed more experience and more conflict before he would be able to go further in his ascent to God, for, says Gregory, 'the knowledge of God (*theologia*) is a mountain, steep indeed and difficult to climb – the majority of people scarcely reach its base'.[11] The multitude of the Hebrews was not able to go up into the mountain, but had to rely on Moses to bring to them what he had learned of God and God's will for his people.

Gregory then goes on to make some interesting and highly mystical remarks about the encounter with God at the giving of the law, and how it compares with the earlier encounter at the bush. He asks:

What does it mean to say that Moses entered the darkness and then saw God in it? (Ex. 20.21). What is now recounted seems somehow to be contradictory to the first theophany, for then the Divine was seen in light and now he is seen in darkness. Scripture teaches by this that religious knowledge comes at first as light. But as the mind progresses and, through an ever greater and more perfect diligence, comes to apprehend reality, as it approaches more nearly to contemplation, it sees more clearly what of the divine nature remains uncontemplated. For, leaving behind everything that is observed, not only what sense comprehends, but also what the intelligence thinks it sees, it keeps on penetrating more deeply, until by the intelligence's yearning for understanding, it gains access to the invisible and incomprehensible, and there it sees God. This is the true knowledge of what is sought; this is the seeing that consists in not seeing.[12]

Gregory is talking here of the inaccessibility of the depth of God, and of the limitless nature of the exploration into God. This is one of the points where Gregory differs from Origen, who thought that the end of the exploration is a static perfection. Gregory has a much more dynamic view of the matter, and about this I shall say more later. But first I shall try to make more acceptable the paradoxes in what Gregory says about our knowledge of God being at the same time an ignorance, and our seeing of God a not seeing. The more we learn of God, the more we realize that there is still more to learn. I think we get some idea of this in our relations with other human beings. We think we know someone we love, yet we are always discovering fresh truths about that person, such as deepen our love still more. As for the vision of God – and we remember that the Bible itself is somewhat ambiguous on this subject (see above, pp. 7–9) – Gregory says, 'This truly is the vision of God: never to be satisfied in the desire to see him. One must always, by looking at what he can see, rekindle the desire to see more.'[13]

I shall not follow in detail Gregory's further mystical interpretations, of the tabernacle, of the priestly vestments, of the stone tables and so on. We have seen enough to show that for Gregory the *Life of Moses* could never be adequately expressed in an objective history, however accurate. Partly from the scriptural traditions about Moses, which Gregory did not doubt had a factual historical basis, and partly from the Platonist and neo-Platonist teaching that the reality with which we have to deal is to be sought beyond the sensible appearances, Gregory, almost anticipating some of the post-modernists of the twenty-first century, has moved from historical research to the text itself as the reality of the *Life of Moses*, namely, as a guide for human beings who are searching for the path to moral and spiritual fulfilment.

What is most distinctive in Gregory's treatise is his belief that perfection is not a static goal to be reached and then simply maintained, but a dynamic and never-ending progression in virtue. 'The perfection of human nature', he tells us, 'consists perhaps in its very growth in goodness.'[14] God is goodness, but God is infinite, so there can be no bound to goodness. There is an echo here of Plotinus: 'Truly, when you cannot grasp the form or shape of what is longed for, it would be most longed for and most lovable, and love for it would be immeasurable. For love is not limited here, because neither is the beloved, but the love of this would be unbounded.'[15]

Undoubtedly the most famous of all Plotinus' Christian admirers was Augustine, later bishop of Hippo and a Doctor of the Church. Peter Brown tells us that in the last days of Augustine, when his diocese was being ravaged by hordes of Vandals, 'in the midst of these evils he was comforted by the saying of a certain wise man: "He is no great man who thinks it a great thing that sticks and stones should fall, and that men, who must die, should die."' Brown comments, 'The "certain wise man" is, of course, Plotinus. Augustine, the Catholic bishop, will retire to his deathbed with these words of a proud pagan sage.'[16]

Augustine (354–430 CE) was born in Thagaste, in modern Algeria, of a pagan father and a Christian mother, Monica. His mother was able to ensure that he received a Christian upbringing but he drifted away from the faith and became a Manichaean. For about ten years he taught in Carthage, Rome and Milan, but became disillusioned with Manichaeism and dissatisfied with his own spiritual condition. It was at this time that he was influenced by the sermons of Ambrose, bishop of Milan, and that he obtained 'certain books' of the Platonists and came to admire the philosophy of Plotinus.

This state of mind culminated in his conversion or reconversion to Christianity in 386. He returned to Africa and about 395 was consecrated, first as coadjutor and later as diocesan bishop of Hippo. The process of conversion from being a disciple of Mani to becoming a bishop of the Church was a complex one, a progression through Manichaeism, neo-Platonism and finally Christianity. I think also that one would have to say that some elements of each stage remained in the one which followed. Thus something of Manichaean dualism continued, in Augustine's doctrine of original sin and his belief in double predestination. Something of neo-Platonism remained in his mysticism and his vision of God.

But the usual question arises – was Augustine truly a mystic? I return the usual answer: Augustine had many roles – theologian, bishop, teacher and writer, ecclesiastic and so on – but no one could read his *Confessions* without acknowledging that there was in this man a powerful mystical drive, which probably motivated and sustained his many activities in different fields.

'Thou hast made us for thyself, and our hearts are restless until they rest in thee'.[17] These often-quoted words of Augustine, taken from the first paragraph of his *Confessions*, already express the heart of his spirituality, and indeed of his entire life and work. There is something at the very centre of a human being that keeps him or her in what I previously called a state of *Angst* until that person finds a right relationship to God. But where does one look, in order to find that relationship?

Augustine, more clearly than any of the mystics or quasi-mystics we have studied so far, insists on the close relation between knowledge of God and self-knowledge; or, to say the same thing in a different way, of the need to turn inward in the search for God (see above, pp. 16–18, where I cited Augustine as a clear example of this inward quest). Dissatisfaction with the teachings of Mani came at the time when Augustine was discovering Plotinus and other thinkers in the Greek tradition. He seems to have entered quite deeply into neo-Platonism, and we have noted that at the end of his life he had kind words for this pagan philosopher. Of the neo-Platonists generally, he says, 'I was warned of them to return to myself; so I entered into my inmost soul under thy (i.e., God's) guidance, thy help enabled me to do so' (see above, p. 17). But it seems that the spiritual stimulus which he had received was transient. Kenneth Kirk comments: 'It was the failure to sustain the high neo-Platonic experience of the vision of God which first turned Augustine's mind seriously to the person of Christ.'[18] Perhaps Augustine was too human, too earthly, to be at home in the highly other-worldly regions of Plotinus. In Augustine's own words, 'I read there that God the Word (Logos) was born not of flesh, nor of blood, nor of the will of man, nor of the will of the flesh, but of God. But that the "Word was made flesh and dwelt among us", I read not there',[19] and 'we might think that thy word was removed from union with man, and despair of ourselves had he not been "made flesh and dwelt among us"'.[20] So the doctrine of incarnation finally brings the former Manichean from his neo-Platonist phase into the full Christian faith, to fulfilment not only as a bishop and one of the four great Doctors of the Church, but as one of the great Christians of all times.

That Augustine owed much to Plotinus and to Greek philosophy, and that he continued even after having become a Christian to respect Plotinus, is something that cannot be denied and ought not to be denied. But Augustine does make clear that he believed Christianity to be (if I may so speak) an advance on the Platonist tradition. When he says that though he found a doctrine of the Logos in the philosophers, but then complained that he did not find the doctrine that the Logos was made flesh, we may think it surprising that he even looked for a doctrine of incarnation there. In Plotinus' view, matter ranked so low in the hierarchy of being that an incarnation would be unthinkable. That may explain why he never discusses Christianity, for its central assertion would seem to him absurd. In later generations of neo-Platonists, thinkers such as Porphyry, Iamblichus and Proclus were indifferent or even hostile to Christianity, and the Emperor Julian the Apostate claimed to be a neo-Platonist. Whatever his debt to Plotinus, Augustine's spirituality relies principally on the Bible and Christian tradition, and he himself gives it an intellectual foundation in his great theological writings.

One further point may be made before we leave Augustine. We have seen that he is one of those mystics for whom knowledge of God and knowledge of self are closely related, so closely that it is by withdrawing into the depths of the self that one comes to encounter God. The great danger arises of confusing self and God. I think Augustine kept well away from such an error. There is nothing here that might suggest that the human soul contains a 'spark', as it has been called, of divinity. There is indeed an affinity between God and humans, and it is for this reason that the human heart is restless until it finds rest in God. The language about a spark brings us very close to pantheism, but Augustine is very clear that in entering into his own inner soul, he saw a light which was 'above me because it had made me, and I was below because I was made by it' (see above, p. 17). My own view is that what Augustine is saying here could be expressed by an adequate theological concept of conscience as the link between human self-knowledge and the awareness of the legacy of the divine image in humanity.

We conclude this chapter by considering a very different exponent of the neo-Platonist interpretation of Christian faith, Dionysius the Areopagite (460–520 CE). It has to be admitted at once that the name given is a pseudonym and the dates highly speculative. The original Dionysius the Areopagite gets a bare mention in Acts 17.34 as an Athenian citizen who became a Christian believer in response to Paul's preaching in the city, and there is a tradition that he became the first bishop of Athens. Beyond that, nothing is known about him. However, there exists a body of Christian writings claiming Dionysius the Areopagite as its author. The said writings bear unmistakable evidence of having been written around the year 500. The name of Dionysius is a pseudonym, and the real name of the author is unknown. It is commonly believed that he was a Syrian monk. The fact that he quotes the neo-Platonist philosopher Proclus, who died in 485, and that Dionysius himself was being quoted at a colloquy in 533, is the basis for dating his work around 500. No stigma attached in those days to writing under the name of a well-known personage, but there can be no doubt that the immense influence which this particular writer came to have in the Church, especially in its spirituality, was due to the belief that he was a disciple of Paul himself. The rise of historical criticism led to suspicion about the claim that the writings go back to the time of Paul, and probably no serious scholar accepts that ascription nowadays. However, Dionysius, as we may call him, is now judged on his merits, without the help he may have got from the alleged association with Paul, and altogether apart from that association, he is recognized as an able defender and expounder of perhaps the dominant form of Christian mysticism.

Of his writings, two are of special interest for our own purpose: *The Divine Names*, which takes up the question of how we can venture to speak of God; and *The Mystical Theology*, which is concerned primarily with the doctrine of God.

Of the mystics we have so far considered, Dionysius is the one who takes most seriously the apophatic aspect of mysticism, the recognition that the depth and otherness of God make it quite impossible to speak of him in the straightforward literal language which we use in talking of the sensible world. *The Divine Names* is a bold and at the same time subtle attempt to come to terms with the ineffability of God. The problem of theological language is still with us, and has in fact been very much to the fore in recent times, because of the linguistic turn of philosophy in the twentieth century. Paul Tillich is a theologian of our time who devoted much attention to the question of language about God, but I believe there is very little in Tillich's treatment of the matter that was not anticipated by Dionysius. In his *Systematic Theology*, Tillich declares that the only literal statement we can make about God is that he is Being itself, and latterly he appeared to doubt that even this is a literal statement. All else that we say about God is symbolic. Only grudgingly did Tillich acknowledge his debt to Dionysius, saying that 'perhaps [he] was the source – unconsciously – of what I wrote at the end of my book, *The Courage to Be*, about the God above God who is the real ground of everything that is, who is above every special name we can give to even the highest Being'.[21] At any rate, Dionysius went surely to the limit in his attempt to marry Plotinian neo-Platonism and Christian theology.

In what he says about God, Dionysius purges his language of anything that might savour of anthropomorphism or even of personality. He avoids the very word 'God', preferring to speak of the 'Thearchy', an impersonal expression which we might compare with the 'Absolute', as used by many philosophers and some theologians during the Hegelian ascendancy, because traditional God-talk was too much contaminated by popular humanist and personalist associations. While this kind of language has its appeal for philosophically minded theologians, including the present writer, it tends to be anathema to those theologians who try to keep as close as possible to the Bible, even in matters of language.

Dionysius' translator and editor, C. E. Rolt, who is also his sturdy defender, justifies his use of impersonal language thus:

> Personality consists in the faculty of knowing oneself to be one individual among others. By its very nature, personality is a finite thing. The very essence of my personal state lies in the fact that I am not the whole universe but a member thereof. God, on the other hand, is suprapersonal because he is infinite. He is not one being among others, but in his ultimate nature dwells on a plane where there is nothing whatever beyond himself.[22]

I am not myself persuaded by this argument, and the ideas behind it will come up again. Rolt ignores the fact that a person is not an isolated individual, but is a person only in relation to other persons. As regards God (or the Thearchy), it is hard to know whether he is being presented here in pantheistic terms as simply the All, the Universe, or, on the other hand, as completely transcendent and 'other'. I have always held that God is both transcendent and immanent, but it is hard to see how that could be true if we accept Rolt's interpretation of Dionysius.

But what does Dionysius himself say? He distinguishes three ways of thinking and talking about God. These are the cataphatic way, the apophatic way, and the symbolic way. Let us briefly consider these three ways.

The *cataphatic* way is the descending way. It is so called because it reads the character of God from the created world; that is to say, from the created beings that have come down or come forth from the hidden reality of God. Although God is so far above the created order, he does not remain wholly unknown. The divine reality 'lovingly reveals itself by illumi-nations corresponding to each separate creature's powers, and thus draws upwards holy minds into such contemplation, participation and resemblance to itself as they can attain'.[23] This is God as we talk about him in terms of our everyday human experience in the world, and as the Bible talks about him – God as good, God as light, God as life, and so on. These are names of God sanctioned by scripture, and we should according to Dionysius confine ourselves to these scriptural descriptions. Even as God has come out of himself into a world, so he has also granted through that world such understanding of himself as finite minds can grasp.

But over against this popular way of thinking about God has to be set the *apophatic* or *negative* way. God is unique and incomprehensible in his essence, and none of these descrip-tions can be taken literally. They point to an ineffable mystery, and each description has to be denied as well as affirmed.

Furthermore, Dionysius seems to place the denial above the affirmation. This is a moment when Christian and Indian mysticism seem to touch: God is not this, not that.

Dionysius is very fond of the Greek prefix *hyper*, meaning 'above' or 'beyond'. Thus, God, or strictly speaking, the Thearchy, is 'above intellect' *(hyper noun)*, 'above being' *(hyperousia)*, even 'above deity' *(hypertheotetos)*. No words ever catch up with him or it.

The negation is not just simple denial, but is meant to point beyond the affirmation to a mystery which is itself inexpressible on our level of thought and language. So here we come to a point that we have already met in Gregory of Nyssa – that the more we learn of God, the more, so to speak, we realize that our knowing is an unknowing and that the light gives way to a divine darkness. But the unknowing is not sheer ignorance, and the darkness is the brilliance of a light beyond our power to endure.

The two opposing ways are resolved in a *symbolic* theology, and it is here that Dionysius provided a basis for God-talk long before Tillich or any other of our modern theologians. We are invited to enter on a critical study of religious symbolism.

Dionysius sees this criticism as a stripping down of the images of God derived from the cataphatic way, even those which are allowed in the Bible, so that as the soul gets nearer to God, it recognizes more strongly the ultimate inaccessibility of the divine depth. He notes that there are two kinds of symbols, both to be found in the Bible. Some symbols, such as light and life, are themselves such exalted entities that we mistake them for God himself and so fall into idolatry. It is important not to be stuck at the symbol, but to see it as always pointing beyond itself. So one might prefer a symbol less obviously suggestive of God, and even apparently remote from God. He does not give an example, but I wonder if he may have had the cross in mind. It certainly needed, and still needs, a revolution in our common conceptions of God to see him in the crucified Lord. Dionysius likens the criticism of symbols to a comparison which goes right back to Plato. It is like the work of the sculptor who chips away the marble and removes 'all the impediments that hinder the clear perception of the latent image, and by this mere removal displays the hidden statue in its hidden beauty'.[24]

This consideration of the stages in reaching a deeper understanding of God can be seen also as stages in the ascent of the soul to God in the mystical life. Already in Clement of Alexandria (see above, pp. 68–9), we met an early version of the threefold mystic way that was later described in terms of purgation, illumination and union. This description is now clearly stated by Dionysius, but his order is different. Purgation appears to come in the middle, between illumination and the final union. However, the stages were never understood as rigidly successive, and are not so much stages as aspects of a development in which they may alternate or even be simultaneous. Dionysius freely uses the word *theosis* or 'deification' for the final state of union with the divine, though there is the danger of understanding this in a pantheistic way.

Dionysius also wrote a work called *The Celestial Hierarchy*, in which he gives a picture of the universe along the lines of Plotinus; that is to say, with the One as the centre and source, from which emanate a whole series of finite beings. Already in Plotinus the series was conceived as a hierarchy, but this is worked out in much greater detail by Dionysius. In fact, if his name is mentioned nowadays, probably a majority of people would associate it with the nine choirs of angels, spiritual beings who, in his view, constituted levels of existence above the everyday sensible world. We may reject these thoughts of Dionysius as baseless speculation, but he was correct in viewing the universe in a hierarchical way. This is not a popular conception in our egalitarian age, but it is almost certainly correct in claiming that the beings which exist fall into a graded order. There are rational beings, sentient beings, vegetative beings, a whole range of inanimate beings down to the lowliest subatomic particle. The human race has its place in this series, but it also has its own inner drive to transcendence, understood by the mystic as the quest for God. We have to note that Dionysius' hierarchy was not a fixed order but a dynamic one, as it already was in Plotinus. The history of the creation, on this view, is a going out (*exitus*) and a return (*reditus*), God going out into creation, the creatures returning in a synergistic response to God, though presumably it is not just a return to the original state but to an enriched condition. It accords well with the biblical understanding of creation, fall, salvation and final redemption.

Does Dionysius, like Origen and perhaps also Gregory of Nyssa, lay all the stress on the soul's freedom to ascend to God, ignoring the need for grace and divine assistance? I do not think that is how we ought to read him. There is a dramatic passage where he breaks free from Plotinus' contempt for the material world and from any Pelagian idea that human beings are able to achieve salvation of themselves. He writes:

And we must dare to affirm (for it is the truth) that the Creator of the universe himself, in his beautiful and good yearning toward the universe, is through the excessive yearning of his goodness transported outside himself in his providential activities toward all things that have being, and is touched by the sweet spell of goodness, love and yearning, and so is drawn from his transcendent throne above all things to dwell within the heart of all things, through an ecstatic power that is above being and whereby he yet stays within himself.[25]

This passage needs a good deal of exegesis and even disentanglement, but it does seem to show that Dionysius' Thearchy is not quite so remote and impersonal as we might have believed, and that Dionysius is finding a place in his theology for God's self-giving and for incarnation.

6

The Dark Ages:

Maximus Confessor, John of Damascus, John Scotus Eriugena

The so-called Dark Ages cover the second half of the first millennium of our era. The term, first used in the eighteenth century by scholars who called their own age the Enlightenment, is used here in a neutral sense, with no value judgement implied. For myself, who belong to the Celtic fringe of Europe and have my origins in the western islands of Scotland, the sixth century CE must be reckoned a time of light, for it was in 563 that Columba, the apostle of these parts, founded his famous monastery on the island of Iona, where it still stands in a restored condition as a centre of Christian spirituality. Let it be admitted, however, that over much of Europe there was indeed a darkening in this period. In 410 the city of Rome itself had been sacked by the Visigoths, a foretaste of the final collapse of the western Roman Empire in 476. The eastern Empire survived much longer than the western, but was also subject to constant invasions or threats of invasion. Then in the seventh century both east and west were confronted with a new threat from the armies of Islam. Whole provinces in the Near East, in North Africa and even in Spain were taken over by the followers of Muhammad. Christianity, which had been extending its hold throughout the Mediterranean region, was checked, and some of the great Christian centres, such as the city of Alexandria, were permanently lost.

I did say in an earlier chapter that mysticism is more likely to arise among persons who have inner conflicts than only in circumstances where everything is quiet and peaceful, but if there is continuous strife and bloodshed, people become hardened and spiritual growth is slowed or even halted. It is, I think, signficant that in the 500 years or so to be considered in the present chapter, there were very few outstanding mystics, compared with both earlier and later periods. Of course, there are many other forms of spirituality and of Christianity in general besides mysticism, and some of them flourished even in the Dark Ages. I have mentioned already the Celtic Church, and I could mention also Benedict who founded his abbey at Montecassino in 529, or Gregory the Great, an outstanding pope who tried to remodel society in line with Augustine's teaching in *The City of God*. But while both of these men had some mystical tendencies (and I have been maintaining that all religious experience has a mystical component), we would not think of them primarily as mystics. No doubt there were quite a few mystics in the half-millennium we are looking at, but only a handful made lasting contributions to the mystical tradition. I propose to consider three, and I am not quite sure that one of them would qualify as a mystic in the commonly accepted sense of the word.

The first of our three exemplars was, I would say, a genuine mystic, Maximus Confessor (580–662 CE) from the Eastern Church. He was born in Constantinople and when a young man served as an official at the court of the eastern Roman Emperor. In 614 he became a monk in a religious house not far from the capital city, but invasions were being experienced at that time, and he was forced to go elsewhere, living at various times in Crete and North Africa, and coming to Rome in 645. Twice he was arrested, and on the second occasion was brought back to Constantinople and put on trial in 661. The charge was treason, he was found guilty, treated – though a man in his eighties – in the most shamefully brutal fashion and banished from the city. Not surprisingly, he died soon afterwards.

I mention this because, underlying the charge of treason, was a theological dispute. It was a controversy between those who said Christ had one will (monothelitism) and those who said that he had two (dyothelitism). Some years ago I had occasion to write a few paragraphs on Maximus in the course of a book on christology, and while I found some things to admire in his treatment of that subject, I criticized his involvement in the dispute between monothelites and dyothelites.[1] I am still of the opinion that this was an utterly speculative and artificial question, not capable of receiving a rational answer, though in fact the Church did, at the Ecumenical Council of 553 (Constantinople III), nearly twenty years after the decease of Maximus, vindicate his teaching that Christ had two wills.

Those who do attempt to answer the question are guilty of attempting a kind of spiritual anatomy of Christ, in an academic exercise which shows theology at its most irrelevant, both in relation to religion and to serious scholarship. But Maximus was almost obsessively opposed to monothelitism. In spite of his apophatic leanings, he not only opposed the monothelites but equally what was called the *typos*, a compromise document favoured by the Emperor, forbidding further discussion of the subject. Now that I am writing briefly about the spirituality of Maximus, let me say that I do not think this is affected one way or the other by his dyothelite views. If he thought, as he may have done, that he was doing more justice than his opponents to the true humanity of Christ, I would reply that this was already being stressed in his 'second Adam' type of christology. Nothing further is to be gained by introducing speculations about Christ's will or wills.

Although Maximus left quite an impressive corpus of writings, he did not write at length or in a systematic way on any topic, but supplied answers to questions that were asked of him by inquirers, real or imaginary. For instance, his *Four Hundred Chapters* (or *Four Centuries*) *on Love* occupy only about fifty pages of print, and many of the chapters consist of only one or two sentences and do not together form a continuous argument. Much the same is true of his *Two Hundred Chapters on Knowledge*. I am afraid that some of his interpreters who have given us neat summaries of his thought have made it seem more orderly than it actually is. Maximus himself disclaims originality for most of the material in his anthologies, telling us that he culled the sayings from earlier writers or from the Bible itself.

Nevertheless, one idea (though it is not very clearly expressed) which we have not encountered in any of the mystics we have so far considered, deserves our notice. It concerns the Word of God or Logos, so important in most of the mystical writers. The Logos (singular, and spelled with a capital L) is identified with the Son, Jesus Christ. But Maximus believes that every finite creature has its logos, and this may be understood as its 'reason for being'. Every human being, every angel, and perhaps everything in the lower ranks of creation, has its logos. These logoi (plural) are the ends, the completions of their being, set before the finite entities. I think they might also be called 'entelechies', a word used by Aristotle but not used by Maximus. I am encouraged to think that Maximus included the lower creation in his thinking, for he is more positive in his attitude to incarnation and the material world than was Dionysius, who was perhaps the major influence in his philosophizing and theologizing. We did note that Dionysius does have a passage in which he speaks of God's self-emptying in the incarnation, but it seems almost an afterthought in the general body of his teaching (see above, p. 95). In the view of Jaroslav Pelikan, Maximus's principal contribution in both theology and spirituality was his correction of Dionysius by introducing a better balance between neo-Platonism and the biblical tradition.[2]

I have mentioned that Maximus had a more positive attitude towards the sensible and material world than did Dionysius and some other mystics in the Platonist tradition, but he certainly embraced a measure of asceticism, and teaches that the love of God displaces all other loves. It is the pearl of great price, for which the wise man or woman will sell everything else. In a striking simile, he says that the love of God causes finite entities to fade, just as the physical eye has no perception of the stars once the sun has arisen.[3] We may ask of Maximus, as of some other mystics, 'Is your teaching only for those who become monks and nuns?' They can never be more than a small minority. Life is only possible for the human race if the vast majority of people live in the world as mothers and fathers, doctors and pastors, practising some useful profession or trade for the benefit of society. But Maximus believed that he was speaking to a wider audience than monks and nuns. His emphasis on love even of enemies applies in everyday life, just as much as it does in the monastery.

Whether he is entirely successful or not, Maximus certainly means to commend a way of life that will shape the careers of those who live in secular society. This becomes clear in his sacramental interpretation of the material world. It is not to be shunned, for it can nourish the vision of God. One of his writings, which brings together several aspects of his teaching, is entitled *The Church's Mystagogy*. Mystagogy is the interpretation of mysteries. According to Maximus, even the church building can serve the purpose. The nave is the sensible world; the sanctuary is the spiritual world and is mysteriously imprinted on the whole sensible world in symbolic forms. Maximus guides his readers through a celebration of the liturgy as it was in his time, each action being interpreted as a stage in the spiritual life. The goal of the liturgy and of the life of faith is deification (*theosis*), and this means 'becoming as much as possible what God is'.[4] The human person is not purely passive in this progression, which is a genuine synergism.[5]

By restoring a christocentric and incarnational emphasis, Maximus also guarded against the tendency to individualism, so common among the mystics. This is where we see the importance of his distinction between Logos and logoi. In a way which is not clear (and perhaps could not be clear), the Logos in reaching its fullest manifestation in Jesus Christ achieves a universal consummation for the whole creation, a reminiscence of Origen's doctrine of an apocatastasis. This would mean deification for human beings, and a corresponding perfection for the rest of creation.

In introducing this chapter, I said that genuine mystics were scarce in the period 500–1000 CE, that I would discuss only three, and that even one of them might hardly qualify as a mystic, if we define that term too closely. The person I had in mind was John of Damascus (665–749 CE). We think of him primarily as a theologian, a kind of Eastern counterpart to Thomas Aquinas in the West and one who came to be respected in the West as much as in the East, for in 1890 Pope Leo XIII declared him to be a Doctor of the Church. We might compare him to Augustine, likewise primarily a theologian, but one who made an important contribution to mystical spirituality. We shall see also that a notice of John of Damascus follows naturally on what we have learned from Maximus Confessor. John's principal theological work, *The Fount of Wisdom*, followed Maximus in strongly criticizing the monophysite heresy, the doctrine that Christ had only a single divine nature, and its spin-off in monothelitism. Maximus's general strengthening of the emphasis on incarnation and the value of the material world as a creation of God was continued and given a more concrete expression in the teaching of John.

In 635 CE the city of Damascus had ceased to be part of the eastern (and nominally Christian) Roman Empire and came under the sway of Islamic rule. John of Damascus's own grandfather had negotiated the surrender, and John, who had been born and grew up in the city, was given a position in the administration of the Caliph, the new ruler. But he soon left the Caliph's service and entered a monastery in Palestine. It is ironical that John, living under Muslim rule, enjoyed theological freedom, whereas Maximus, in the Christian city of Constantinople, was condemned by his fellow Christians to punishments so cruel that even the most barbarous tribes would be ashamed to inflict.

John, like Maximus, became involved in a theological controversy, but one which, in my opinion, had more substance to it than the dispute between monothelites and dyothelites. The new controversy was over the question of icons. The English word 'icon' is simply an anglicization of the Greek word *eikon*, meaning a 'picture' or 'image'. Paul writes of Jesus Christ that 'he is the image [*eikon*] of the invisible God' (Col. 1.15).

If there is a theme that almost dominates the Old Testament, it is the condemnation of worshipping images of the gods. But in the Christian Church, it was felt that the ban no longer applied. The Word had become flesh, in some sense the very life of God had entered the sensible world in the bodily form of Jesus Christ. In the new religion, it was felt to be permissible and even praiseworthy to make visual representations of Jesus Christ. This activity was both an expression of devotion to him and also a means of awakening devotion. Especially in the Eastern Church, icons began to play a major part in spirituality. The picture, itself a material object, became a focus from which flowed new insights into the understanding of the Jesus of the Gospels. People prayed before the icons or lit candles to honour them. It will be remembered that Maximus had said that the nave of a church represents this earthly world, the sanctuary is the heavenly or spiritual world. In Eastern churches, the sanctuary is screened from view by a partition across the church. This partition is called the iconostasis, because on it are displayed icons or pictures of Jesus and the saints, affording glimpses, as it were, into the spiritual realm.

About the beginning of the eighth century, there arose a strong reaction against the veneration of icons. There were several reasons for this. The monophysite heresy had minimized the humanity of Christ (and this may be some excuse for Maximus and others who engaged in the one-or-two wills controversy); or it may have been the Manichaean view that all matter is evil (and even Augustine had for a time accepted this); or it may have been the new influence of Islam which has from the beginning been resolutely against any visual representation of God or even of Muhammad (for the very birth of Islam may be traced to the dramatic moment when the Prophet entered the Ka'aba and destroyed the images of the old gods of Mecca). In any case, in 726 the Emperor Leo III condemned the use of images and ordered their destruction. He is said to have believed that they were hindering the conversion of Jews and Arabs.

John of Damascus emerged as the leading defender of the icons, and before he wrote his major theological works he had produced three treatises entitled *On the Holy Icons*. He wrote, 'I shall not cease to honour matter, for it was through matter that my salvation came to pass. Do not despise matter, for it is not despicable; nothing is despicable that God has made.'[6]

John's defence of the icons is twofold. First, he rejects the accusation that the respect paid to the icons is a form of idolatry. 'I do not worship matter, but I worship the Creator of matter, who for my sake became material and deigned to dwell in matter, who through matter effected my salvation.'⁷ We human beings cannot live as if we were purely spiritual creatures. We are not and should not make the attempt. That would be the sin of angelism. I think that John's point here would nowadays be extended by many people beyond the Christian faith. Even in the nineteenth century, a popular hymn contained the words: 'The heathen in his blindness bows down to wood and stone'. But the heathen is not so stupid, nor are the Christians who venerate the icons. Second, living in an age when many people were illiterate, John saw the educational value of the icons. 'If a pagan asks you to show him your faith, take him into church and place him before the icons.'⁸ Truths are conveyed not only by words. It would, I think, be fair to say that John's mysticism is of a sacramental type. The physical becomes an opening into the spiritual, and John is at this point continuing Maximus's correction of the one-sided concern with the spiritual and the accompanying contempt for the material that were weaknesses in Dionysius and the neo-Platonist inheritance which he had taken over.

Mention of the sacraments draws attention to the parallel between the Eastern appreciation of icons and the Western practice of praying in the presence of Christ in the reserved eucharistic body. In both cases, a physical object, in the one an icon, in the other the consecrated bread, awaken the spiritual susceptibilities of the worshipper. These physical objects are in their different ways the bearers of many connotations, and lead into that contemplation in which the human soul experiences communion with God.

While I believe myself that there is a close resemblance between religious experience and aesthetic experience, it is a symptom of the superficiality of our own epoch in history that icons have now become largely aesthetic articles and are collected by the chattering classes, much as postage stamps are collected by schoolboys. Icons are primarily religious items and lose their deeper significance if treated only as works of art, though sometimes it comes about that the inherent influence of the icon can bring even the careless collector to a deeper understanding of its significance; that is to say, can bring him or her to the threshold of a mystical experience.

It took thirty-eight years after the death of John of Damascus before his defence of the icons was vindicated, when the Seventh Ecumenical Council (Nicaea II) decreed that icons were to be kept in the churches and venerated as in the past. Even then iconoclasm continued to have its supporters, and only in 843 CE was the victory of the icons complete. Bishop Kallistos Ware explains that 'the final victory of the holy images in 843 is known as "the Triumph of Orthodoxy", and is commemorated in a special service celebrated on "Orthodoxy Sunday", the First Sunday in Lent'.[9]

For our third representative of the mystical way in the 'Not So Dark Ages', we have to go from the Eastern Church to the furthest west of Europe, to the Celtic Church, which during those centuries did much to keep alive both faith and learning. John Scotus Eriugena (810–877), nowadays often called simply Eriugena, is probably the greatest Celtic thinker who has ever lived. He was known in his lifetime as John the Scot, but there were very many men with that name. He is distinguished by the additional name of Eriugena, meaning 'Irish-born'. At that time the Scots occupied a large swath of the British Isles in both Scotland and Ireland. Another John the Scot from a later time was John Duns Scotus, an actual native of Scotland, distinguished like his Irish counterpart by an additional geographical name, Duns being a parish in the south-east of Scotland.

Although Eriugena came from a western outpost of Europe, he seems to have had a good education, perhaps obtained at Clonmacnoise, which was something like an early Celtic university in Ireland. At any rate, however he got it, he acquired a good knowledge of neo-Platonism, and that combined very well with his native Celtic spirituality. He was also proficient in Greek, a very rare accomplishment in western Europe at that time, and translated into Latin writings of Gregory of Nyssa, Dionysius the Areopagite and Maximus Confessor. From about 850, he was teaching in the University of Paris. His own writings comprise a lengthy metaphysical and theological work, called *Periphyseon* or *De Naturae Divisione*, and exegetical works on the Bible, especially John's Gospel.

Although Dean Inge included Eriugena in his book, *Christian Mysticism*, he does in a footnote say, 'For us, Eriugena's defect as a mystic is to be sought in his extreme intellectualism'.[10] I was rather surprised to read this note, since I would have thought that Inge would welcome intellectualism, which is certainly needed among the mystics if they are to avoid the dangers of emotionalism and even sentimentalism. But perhaps if one lingers too long among the scholastic distinctions which Eriugena makes in the *Periphyseon*, one does experience a sense of dryness. I would be inclined to say that Eriugena, though his style of argument would not be readily acceptable today, does provide a remarkably solid philosophical framework to support a mystical theology.

Perhaps the best way to come to grips with Eriugena is to plunge in at the deep end and try to understand the metaphysical framework within which both his theology and his spirituality find expression. He uses the term Nature (*Natura*) for the totality of things. Nature includes not just the material world but the spiritual world, even God himself. I think it would correspond roughly to what idealist philosophers called the Absolute, and Eriugena sometimes calls it the Universe. He says that it covers both the things that are and the things that are not, a phrase which will call for some explanation. Within Nature, he distinguishes in a decidedly scholastic manner four divisions.

1 That which creates and is not created. Obviously this includes God, though we shall see shortly that a qualification is needed.

2 That which is created and also creates. This division is less obvious than the first. It is derived from the Platonist or neo-Platonist element in Eriugena's thinking, and refers to the eternal forms, ideas or species, also called volitions and participations in the one Cause of all things, which constitute a spiritual realm above the realm of space and time. These ideas are themselves causes, in the sense that they determine what can possibly be brought into the universe (laws of Nature?), so they have a creative agency although they have themselves been created by the divine will.

3 That which is created and does not create. This is the logical opposite of the first division, and is intended to include the finite beings of the sensible world, including human beings.

4 That which neither creates nor is created. This fourth division would seem to include nothing at all, but by a somewhat artificial twist, Eriugena equates it with the first division. This is another way of talking about God, a negative way. God is in Nature, but not as another item in Nature, so that in a sense he is nothing (no thing). As Creator, he stands outside in total differentiation. Expressed otherwise, it could be said that as Creator, God brings forth the universe, but all things are determined to return to God and to come to rest in him,

so that viewed *sub specie aeternitatis*, one could say that God will finally cease to create and so be the One who neither creates nor is created.

But surely Eriugena in his scholastic zeal has overshot himself at this point. In fact, he appears to contradict himself elsewhere in his text, for he states that God and his making are co-eternal, that for God 'to be' and 'to make' are one and the same, and that God did not exist before he created a world, if one could speak of such a time.

God and the world are inseparable, each implies the other, in some sense they constitute one entity rather than two. That explains why I said that in modern philosophy, what Eriugena calls Nature would possibly be called the Absolute. The question then arises whether Eriugena teaches a form of pantheism, and we have seen that such an aberration is constantly hovering around the mystics. He escaped censure during his lifetime, but the Church has a long memory in such matters and his views were condemned more than three centuries after his death.

Eriugena cannot justly be called a pantheist, and like many other so-called heretics of the past, he has been receiving a certain amount of rehabilitation in our more tolerant age. What he is trying to do, and certainly it is something very difficult, is to express a genuinely dialectical understanding of God, one that will include both his immanence in all creation and his transcendence. Both of these are essential to divine Being, at least, as Christians believe. So if our exposition of Eriugena has so far emphasized God's presence *within* Nature, let us hear the other side of his thought. He writes, 'Among the divisions of the created Universe, I certainly would not place [God], but for placing God within the divisions of that Universe which is comprehended by the term "Universal Nature", I have not one reason but many. For by that name

"Nature" is usually signified not only the created universe but that which creates it.'[11] He states clearly the difference between 'the divine Nature, which through itself, in itself and by itself is essence, life, wisdom and power, and the created nature which has being and life only by participation'.[12] Is this divine Nature then some kind of God beyond God? I doubt if we need to introduce such a difficult and dubious idea. The expression could just as well be interpreted as referring to the inaccessible depths of God. Yet after all these affirmations of the transcendence of God, he can also say, 'God is in all things everywhere.'[13] God is a paradox, a *coincidentia oppositorum*, a belief that goes back as far as Heraclitus. Among modern thinkers, the one who possibly comes closest to Eriugena is Alfred North Whitehead, who conceives God as having both a primordial nature which is unchanging and complete, and a consequent nature which emerges in the history of the world. It is something like that which lies behind Eriugena's cryptic words that God both creates and is created.

There is also a sense in which God belongs to the things that are not. This does not mean that God is bereft of any reality, but is a recognition that he is not another being in addition to all the things that make up created nature, but prior to them as their Creator. He is therefore nothing, in the literal sense of the English 'no thing'. Following Dionysius, Eriugena is saying that our language cannot be understood literally of God, even when we say, 'God is'. His mode of being is unique and beyond what we understand by such words as 'is' and 'exists'. Philo had said that God is *ho on*, an expression which Thomas would later translate as *Qui est*, 'He who is', though he well understood that God is in a manner different from that in which everything else may be said to be. Eriugena had already before Aquinas used a more satisfying (if more mystifying) expression, when he did not say God is 'He who is', but that God is 'He who is more than being'

(*Qui plus quam esse est*), but carefully adding that when we say 'God "is" more than being, what that "is" is, we cannot say'.[14]

We might expect then that Eriugena's mysticism would be in the last degree apophatic, but not so. God is not simply distant and unknown, but has descended into his creation and shown himself in theophanies. Here he is continuing ideas which we have already met in Maximus and Dionysius. But for Eriugena, the great theologian was John the Apostle, or at any rate, the person who wrote the Gospel of John. From early times, each of the four evangelists was associated with an emblem, one of the four angelic creatures seen in a vision by Ezekiel and likened severally to a man, a lion, an ox and an eagle. John was seen as the eagle, and Eriugena calls him 'the mystic (*spiritualis*) eagle'.

> The mystical bird – I am speaking of John the theologian – rises above the whole creation visible and invisible, penetrates every thought, and, deified, enters into the God who deifies him ... No, John was not only a man, but more than a man when he rose above himself and above all the things that exist, and, transported by the ineffable power of wisdom, penetrated into what is above everything; the secret of the unique essence in three persons, and of the three persons in the unique essence.[15]

I quote these sentences from the opening pages of Eriugena's *Homily on the Prologue of John* just to give a flavour of the kind of interpretation which he put on the Johannine writings. John emerges as the great theologian, but his ideas are expressed within what I called the 'metaphysical framework' of Eriugena's own mystical theology of which, if one were to accept Eriugena's hermeneutic, the Johannine writings would be the ideal exposition.

Eriugena would not get very high marks for his exegesis, for he reads his own philosophy of neo-Platonism into the Johannine writings. It is not that he was wrong in imputing mystical leanings to John. For instance, the important mystical insight that there is or can be a 'mutual indwelling' of God in man and man in God is first clearly set out in the Gospel of John, e.g., Jn 17.20–26. When, early in this book, I wanted to give an example of mysticism in the New Testament, I thought of John's Gospel, but in fact I chose Paul. I did so because we have Paul's own testimony in his letters and an outline of his career in Acts, and so, while we would think of him primarily as a missionary, we were, I think, able to discover enough in his experience to justify the claim that he was also a mystic. On the other hand, though we might have discovered mystical elements in the Fourth Gospel, there is so much doubt about its date and authorship that Paul seemed a better choice for our purpose. We may take note of the claim made by Deissmann that John was Paul's greatest disciple, but there is no serious evidence to support this view.

Eriugena's own importance does not depend on his work on the Johannine writings, though this is not to be simply dismissed, but on his attempt to provide mysticism with a sound intellectual basis that safeguards it against falling into emotionalism or sentimentalism.

The Early Middle Ages:

Symeon the New Theologian,
Bernard of Clairvaux, Richard of St Victor

When we talk about Dark Ages, or Middle Ages, or the Renaissance, or modern times, we are using only vague expressions, and should not try to define them too precisely. These expressions do have meaning. There is indeed a type of society that we call medieval, and we can list some of its characteristics, but it changed only gradually into a different type, just as it had emerged gradually, and I think it is a mistake to say that it began or ended in such and such a year. We have found in the preceding chapter that the Dark Ages were not so dark as some people have believed. I suggested that roughly the half-millennium from 500 to 1000 CE, when Europe was undergoing fundamental and often violent changes, could be distinguished from the times before and after, but there was nothing magical about the year 1000. Some people were possibly expecting the end of the world, but the world kept going, just as happened again when the year 2000 came and then departed into history.

Even so, in the field which is our special interest, Christian mysticism, a subtle change was taking place around 1000 CE. In mysticism, as in other areas of experience, there are always tensions, when conflicting tendencies pull in opposite directions. In mysticism, there is the intellectual or noetic pull in tension with the emotional or affective pull. Or, to express the matter in another way, theology, the attempt to give an intellectual or even scientific account of religion, may find itself in conflict with some of the beliefs and practices of the adherents of a religion. A right balance has to be struck between these conflicting tendencies. If the intellectual interpretation of religion becomes the dominant influence, then religion loses its popular appeal and becomes a dry and abstract affair. On the other hand, if the emotional and affective influence is not controlled or limited by intellectual criticism, it tends to assume extreme forms, varying from fundamentalism to speaking with tongues, and the whole religious enterprise is brought into disrepute.

In the three chapters preceding this one, we have seen how the influence of Greek philosophy, mainly Platonism and neo-Platonism, constructed a form of mysticism with an intellectual basis which was certainly a strength but which tended to restrict mysticism to the mature so-called gnostics (see above, pp. 69–70). This provoked a reaction, aimed at finding God in the sensible world, as we found in the work of Maximus, John of Damascus and Eriugena. But in the last-named, despite his talk of theophanies, the intellectual element and the method of scholastic argument still dominated. In the mystics whom we have to consider in the present chapter, the pendulum is swinging back, so to speak, and we find the affective influences in spirituality reasserting themselves and even openly challenging the claims of academic theology.

Our first example in this chapter is taken from the Eastern Orthodox Church, Symeon the New Theologian (949–1022 CE). The very designation, 'the new theologian', suggests a fresh beginning, but its origin is obscure. Gregory of Nazianzus had been referred to quite often as 'the theologian', and some scholars believe that in calling Symeon 'the new theologian', it was the case that the Church was recognizing Symeon as worthy to be placed alongside Gregory. John the Apostle, traditionally regarded as the author of both the fourth Gospel and the Revelation, was considered the greatest theologian, and Revelation is known as 'The Revelation of John the Theologian', a title translated into English as 'John the Divine', where the word 'divine' is not an adjective but a noun, meaning 'theologian' or 'expert in divinity' (see the exaggerated comments of Eriugena on John, p. 111 above). So perhaps Symeon was even being compared in a moment of enthusiasm to John! More soberly, Symeon may have acquired his title because his method was new and innovative in the sense that it opposed the abstract official theology prevailing in the upper echelons of the Church with what Symeon believed to be the pristine Christian experience 'as a wisdom infused by the Holy Spirit into the believer'.[1]

Symeon was born in Galatia in 949, and even in his youth felt an attraction to the life of a monk. He had a spiritual director, also called Symeon, who advised him to wait until he was older, so he was engaged in secular employments until he was twenty-seven. Then he had his first vision, which he describes for us himself, writing about himself in the third person, as many mystics do:

> One day, as he (Symeon himself) stood and recited 'God have mercy on me, a sinner', uttering it with his mind rather than with his mouth, suddenly a flood of divine radiance appeared from above, and filled all the room. As this happened, the young man lost all awareness of his surroundings and forgot that he was in a house and under a roof. He saw nothing but light all around him and did not know whether he was standing on the ground. Oblivious of all the world, he was filled with tears and with ineffable joy and gladness. His mind then ascended to

heaven and beheld yet another light, which was clearer than that which was close.[2]

The imagery of the light in his own mind contrasted with the light above him is bound to remind us of the experience of Augustine (see above, p. 17). Symeon adds the detail that in the light he was able to discern the figure of the other Symeon, his spiritual director.

After the experience described and possibly others like it, Symeon entered the Stoudion Monastery in Constantinople. But he still had the zealous enthusiasm of his adolescence and offended his fellow monks by insisting that his own interpretation of Christian discipleship was the correct one and inspired by the Holy Spirit. We can recognize in this attitude what we can still observe today in charismatics, who set their own inward experiences above the authority of the Church or even the Bible. Not surprisingly, the abbot asked him to leave after a few months. But his old mentor still had faith in the young man, and placed him in the nearby Mamas Monastery, where he very soon became abbot at the age of thirty-one. Perhaps he had an abrasive manner, but his attempts to impose a stern ascetic discipline in the name of the Holy Spirit led to a rebellion among the monks and eventually to a falling out with the leading Byzantine theologian of the time, who feared that Symeon's enthusiasm was threatening the stability of the Church by putting individual judgement above the teaching of the institution. On his side, Symeon felt that the Church had become too formalized and was stifling the message of Jesus Christ.

In his exile Symeon formed a small monastery of his own on the Bosphorus not very far from Constantinople, and there he spent his years teaching and writing until his death in 1022, and declining an invitation to return to the capital city. His secretary, Nicetas, records that 'while the blessed Symeon was still living, he was writing, even in spite of himself, night and day, the mysteries that the divine Spirit was confiding to his intelligence. The Spirit that was stirring and leaping within him was not allowing him any repose until he had put into writing his words and interior operations.'[3] His message was on one side negative, with stress on withdrawal from the world and continuous penitence; on the other side, the affirmative opposite, his great symbol was light, as we might expect after his early vision, but it was no impersonal light. The light was somehow personal, if one can so speak, the light was Jesus Christ, and Symeon was bound to Jesus in bonds of personal love. To live in the light was to live in Christ, and that was in turn to live in the Holy Trinity in a union in which the soul itself was deified. Even the light of his early vision disclosed a person in it, his old teacher.

Let me now illustrate these points in his teaching in a *catena* of quotations, selected from these voluminous writings which took up his energies night and day.

Let us then, dear brothers [and sisters], flee from the world and 'the things that are in the world' (1 Jn 2.15). For what have we in common with the world and the people who are in the world? Let us run, let us pursue, until we have laid hold on something that is permanent and does not flow away ... But what is the world? What are 'the things that are in the world'? Not gold or silver, horses or mules, not meat nor bread nor wine, not houses or fields or vineyards. All these things serve our physical needs. The 'world' is sin and attachments to things and passions. Let John the Theologian speak of 'the things that are in the world': 'all that is in the world, the lust of the flesh, and the lust of the eyes, and the pride of life, is not of the Father but is of the world' (1 Jn 2.15–16) ... For this reason let penitence be the task of us all, a task that not only accompanies all others but takes precedence over them all. With it is joined weeping and the tears that follow on it, and let no one say that it is impossible to weep daily ... Let no one deceive you. 'God is light' (1 John 1.5), and to those who have entered into union with him he imparts of his own brightness to the extent that they have been purified. When the lamp of the soul, that is, the mind, has been kindled, then it knows that a divine fire has taken hold of it and inflamed it. How great a marvel! Man is united to God spiritually and physically. He is a single god by adoption with body and soul and the divine Spirit, of whom he has become a partaker. Then is fulfilled what was spoken by David, 'You are gods, all of you, children of the most High' (Ps. 82.6).[4]

These are certainly bold words combining in one existence the life of the charismatic and of the mystic. One may criticize some things in Symeon's ideal of the Christian life; for instance, his individualism, his harshness towards those in authority and those who took a different view from his, his extreme otherworldliness, a possibly exaggerated idea of deification, but it may have been a healthy corrective to the prevailing theology and practice in his day.

Moving now from the Eastern Church to the Western, we have to remember that the final separation of East and West was still in the future, and we find tendencies in the West not dissimilar from those we have observed in the East. The career of Bernard of Clairvaux (1090–1153) shows some surprising parallels to that of Symeon, though one difference is the impression that Bernard had much the sweeter temperament of the two! But, like Symeon, Bernard is remembered for his unsophisticated love of Jesus Christ and his distrust of what he took to be the formalism of scholastic theology, as exemplified in the West by the work of Abelard. Bernard was for long the reputed author of the hymn, *Jesus, dulcis memoria*, which, in the English translation by John Mason Neale, begins

> Jesus! the very thought is sweet!
> In that dear name all heart-joys meet;
> But sweeter than the honey far
> The glimpses of his presence are.

Although Bernard is no longer believed to have been the author of this hymn, it comes from around his time and expresses thoughts that were typical of him. But if we take this hymn in isolation, it may exaggerate our impression of the affective side of Bernard's spirituality, and we then have to remember that he was not just a sentimentalist but a man of intellect, as was shown by Etienne Gilson,[5] and when required, a man of affairs.

He became a monk at twenty-one, and three years later was appointed abbot in the new Cistercian monastery of Clairvaux, from which he got his name or title. He was less opposed to scholasticism and certainly less anti-intellectualist than he is sometimes represented, but his main contribution was in stressing the affective and devotional aspects of the Christian life, and his spiritual writings are the ones for which he is chiefly remembered.

His first important writing, composed about 1126 when he was already a mature man of thirty-five, was a short treatise entitled *The Steps of Humility and Pride*.[6] It owes its inspiration to the Rule of Benedict, and uses such familiar mystical themes as the ascent to God, the image of Jacob's ladder, and the threefold path of purgation, illumination and union, but it is an original and skilfully constructed piece in which Bernard places his own interpretations on these themes.

Bernard, who came of an aristocratic French family, 'was not humble by origin, nature or temperament', according to

Basil Pennington, who wrote an introduction to the work. Therefore we must suppose that a deep personal experience lay behind his plea for humility, and that there is genuine conviction behind it. Humility is defined as 'a virtue in which a man has a low opinion of himself because he knows himself well'. By contrast, pride (and here Bernard follows Augustine) is 'love of one's own excellence'.[7] Humility, described as 'bitter but medicinal', is needed if one is to get on to the first rung of the ladder of ascent to God. But we are not there already. Bernard considers that he himself and presumably most of us are infected with pride in varying degrees, so that as we begin to climb the ladder of humility, we have to descend from the ladder of pride. There are seven steps on that ladder of humility, and seven on the ladder of pride. So we have to come down seven steps of pride in order to ascend the seven steps of humility. The proud person is curious, the humble person keeps the eyes down; the proud person shows levity of mind by much talking, the humble person speaks few and reasonable words; the proud person is given to 'silly mirth' (the kind we hear nowadays on television), the humble person is 'not over-ready to laugh' ... and so it goes on, some of the points applying to everybody, others primarily to monks and nuns.

Jesus, Bernard tells us, is the Way that leads to the Truth; he is the Truth that promises the Life, and he is himself that very Life (Jn 14.6). Here we have another statement of the threefold path – humility leads to truth and illumination, the illumination of truth promises life, and life itself is the goal, union with God. He also associates the three stages with the persons of the Trinity: humility with Jesus Christ, illumination with the Holy Spirit, and the union in love and contemplation with the Father. One begins to wonder at this point whether, with these possibly over-precise distinctions, Bernard is himself in danger of toppling over into scholastic theology! But they do not diminish the powerful spiritual impact of this early work on humility.

On Loving God is another spiritual treatise which has a scholastic shape. Bernard distinguishes four stages on the way to a more perfect love.

1 There is the love of oneself for the sake of oneself.
2 There is the love of God for the sake of oneself; that is to say, for what rewards it may bring.
3 Then there is the love of God for God's sake.
4 Finally, there is the love of oneself only for God's sake, a quite revolutionary advance, in which one's own self is at last eclipsed.

We pass on to Bernard's principal work on spirituality, his four-volume commentary, *The Song of Songs*. We have already noted the fascination of this book of the Bible for mystics and seen how Origen made use of it. Bernard goes much further in employing erotic imagery to expound the mystical experience. His commentary includes no fewer than eighty-six sermons on the *Song*, and goes into great detail in elaborating the allegorical significance of its images. We are brought up sharply to face the question about the appropriateness of such imagery for elucidating the divine–human relationship.

Bernard assimilates this imagery to the wider doctrine of a threefold path to God. That path is represented by him under the form of the three kisses. These are the kisses of the feet, the kisses of the hands, and the kisses of the mouth. Obviously, these three kisses stand for three stages of intimacy in the approach of the soul to God. The kisses of the feet belong to the moment of humility before God, those steps by which one begins the ascent. Even at this stage, Bernard is careful to maintain that the ascent is made not in the strength of the soul itself, but with the assistance of divine grace. Next come the kisses of the hand. This is not quite clear but leads into illumination by the truth, learning more of God, moving more easily in the presence of God, perhaps even making a commitment, a kind of betrothal to God. The kisses of the mouth represent the climax, the most intimate union with God.

It would be going beyond the scope of this book to follow all the details which Bernard finds in or reads into the text of the *Song*. But a short excerpt will make his method clear and also his justification for using erotic language and imagery.

'Let him kiss me with the kiss of his mouth,' she said [*Song* 1.23]. Now, who is this 'she'? It is the bride. But why the bride? Because she is the soul thirsting for God . . . She is the one who asks for a kiss, she is a lover. Among all the natural endowments of man, love holds first place, especially when it is directed to God, who is the Source whence it comes. No sweeter names can be found to embody that sweet interflow of affections between the Word and the soul, than bridegroom and bride. Between these all things are equally shared, there are no selfish reservations, nothing that causes division. They share the same inheritance, the same table, the same home, the same marriage-bed, they are flesh of each other's flesh . . . Therefore if a love relationship is the special and outstanding characteristic of the bride and groom, it is not unfitting to call the soul that loves God a bride. She does not resort to the arts of seduction, she makes no devious or fawning solicitations for the prize that she covets. No, but with a spontaneous outburst from the abundance of her heart, direct even to the point of boldness, she says, 'Let him kiss me with the kiss of his mouth'.[8]

I have no difficulty in accepting that the love of a human couple is perhaps as near as we can get to understanding what is meant by the mutual indwelling of one soul in another, including the relation of God and a human being, or even the perichoresis of the persons of the divine Trinity. But no analogy is ever perfect, and I have one important reservation here. The relation of two human beings in marriage is a relation of equality as well as of the deepest intimacy, and this equality is clearly stated in Bernard's description of the relation. When one of the partners is God or Christ, I do not think that one can speak of equality. Sometimes mystics come close to it, and take deification or union with God to mean that somehow they become God or a part of God, if one may speak of a 'part' of God. Certainly, there is a deep affinity between God and the human person, otherwise mysticism or any form of spirituality or even incarnation itself would not be possible. But alongside the affinity there is the otherness between the Infinite and the finite, the Creator and the creature. The language of erotic love can obscure or even abolish the difference between God and humans.

Bernard died in 1153, but his influence has remained down to the present, and he is perhaps the most popular of all the Christian mystics. That influence, with some modifications, was already strong in Bernard's own time. The once-famous abbey of St Victor had been founded near Paris in 1113, and several of the monks – Victorines, as they were known – cultivated a form of mysticism not dissimilar to that of Bernard.

One of the best known was Richard of St Victor (1125–73). The date of his birth is uncertain, but must have been quite close to the one cited here, as he was still a young man when he came to the abbey around 1150, going on to be Prior (second to the abbot) in 1162. His country of origin is also uncertain; he is described as a Scot, which is usually taken to mean he was from Scotland, but possibly he was from Ireland. He wrote two lengthy works on spirituality, known by the names *Benjamin Minor* and *Benjamin Major*, or, somewhat more descriptively, as *The Twelve Patriarchs* and *The Mystical Ark*.[9] In these works we see a form of biblical exegesis which goes far beyond what we met in Origen and other earlier writers, as Richard tries to penetrate even beyond the allegorical meaning of the text to what is called the 'tropological' meaning; that is to say, its meaning or alleged meaning for the stages of the soul's pilgrimage to God. Admittedly, as we shall see in a moment, Richard has to exercise his imagination quite a bit in discovering these arcane meanings. But it is remarkable how the text lends itself to his treatment. He does have some enlightening things to say, and we find ourselves asking whether he could have discovered such meanings if there were not, below the surface text, unconscious thoughts and desires not present to the author, but now being brought to light. It is at least conceivable that this could be the case.

In *The Twelve Patriarchs*, Richard considers the twelve sons of Jacob, the supposed founders of the twelve tribes of Israel. Richard leans more than did Bernard towards the intellectual side of mysticism and the rising scholastic philosophy, but in the final stage of the pilgrimage, reason surrenders to ecstasy. In his interpretation, Jacob is the rational spirit of a human person, Rachel his wife is reason, Leah, his other wife, represents the 'ordered affections'. The sons born of Leah prepare the way for the mystic: Reuben, the eldest, represents the fear of God (holy awe), Simeon represents sorrow for sin, Levi hope of forgiveness, and so on. These are the early stages on the way (we can recognize purgation), and are achieved by human effort. But the final stage needs the divine action. God lifts the soul to a new level, into ecstasy or, as Richard calls it, *excessus.* At this climactic moment, reason is superseded by contemplation, an event represented in the Old Testament narrative by the death of Rachel (reason) in giving birth to Benjamin (contemplation).

Interspersed through Richard's tropological exegesis of the characters of Jacob's sons are several passages of a more scholastic nature, in which he offers analyses of some of the basic phenomena. Thus he distinguishes six kinds of contemplation: purely imaginative, imaginative in a rational manner, rational contemplation that makes use of visible things, purely rational contemplation without imagery, suprarational contemplation, contemplation that is (or appears to be) contrary to reason. Some of the distinctions are not quite clear, but Richard's scheme was taken up by some later mystics (see below, pp. 132–3, on Bonaventure). There are three heavens, corresponding to three stages in the knowledge of God: faith, reason and contemplation. The soul may actively ascend to the first and second, but the third and highest heaven is attained only when the soul is caught up in ecstasy (as was Paul, see above, p. 57). The analogy which underlies much of *The Twelve Patriarchs* is that of climbing a mountain, and this is identified with the mountain of Christ's transfiguration. The top can be reached only with Christ as guide. The soul is enveloped in the light of Christ, and his shining garments stand for a new level of teaching that can be had only at the mountain-top. Here we again meet the suggestion that there is a special kind of enlightenment that will be granted only to a few, though I do not think that Richard uses the word 'gnostic', which by this time had perhaps come to be reserved for members of the gnostic sects.

It is at the top of the mountain also that the soul attains the highest degree of self-knowledge, for the peak of the mountain not only reaches into the mystery of God, but seems to be at the same time the apex of the human soul;

hence the controversial doctrine that there is a divine spark in the soul, or that something in the human soul is divine and uncreated (see below on Eckhart, p. 137). The relation between self-knowledge and the knowledge of God is brought out even more strongly in the rather different analogy in *The Mystical Ark*. In this writing, the climax is reached not at the top of a mountain but by penetrating to the inmost depth, the Holy of Holies. Here we meet again the idea prominent in Augustine and other mystics that God can be found in the depth of the self. Like a treasure hidden in a field, so the image of God is hidden in the centre of the soul. In another simile which Richard uses, the soul is understood as a mirror which, if we keep it clean and look on it long enough, we can see the divine light that comes from its origin. I would fear myself that in the average human being, the divine image has been so obscured that there would need to be extraordinary progress in purgation and illumination before it became even dimly discernible. But on this, more later.

If we enquire further about the ecstasy of which Richard speaks, we find him illustrating it from human love, as expressed in the *Song of Songs*. There are three causes which may trigger an ecstasy. The first is the burning desire of love – not, in this case, sexual love but 'heavenly desire', though clearly Richard sees an analogy between them: 'Who is this who comes up from the wilderness like a column of smoke, perfumed with myrrh and frankincense, with all the fragrant powders of the merchants?' (*Song* 3.6). The second is wonder, the soul is overwhelmed by a sublime vision: 'Who is this who comes forth like the rising dawn?' (*Song* 6.10). The third cause is 'greatness of joy and exultation'. 'Who is this who comes up from the desert, flowing with delights, leaning upon her beloved?' (*Song* 8.5). Richard offers no excuse for this imagery, claiming that human love is indeed our best clue to the divine love.[10]

The modern reader may find Richard's tropological hermeneutics rather too much for his or her tastes, but that may be simply because we have become so literal-minded that our imaginative faculty is impoverished. A master of the imagination, the poet Dante, described Richard of St Victor in admittedly exaggerated terms as one 'who was in contemplation more than human' (*che a considerar fù piu che viro*).[11]

8

The High Middle Ages:

Bonaventure, Meister Eckhart

I have entitled this chapter 'The High Middle Ages' for it was in the thirteenth and early fourteenth centuries that European Christianity reached its heights. The thirteenth century was the time of Francis of Assisi, possibly the greatest saint in Christian history; Thomas Aquinas, the greatest Christian theologian; and Dante, the greatest Christian poet. Christian mysticism too was at its peak. We shall discuss two of its representatives, one an early Franciscan, the other a Dominican and therefore in the same order as Thomas.

We begin with the Franciscan, generally known by his religious name of Bonaventura or in English Bonaventure (1217–74). It was only late in my life that I became acquainted with the work of this great mystic, but in one respect I could not have been more fortunate, because I was directed to him through my friendship with Dr Ewert Cousins of Fordham University. Dr Cousins has been a lifelong student of Bonaventure, and is editor and translator of a volume containing his biography of St Francis and his major spiritual writings.[1]

Bonaventure (as we shall call him, leaving aside his original name) was born in central Italy, and was a boy of only nine when Francis died in 1226. At that time the new Franciscan Order was expanding rapidly. Bonaventure went to study in the University of Paris, and found the Franciscans already well established there. He entered the Order in 1243, became head of the Franciscan school in Paris in 1253, and then Minister-general of the Order in 1257. In spite of being involved in ecclesiastical affairs, he kept up his studies and writing. He died at the Council of Lyons in 1274, was canonized in 1482 and declared a Doctor of the Church in 1588.

Bonaventure's principal spiritual writing is *The Soul's Journey into God*. It was in 1259, two years after becoming Minister-general, that Bonaventure, 'under divine impulse', as he believed, and 'seeking a place of quiet and desiring to find there peace of spirit', went to Mount La Verna in Tuscany, the spot where the revered St Francis had had a vision and received the stigmata. As he reflected on Francis's vision in that place, Bonaventure himself received the inspiration for his treatise, in which six chapters, broadly corresponding to the six kinds of contemplation that had been described by Richard of St Victor (see above, p. 125), and the six wings of the seraph seen by Francis, trace the stages of the soul's journey to God, and a seventh the final rapture. After a brief introduction, Bonaventure addresses the following invitation to his reader, and I would say that even if he had written nothing else, this invitation alone expresses so much of the meaning of mystical thinking and of prayer in general that in itself it has classical status and entitles its writer to the deepest respect:

First, therefore, I invite the reader to the groans of prayer through Christ crucified, through whose blood we are cleansed from the filth of vice – so that he does not believe that reading is sufficient without unction, speculation without devotion, investigation without wonder, observation without joy, work without piety, knowledge without love, understanding without humility, endeavour without divine grace, reflection as a mirror without divinely inspired wisdom.[2]

These words, and the remainder of the invitation which is too long to quote here, seem to me an ideal statement, combining in a wonderful way intellect and passion, understanding and will, human endeavour and human passivity before the mystery of the spiritual adventure.

I have written elsewhere that 'prayer is thinking', but *passionate* thinking that is suffused with longing and will for fulfilment, the opposite of that so-called 'value-free' thinking which some scientists and philosophers have advocated. I doubt very much if any thinking can take place without some admixture of feeling, and I am sure that if we do not wish to fall into a kind of schizophrenia, 'value-free' thinking should be avoided. Truth cannot be pursued in isolation from goodness, or at least ought not to be isolated. If we sometimes complain that scientific discoveries are used for bad purposes, that must be laid at the door of those who isolate the pursuit of truth from other human interests. Science and its applications have to do with means, not ends, and means without ends can be very dangerous. The situation is a complex one, and we cannot go fully into it here. While I criticize 'value-free' thinking as irresponsible, this does not in the slightest degree diminish the duty to be intellectually honest, which demands that we represent things to be what we have found them to be, not what we would like them to be.

But to return to the mystic and his or her prayer, there is no pretence here, the thinking is not value-free but suffused with a longing for ends that inspire passion and desire. 'Thy kingdom come' is perhaps the passion that accompanies all Christian prayer. We could say, recognizing that our language is being stretched into the symbolic mode, that the passion or *pathos*[3] of God himself is expressed in this prayer, his own longing for the fulfilment of the end or purpose of creation. This is what one is trying to say when we speak of the Holy Spirit praying in men and women, or when the mystic speaks of his or her union with God. This is not a 'substantial' union, so to speak; that is to say, the mystic does not become God or part of God, but the will and desire of the mystic are unified with the divine purpose. Also, in this mystical thinking, the active, investigative thrust in our ordinary thinking seems to be dimmed down, so to speak, and is replaced by a passive, receptive frame of mind which does not grasp at the truth but rather submits to it and absorbs it.

I have laid stress on this passage in Bonaventure because I think that it expounds the mystical way of thinking just about as clearly as possible to persons like myself who are not mystics and who have never had visions or ecstasies, but who can react sympathetically to what Bonaventure is saying and even feel that to at least some degree they can share in his experience.

Another remarkable passage comes at the fifth stage of the jouney into God when Bonaventure reflects on God as Being, his most proper name, and describes this ultimate Being in a series of opposites:

> You have something here to lift you up in wonder. For Being itself is first and last; it is eternal and most present; it is utterly simple and the greatest; it is most actual and most unchangeable; it is most perfect and most immense; it is supremely one and yet all-inclusive. If you wonder at this with a pure mind, you will be flooded with light when you see further that it is last because it is first, necessarily the beginning, the end and the consummation, the Alpha and the Omega.[4]

As I mentioned earlier, I came to Bonaventure only late in my career through the influence of Ewert Cousins, but when I first read this passage, I had the feeling that I had read it before! So I wondered about it and eventually remembered that there is a very similar passage in Heidegger's book on Nietzsche: 'Being is both utterly void and most abundant; most universal and most unique; most intelligible and most resistant to every concept; most in use and yet still ahead of us; most available and most abyssal; most forgotten and most memorable; most mentioned and most reticent.'[5] The resemblance between the two passages is not exact, but both in form and content it is sufficiently close to make us suspect that it is not due simply to chance. Of course, the idea that we speak of God in a conjunction of opposites goes back to ancient times, and I have already cited Heraclitus on the subject (see above, p. 81). Heidegger may have picked up the idea from quite a number of writers. But I remembered that in his early years at Freiburg, before he went to Marburg, he was a professor of scholastic philosophy. What he has written may well be an unconscious reminiscence or an inexact quotation from memory of words which had first impressed him when he was teaching medieval thought. In any case, whether one speaks of God, Being, the Absolute, the Logos or whatever term is used, the notion of a *coincidentia oppositorum* is here clearly presented by Bonaventure as part of his mystical thinking about God.

The six stages on the journey into God are not always completely clear. They reflect not only the six kinds of contemplation taught by Richard of St Victor but also the imagery of the six-winged seraph of Isaiah's vision (Isa. 6.2). A very inadequate summary would mention the following points.

The first two stages refer to the traces of the Creator to be read in the works of the creation; in other words, a natural theology. Through the light that shines from his works, we are led to the eternal Light.

In the third and fourth stages, we turn away from the external world of the senses to look within the human mind itself, first in its natural powers, then as purified by divine grace. There we find or hope to find the image of God. Bonaventure exclaims, 'It seems amazing, when it has been shown that God is so close to our souls, that so few should be aware of the First Principle within themselves.' His teaching here is close to that of Richard, but I did criticize Richard on the ground that the divine image in man is more severely damaged than perhaps he allowed. Bonaventure is more aware of the danger. However one may explain it, whether 'clouded by sense images' or 'allured away by concupiscence', the human soul in its natural condition is not a persuasive representation of God. The human being needs grace, a helping hand, and this is where Jesus Christ enters as the Mediator.

> He says, 'I am the door. If anyone enters through me, he will be saved, and he will go in and out and find pasture' (Jn 10.9) . . . But we do not draw near to this door unless we believe in him, hope in him and love him. Therefore, if we wish to enter again into the enjoyment of Truth as into paradise, we must enter through faith in, hope in and love of Jesus Christ, the Mediator between God and men, who is like the tree of life in the middle of paradise.[6]

The human soul therefore needs to be renewed by the Christian virtues of faith, hope and love, and so the image of God in the soul is purified and perfected. Bonaventure refers at this point to the *Song of Songs*, and repeats the three verses from that writing which we have already seen quoted by Richard of St Victor (see above, p. 126).

In the fifth and sixth stages, the soul begins to enjoy the vision of God. We have already seen how God as Being is understood as the coincidence of opposites. At the sixth stage, God is contemplated as the Good. God is not only Being but shares the gift of being, first within the Trinity through the begetting of the Son and the procession of the Holy Spirit and then with all his creatures in an act of self-diffusion. Here Bonaventure is echoing the words of Dionysius (see above, p. 95).

The seventh and final stage of the journey brings the soul to rest in God, just as the seventh day of the creation brought rest after the six days of work. I hope that I rightly interpret Bonaventure at this point, but I cannot be quite sure that I understand him. He does tell us that now we must give up all intellectual efforts and surrender ourselves to the affections. We contemplate but do not comprehend the coincidence of the opposites in God, where they co-exist in an ineffable unity. 'If you wish to know how these things come about, ask grace, not instruction; desire, not understanding; the groaning of prayer, not diligent reading; the Spouse, not the teacher; God, not man; darkness, not clarity; not light, but the fire that totally inflames and carries us into God by ecstatic unctions and burning affections.'[7] He speaks of this final union as a kind of death – does he mean that the individual soul ceases to exist as a distinct person, and becomes somehow absorbed into God, 'a pulse in the eternal mind'?[8] It is hard to know, but perhaps this is implicit in Bonaventure's choice of preposition. He speaks of a journey *into* God, not to God.

It might be asked whether the Christ of *The Soul's Journey into God* has not been excessively spiritualized by Bonaventure. I do not think that this is the case; but even if it were, one would still need to take account of Bonaventure's further treatise, *The Tree of Life*. Here he explores the story of the earthly historical Jesus as depicted in the Gospels and invites the reader to accompany Jesus Christ through the several events of his life. Professor Cousins sees this work of Bonaventure as an anticipation of the method of Ignatius Loyola (see below, p. 165); or, if I may add an example nearer our own time, to the existential interpretation employed by Rudolf Bultmann.

Among the mystics whom we have examined in our survey up to this point, Bonaventure takes a very high place, perhaps the highest, when we consider the clarity, the completeness, and the sanity, balance and moderation of his exposition. But he had a near contemporary who rivalled him in these matters, and possibly excelled him in intellectual power. Quite appropriately, this rival was a Dominican, and the Dominican order vied with the Franciscan in its attempts to witness to Christian truth at that period of history. I am referring to Meister Eckhart (1260–1327). It is said that his Christian name was John, but this is doubtful and I shall call him by the title commonly used, Meister Eckhart. He was a native of Thuringia, in south-west Germany, and in his teens entered the Dominican order. He studied at Paris and Cologne, and read the works of the great Dominican theologian, Thomas Aquinas. After giving service to the order, he began to teach in Paris in 1311, but after two years he went to live first in Strasbourg, then in Cologne, and built up an impressive reputation as a preacher. In 1326 he was accused of heresy by the archbishop of Cologne. He was tried in Cologne but appealed to the pope, then resident in Avignon. In that city Eckhart died in 1327, two years before the pope pronounced his verdict. This was to the effect that of twenty-eight propositions about which a complaint had been made, seventeen were heretical, and eleven, though not definitely heretical, were to be deplored for their tone. From the records of his trial which are still extant, one gets the impression that the proceedings were reasonably fair by the standards prevailing at that time, but nowadays we probably would make much more allowance for Eckhart's sometimes careless use of language, and for the vagueness and ambiguity of some of the matters under discussion.

As happened with Origen, Eckhart continued to have admirers even after the Church's judgement had gone against him, and in fact he has had quite a revival in recent years. However, he remains a figure of controversy, and we must now turn to his own writings and judge for ourselves the value of his contribution to Christian mysticism. The comparison of Eckhart with Origen is quite a useful one. Origen could be considered as a Christian Platonist or as a Platonic Christian, depending on how one looks at him, and what one's own convictions are. Similarly, I believe, Eckhart could be considered in one light as a philosopher with theological interests, but in another as a Christian mystic and theologian who believed it to be his duty to respect the rational procedures of philosophy and to work towards a *rapprochement* between faith and reason. Even on specific questions as well as on their general attitudes towards secular knowledge, Eckhart and Origen were quite close. For instance, we noted that for Origen God's very nature is to create, so there never was a time when God existed in sheer isolation, and even the finite souls were eternal. A similar view is found in Eckhart. In the bull of condemnation of 1329, *In agro dominico*, we read: 'When someone asked [Meister Eckhart] why God had not created the world earlier, he answered, as he does now, that God could not have created the world earlier, because nothing can act before it exists, and so as soon as God existed, he created the world.'[9]

Also like Origen (see above, p. 74) he had no desire to be a heretic. In his *Defence*, he stated a truth worth remembering whenever heresy is mentioned: 'I can be in error, but I cannot be a heretic, because the first belongs to the intellect, the second to the will.'[10] As regards those propositions of Eckhart which were deemed to be not heretical though not very acceptable either, Pope John XXII acknowledged that although they were 'rash', they might with many additions and explanations be given an acceptable catholic meaning.

Like other mystics, Eckhart tried to do justice to both the transcendence of God over the creation, and his immanence in it, and here it must be acknowledged that some of his language was not well chosen, and seemed to verge on pantheism and to obscuring the distinction between God and human beings, as when he speaks of an 'uncreated light' or a 'divine spark' in the soul, and says that the soul 'wants to go into the simple ground, the quiet desert', the distinctionless essence of God beyond the Trinity of Persons.[11] He undoubtedly had a habit of making broad generalizations which, as the pope said, might be found acceptable if there were offered 'additions and explanations', but which stated without explanatory comment could be highly controversial. An example is his claim that 'Moses, Christ and the Philosopher [Aristotle] teach the same thing, differing only in the way they teach'.[12] It would be possible to show that there is common ground among these three, but this would require considerable work and ingenuity, and would fall far short of what Eckhart asserts. So however sympathetic we might feel, we would have to admit that he brought many of his problems on himself.

Let me then try to set out the salient points in Eckhart's understanding of the mystical and metaphysical relation between the divine and the human, stating it in the strongest terms I can find, but drawing attention to those features of his account which are questionable. As far as possible, he dispenses with the imagery which we have met in one mystic after another, and bases himself on intellectual rather than on affective grounds.

First then, let us enquire about the affinity between God and the soul, as this seems to be an assumption in all forms of mysticism. The soul has come from God and seeks to return to God. This in turn carries the assumption that God is immanent in the world of finite entities, including human beings, and we have several times been aware that particular mystics have been moving near to pantheism. There is a difference in the spirituality that relies on a strong sense of divine immanence and any spirituality which goes with a classical and more biblically based theism, in which divine transcendence is stressed more than divine immanence. A more intimate relation to God is possible to the mystic than to a believer whose sense of God is dominated by thoughts of transcendence and sovereignty. In the latter case, there may be reverence and even love towards God, but it begins to approach the homage due to an exalted ruler. Again, the underlying model of a sovereign God tends to foster an understanding of prayer as primarily a petition addressed to a superior power on whose will everything depends. The mystic, in Eckhart's understanding, prays not so much to a God 'out there' as rather one who is open to God's Spirit within him and joins in the prayer of the Spirit. The mystic, however, remains aware of the final mystery and incomprehensibility of God, and if there is a danger among some Christians of treating God as a kind of magnified imperial ruler (a 'Louis XIV of the heavens', as William James put it), there is a danger among mystics of putting themselves on an equality with God, as we noted in criticizing some forms of erotic imagery. In Eckhart's case, we do not find erotic imagery, but we do find extremely bold language.

One of his central ideas is *Abgeschiedenheit*, 'detachment', or perhaps more literally, 'saying goodbye to'. To come to God, one must say goodbye to worldly things. This sounds like withdrawal from the world, but it is not intended in a negative sense. The things of the world are to be seen in their relation to God and evaluated accordingly. Eckhart is an example of the God-intoxicated man: he sees God in everything. He says, 'True detachment is nothing else than for the spirit to stand immovable against whatever may chance to it, of joy or sorrow, honour, shame or disgrace, as a mountain of lead stands against a little breath of wind.'[13] This brings the human soul into a true relation to God. It does not mean a forsaking of the world but a right valuation of all things. So Eckhart could also say, 'No person in this life may reach the point at which he may be excused from outward service. Even if he is given to a life of contemplation, still he cannot refrain from going out and taking an active part in life.'[14]

The return of the soul to God takes place in two stages. The first is the birth of God in the soul, or the birth of the Son or the Logos in the soul. A person who has achieved a sufficient level of detachment is ready for the intimate entry of God into the centre of his or her life. The union is so close that there takes place a deification of the soul. Now we come to that extremely bold language of Eckhart which I mentioned two paragraphs above. 'If my life is God's being,' he says, 'then God's existence must be my existence and God's isness is my isness.'[15] One might think this language could not be exceeded for boldness, but Eckhart does exceed it, for further on he says, 'The Father gives birth to the Son without ceasing; and I say more: he gives birth to me, his son and the same Son. I say more: he gives birth not only to me, his son, but he gives birth to me as himself and himself as me and to me as his being and nature.'[16] These are the words of a man who seems to have transgressed the limits not only of orthodoxy but even of sanity, yet the idea that through baptism the Logos is born in the soul of the believer is one that reaches far back in patristic theology, and the New Testament recognizes that the believer becomes a son or daughter, albeit by adoption. The eminent ecclesiastical historian Hugo Rahner claimed, after meticulous study, that Eckhart's teaching can be shown to be compatible with Christian orthodoxy, though others would disagree.[17] It might be urged, for example, that there is little room left for Jesus Christ as Mediator, certainly much less than in Bonaventure's mysticism.

But the birth of the Logos in the soul of the believer is not the end of the matter. There is a second stage in the return to God, the 'breakthrough' (*Durchbruch*). We must become detached even from God, as he has been imaged. Even our best images, in Eckhart's view, are anthropomorphic in a bad sense and do not respect the ineffability of God. Therefore, the Christian must break through even the doctrine of the triune God to the divine essence underlying the three Persons. This is the meaning of Eckhart's often-quoted saying that 'man's last and highest parting takes place when, for God's sake, he says goodbye to God'.[18] Sometimes the words have been taken to mean that Eckhart had embraced atheism, but that is a very superficial reading. Rather, what we have here is apophaticism carried to a very high degree, a version of the 'God beyond God' doctrine. Many people have been driven to atheism because the Church's ways of speaking about God were too anthropomorphic. But that was not the case with Eckhart.

But is Eckhart going too far? In seeking to penetrate to the essence of Deity beyond the Trinity, an essence in which all distinctions vanish, so that it is like a wilderness or the void of Eastern mysticism (see above, pp. 15–16), has he left any content to the word 'God'? I really wonder whether, with the utmost ingenuity, this teaching can be contained within the bounds of Christian doctrine. Does he leave any place for incarnation, let alone the doctrine of the Trinity? Or does he acknowledge the receptiveness of the soul in its approach to God, seeming to suggest rather that human beings must storm their way into the Holy of Holies?

Apart from the question of a strict orthodoxy which, I must confess, would not trouble me too much, there is also a question here about the logic of Eckhart's argument. I think he is guilty of a category mistake, in putting the three Persons and the divine essence on the same logical level, as if they were all comparable entities. There are, I believe, two major ways of understanding the Trinity. In the Western way, traceable back to Tertullian, the three Persons (*hypostases*) share in the one being or substance (*ousia*); in the Eastern way, the Father is the Source (*pege*) of Deity, and the other Persons of the Trinity are God because they have derived their Deity from the Father. I prefer this Eastern version; but if we accept it, we see that Deity or Godhood is found only in the Persons, and is not some fourth entity to which the soul might directly relate. To give a simple illustration (recognizing that this analogy is inadequate, and any analogy would be inadequate), let us imagine three gold coins. There are three coins and a single substance, gold. But there is no gold apart from that which is in the coins. So it does seem to me that Eckhart's idea of breaking through even the Trinity to the ultimate essence of Godhood is inadmissible.

However, I would not like to think that in using the word 'inadmissible' I am dogmatically throwing out Eckhart's arguments. In an earlier discussion of him in my Gifford Lectures, I tried to rescue his position by pointing out that just as there are two stages by which the soul returns to God, so in Eckhart's thinking there were two stages in the coming forth from God. The first stage he called a 'boiling' (*bullitio*), a process of emanation within God, whereby from the primal

Source (whether it be the Father or the essence), there came forth the Persons of the Trinity. But then there was a second stage, called a 'boiling over' (*ebullitio*), which brought forth the world of finite entities on a lower level of existence. Where is the human soul in this scheme of things? Sometimes Eckhart speaks as if the soul has in it something of divinity, and this belief was one of the errors of which he was accused by the church authorities. But it is not necessary to interpret his teaching as a form of pantheism. The metaphysical background of his thought falls clearly within the neo-Platonist or Plotinian pattern, and I would be willing to regard it as an example of what I call 'dialectical theism', a form of theism which seeks to combine the transcendent and immanent aspects of divine Being.

Although Eckhart has been described here as a God-intoxicated man, like most religious people he must have had his times of dryness, when the sense of the divine Presence forsook him. No doubt these times are in part due to human sinfulness, but Eckhart, in common with some other mystics, believed that there are times when God withdraws himself. 'The vision and experience of God', he claimed, 'is too much of a burden to the soul while it is in the body, and so God withdraws intermittently, which is what Christ meant by saying, "A little while, and you shall not see me; and again, a little while and you shall see me." '[19] Eckhart may or may not be correct in suggesting that God himself is the source of such experiences of absence. Certainly they occur even in the most sincere believers, and sometimes in nations or cultures *en masse*. Did not Jesus himself know the absence of the Father at the crucifixion, when 'at three o'clock [he] cried out with a loud voice, "My God, my God, why have you forsaken me?" ' (Mk 15.34). Are we ourselves living in a time when God has hidden his face? Eckhart offers a reason for thinking that such times have a part to play in spirituality. If God were always clearly manifest, there would be no need to seek him, and the quest for God would come to an end; if he were always absent, we would give up the quest through discouragement. But, as Gregory of Nyssa maintained, the quest never comes to an end (see above, pp. 84–5).

Eckhart eschews erotic imagery, but at this point he seems to suggest something like a love affair between God and the human race. There is an alternation of consolation and desolation, and it is in this way that the finite beings are being constantly drawn into the infinite depths of the divine.

9

Women Mystics:

Julian of Norwich, Catherine of Siena, Catherine of Genoa

In the early centuries of Christian history, there is not much mention of women, apart from those who were martyred in times of persecution and then in due course canonized by the Church. But in the years following 1100 CE, there began to emerge quite a large group of women mystics and visionaries. Among the first was Hildegarde of Bingen, and then there is a long line stretching through the Middle Ages and into modern times. It is interesting to speculate why this was so. Perhaps it was the real or alleged intuitive powers of women that attracted them to a form of spirituality where God is known directly by a kind of spiritual perception. It was left to men to work out by discursive reason 'proofs' of God's existence, though such proofs have never been quite satisfactory and have often raised more questions than they have answered. Another possibility is that, as we have already noted, the language of mysticism spoke of the soul of the believer, whether man or woman, in the feminine gender. Whether one is thinking of an individual soul or of the Church in its corporate being, it is said that *she* is the bride of Christ, and this language goes right back to the New Testament (Eph. 5.25–33). Whatever the reason, women mystics continued to appear. Some of them won very high respect and exerted great influence, not only in opening up the life of the spirit, but in the practical affairs of the Church and the world. In medieval times and later, there were women mystics whose lives and writings place them in the very first ranks of those who have contributed to Christian spirituality.

Our first exemplar, incidentally the first English mystic to be mentioned in this book, is Julian of Norwich (1342–1416). She is an example of a Christian who chose in her lifestyle the religious life in its most rigorous form. I deliberately say 'rigorous', not necessarily 'best' or 'highest'. I do not think that Christianity should have its gnostics, considered as a higher rank of believers. I pointed out earlier the obvious truth that if we all became monks or nuns or celibates, the human race (or at least the Christian part of it) would come to a speedy and inglorious end. That is not to say that we should not admire those who have chosen a sacrificial way of life, but sacrifice is demanded also of those who live in the world. Christian conviction is to be judged not by lifestyle but by faithfulness in whatever honourable work or vocation a person may be placed.

Julian spent her entire life in or near the city of Norwich. She was often called 'Lady Julian', so it is likely that she came of a noble family, as many nuns did. It seems that she even retained a servant as a kind of housekeeper after she retired from the world to a life of prayer! We know very little about her life, and what we do know is gathered mainly from her own writings. She must have received a fairly good education, and at an early age she felt an attraction to the religious life in the full sense of the expression, a life devoted to prayer and contemplation. Grace Jantzen tells us,

In her youth Julian had prayed specifically for three things. Her first prayer was for an understanding of the passion of

Christ, not merely at an intellectual level, but at a level of personal participation. Secondly, she prayed for a physical illness so severe that she and everyone around her would think she was dying. Her third prayer was for 'three wounds': true contrition, loving compassion and the longing of the will for God.[1]

Whether or not it was an answer to her prayer, she did have a very serious illness when she was thirty years old. For several days she was near to death, and the parish priest was summoned to give the last rites. But quite suddenly her illness left her, and it was followed by a series of deep religious experiences, including both visions and locutions. She wrote down these visions in English so that they could be shared with as many people as possible. She claimed to have sixteen visions, and these formed her book, *Showings* or *Revelations* or *Revelations of the Love of God*.[2] She mentions that it was in May 1373 that her visions began, and that she was at that time halfway through her thirty-first year, and this indicates 1342 as the year of her birth.

Just when she took up the religious life is uncertain, but a likely guess would place the event after her illness and the visions, which she may have interpreted as a vocation. At any rate, she became an anchoress, defined in the *Oxford Dictionary of the Christian Church* as 'a person who withdraws from the world to live a solitary life of silence, prayer and mortification'. The anchoress (or, in the masculine form of the word, anchorite) would spend the rest of his or her life alone in a cell, often built against the wall of a church, as in Julian's case. If this sounds like a prison, we should note that there were a few amenities. There were three openings from the cell: one was a window, opening to the outside world, normally curtained, but at certain hours the anchoress would come to the window and give counsel to any who sought it; the second opening was a narrow aperture called a 'squint', affording a view into the church so that the anchoress could see and hear the mass, and receive communion;[3] third, there was a door leading to a smaller room where Julian's helper lived and could go out into the city for supplies of necessities. The helper did the housework, cooking, shopping and the like, while Julian spent her time in prayer, contemplation, writing, and, at set times, counselling people from the window: a 'Martha and Mary' arrangement.

In theory, the anchorite or anchoress had died to this world and was already at least halfway to the next. This was symbolically enacted at an installation, when a requiem mass was said in the church, followed by extreme unction. The anchoress was then conducted by the bishop to her cell where she might remain to her dying day. There could be some alleviation; for instance, in an illness it would be permissible for her to take the air in the garden. It was not exactly solitary confinement for, as we have seen, she was expected to present herself at the window, and she had some company in her helper. The diet was very plain, but there was no severe fasting, as she had to be available for people who needed her counsel and encouragement. We know these details because there survives from the Middle Ages the Ancrene Rule, regulating the lives of anchorites and anchoresses.

So what was it that Julian saw in her visions or heard in those moments when, as she believed, God spoke to her through an inner voice? As we have noted, she wrote them down in English so that they would be available to many people. There are two editions of the *Showings*. The first edition dates back to the time of the original experiences. It seems that in the beginning there were many things in the visions that she did not understand, and for twenty years she meditated on what she had seen and heard. About 1393 she rewrote her book in a longer version, repeating the visions and locutions but adding explanations and interpretations.

The record of her experiences enables us to have glimpses into the life of a mystic or visionary. I, and presumably most of my readers, believe that we have some contact with God through prayer or through reading of the Bible or through the sacraments, but perhaps we can only imagine what that contact is like for a person wholly given to contemplation, a contact which is for most of the time intense and constant. In many of her visions, Julian saw the suffering Christ, and though it may be somewhat shocking to some people, dwelt particularly on his blood freely flowing for those he loves. We wonder whether there is something morbid in dwelling on the Lord's sufferings. Julian herself may have wondered about this, for she tells us that she was tempted to look away from the suffering Christ to the exalted Father in heaven. To quote her words: 'At this time, I wanted to look away from the cross, but I did not dare, for I knew well that while I contemplated the cross, I was safe and secure. Then there came a suggestion to me, seemingly said in friendly manner, "Look up to heaven, to his Father!" Then I answered with all the power of my soul, "No, I cannot, for you are my heaven." '[4] The crucified Christ was Julian's heaven, for in his suffering he was God's eternal love brought down to mankind on earth. It is precisely in the self-giving of the crucified Lord that we see the glory of the Father. Julian was living in a perilous time when all Europe was wracked with suffering. It was the century of the Black Death and of the Hundred Years War. A God exalted high in the heavens could hardly speak to men and women of that time, but a God who shared their suffering to the utmost might be heard. The God who took the sin and suffering of his people into his own experience showed himself to be a God of infinite love. Jesus Christ brought hope and even joy into a desperate situation. Life is always a battleground between hope and despair, but the very suffering and self-giving of Jesus gave the confidence that God is on the side of humanity. So Julian could say, in words that are often quoted, 'Sin is necessary, but all will be well, and all will be well, and every kind of thing will be well'.[5] Taken in isolation (as unfortunately they often are) these words about 'all will be well' can easily be misunderstood as an empty and insensitive optimism, but put into the context of Julian's life and of the fourteenth century, they take on a profound meaning.

God's love embraces everything, even the whole world which seems to us so inconceivably vast. God can metaphorically hold that world in his hand and protect it. Julian tells us about another vision of hers:

> He showed me something small, no bigger than a hazelnut lying in the palm of my hand, as it seemed to me, and it was as round as a ball. I looked at it with the eye of my understanding, and thought, 'What can this be?' I was amazed that it could last, for I thought, because of its littleness, it would suddenly have fallen into nothing. And I was answered by my understanding, 'It lasts, and always will, because God loves it; and thus everything has being through the love of God.'[6]

The ultimate reality for Julian is the love of God, a love of everyone and everything, a love manifested in the sacrificial death of Christ. Her ways of speaking of that love are unconventional. She uses human love as her analogy, but not only married love, as in the mystics' favourite *Song of Songs*. Julian is more inclusive, and tells us that 'God is our Father and our Mother and our Spouse'; and in even more startling language she says, 'Jesus is our true Mother. We have our being in him from whom true motherhood begins, with all the sweet protection which endlessly follows.'[7] God, of course, is far beyond our human distinction of sex, and Julian is not a feminist; but she does think that our human love in its various forms, parent and child, husband and wife, brother and sister, friend with friend, are all analogies which, even when added together, fall short of the love of God in Jesus Christ.

It is not inconceivable that Julian herself had been a mother, for people married young in those days, and we do not know what Julian was doing before she became an anchoress at about thirty years of age. There is a passage in her book where she speaks as if she had known motherhood from the inside: 'To the property of motherhood belong nature, love, wisdom and knowledge.'[8]

What do we think then of Julian? Although she chose the solitary life of an anchoress, she was the very opposite of being self-centred. Her deep awareness of the love of God and of Christ had given birth in her also to a love for all human beings and for the whole creation.

In spite of the disease and violence that were prevalent in her time, Julian lived on into her seventies. In 1413 she was visited by a young woman named Margery Kemp, who herself became something of a mystic. In 1416 a citizen of Norwich left Julian in his will the princely sum of thirteen shillings and fourpence, plus a shilling for her attendant. That is the last mention of her, and it is believed that she died soon afterwards.

Only five years after the birth of Julian, there was born in Italy another woman mystic who was destined to have great influence. This was Catherine of Siena (1347–80). She grew up near a house of the Dominicans and seems to have been attracted to the religious life at an early age. So when her parents began to arrange a marriage for her, she resisted, won her point, and, at the age of eighteen, entered the Dominican Third Order, which allowed her to continue to live at home. In some respects, Catherine is a contrast to Julian. Whereas the latter chose a life of solitude, Catherine has been called a 'social mystic', for she alternated her times of contemplation with sallies into the world of affairs. This was the time of the Great Schism, when the Church was deeply troubled. Those considered to be the authentic popes had been forced out of Rome and lived in Avignon, while a line of anti-popes established themselves in Rome. Catherine helped to rally support for the Avignon line and is credited with having persuaded Pope Gregory XI to return to Rome. She herself spent her last years in Rome, worn by very poor health and eventually dying at the age of only thirty-three – again a contrast to Julian who lived to seventy-four, which at that time was considered quite a great age. It is something of a miracle that Catherine was able to achieve so much in such a short lifetime. She was canonized in 1461 and very belatedly declared a Doctor of the Church by Pope Paul VI in 1970. She was one of the first two women in history to receive the latter distinction, the other being Teresa of Avila (see below, p. 167).

Catherine was about thirty when she began to write a very substantial book entitled *The Dialogue*. It runs to about 350 pages in the English translation, and the writing of it occupied the remaining years of her life. This writing takes us right into the mystical life, being a conversation between a soul (Catherine herself, writing about herself in the third person) and God, sometimes apparently the Father, sometimes Jesus Christ. Much of the book is said to have been dictated while the author was in ecstasy. One of her helpers, Caffarini by name, tells us how the book was composed:

I have very often seen her rapt beyond her senses except for speech, by which she dictated to various writers in succession sometimes letters, sometimes the book; and in different circumstances, sometimes as she walked about the room, sometimes kneeling on the floor, but always with her face lifted toward heaven.[9]

But although both Catherine and her helpers testify to periods of ecstasy when her senses of sight, hearing and the rest were suspended, one gets the impression that she had a good deal of common sense, and did not lose touch with what most of us consider to be the 'real' world. She also held that if someone was in need at a time of prayer, the prayer should be interrupted in order to help that person in need. From time to time she might be called away to act as a mediator in a dispute or to advise some churchman on a problem, but even if away for several days, she would take up the work of writing again at exactly the point where she had left off. Probably because of these interruptions, *The Dialogue* is less systematic than it might have been. In my exposition of its teaching, I have sometimes taken the liberty of rearranging the material, but I have preserved the general progression of her ideas and I hope my account is reasonably accurate.

She begins with a prologue[10] which has as its opening words, 'A soul [Catherine herself] rises up, restless with desire for God's honour and the salvation of souls'. The starting point is affective rather than intellectual, it is humble prayer, and this leads to love conceived, as with other mystics, to be some kind of union with God. He makes of the soul 'another himself'. She quotes, in her somewhat free rendering, a verse from John's Gospel: 'If you will love me and keep my word, I will show myself to you, and you will be one thing with me and I with you' (Jn 14.23). She comments that by love's affection the soul becomes 'another himself'; that is to say, 'another Christ'. This is very bold language, though we find it in many other writers, including Luther who had a decidedly low view of mystics. And already at this early stage, we see why Catherine has been called a social mystic, for the union with God or Christ implies a union with other finite souls who have united with God, and of whom the Word says, 'They are another me, for they have lost and drowned their own wills, and have clothed themselves and united themselves and conformed themselves with my will.' Just what is this union? Is it absorption? We must come back to the question.

Catherine then tells us that she had four petitions to offer to God: first, for herself, for unless she attained virtue, there was nothing she could do for God or for other human souls; second, for the reform of the Church, which in her time was divided and at war with itself; third, for the peace and well-being of the whole world; fourth, for providential intervention in a particular case, but as this fourth petition was private and personal, we can only guess about it and it may be disregarded.

As to the first petition, the eternal Truth (a name which she applied to God and Christ) assures her that her desire to offer herself is accepted. She is told:

> You ask for the way to know and love me, Supreme Truth. Here is the way, if you would come to perfect knowledge and enjoyment of me, Eternal Life. Never leave the knowledge of yourself. Then, put down as you are in the valley of humility, you will know me in yourself, and from this knowledge you will draw all that you need.[11]

Here we come again to the idea that knowledge of God and self-knowledge are closely linked. But Catherine introduces an image which we have not met before – the soul is in God and God is in the soul as a fish is in the sea and the sea in a fish. It is an odd metaphor, but it seems to indicate clearly that for

Catherine the soul is not simply absorbed into God, and their unity is not, so to speak, a substantial unity, in spite of such talk as 'you will be one thing with me'. They remain distinct, though in an intimate relation of love. Just how intimate can be judged from the following words:

> She felt her emotions so renewed in the eternal Godhood, that the force of the spirit made her body break into a sweat. Her union with God was more intimate than the union between soul and body. The holy fire grew so great within her that its heat made her sweat water, but that was not enough, she wanted to sweat blood.[12]

It is important to note also that for Catherine the human soul is not in its ordinary fallen condition a revelation of God. It needs to be washed and cleansed through the mediation of Christ, 'made a new creation in the blood which my Son poured out'. Again, in spite of the intimacy, there is no confusion of the finite soul and God, the former being like a tiny fish in a vast ocean.

The second petition had to do with the Church. It seems clear that for Catherine it is the Church rather than the individual soul that is the 'bride' of Christ. But even the Church needs healing and renewal. 'Look how my bride has disfigured her face!' The individual is not called in his or her individuality to be the bride of Christ, but rather 'to wash the face of the bride', to restore the Church to the exemplary position which it ought to manifest in society.[13]

The third petition was for the world as a whole, and here Catherine introduces a new image, which she develops at considerable length. This is the image of Christ as the bridge. The bridge stretches from earth to heaven and replaces a broken road, presumably the road by which humanity in its original condition as bearer of the image of God would have found its way naturally to God. But in their sinful condition, only foolish human beings would attempt to cross the dangerous terrain of this world and neglect the bridge which God has provided. They will perish on the broken road or drown in the river which they might have crossed by the bridge. A new image of the Church is introduced. The Church is like a hostelry on the bridge, where through the sacraments she supplies sustenance to the souls who are crossing. At this point, Catherine also praises the accredited ministers of the Church for their work.

Catherine, like many of the other mystics, believed that salvation depends on a synergism between God and human beings. There is no purely human way to salvation and wholeness (the road is broken) but equally there is no arbitrary divine manipulation or predestination (the human being has to give free consent and co-operation). Though God created us without our help, she says, he will not save us without our co-operation. In an incredible burst of boldness, the soul in her dialogue with God addresses him thus:

> O mad lover! It was not enough for you to take on our humanity. You had to die as well. Nor was death enough. You descended to the depths to summon our holy ancestors and fulfil your truth and mercy ... You deep well of charity! It seems you are so madly in love with your creatures that you could not live without us. What could move you to such mercy? Not duty or any need, but only love.[14]

This, I said, is bold language, but I think it is far more aware of the love of God than that of some theologians who have said that the world could go out of existence and God would not be affected.

There is no corresponding elaboration of the fourth petition for, as I mentioned earlier, it was private and personal, and we need not try to probe into it.

Perhaps it was after one of her absences on practical concerns that Catherine came back to the imagery of the bridge, but her continuation is difficult to disentangle. We are told that the bridge has three stairways. We have already been told that the bridge is Christ himself, so that the ascent of the three stairs is a threefold advance in the love and understanding of Christ. Here Catherine makes it clear that she avoids the danger to mystics of thinking that Christ is a purely spiritual being. She asserts his humanity. He is not an angel; his feet are on the ground, even if he is the bridge that reaches up to heaven. The soul begins its ascent from his feet: that is to say, in humility and even fear which increasingly become love. We may remember at this point the three kisses described by Bernard of Clairvaux – the kisses of the feet, of the hands and of the mouth. Catherine's pattern is similar, but she develops it differently. From the feet, one advances not to the hands but to the heart of Christ. This is approached by the second stair, and progress on this stair demands perseverance, for sometimes Christ withdraws so that we may know our own weakness. Here we meet again the idea noted in Eckhart that the withdrawal of the divine presence can be a spur to a new seeking on the part of the soul. But in Catherine's account, the ascent of the soul does not end even at Christ's heart. The third stair leads from his heart to his mouth. For Bernard, the kiss of the mouth was the culmination, the moment of intimate union. In Catherine, the teaching is that one may not rest in the consolation of Christ. In *The Dialogue* God says, 'Now that [the soul] has arrived at his mouth, she shows this by fulfilling the mouth's functions. First, she speaks to me in holy and constant prayer ... externally, she proclaims the teaching of my truth.'[15] At this point, Catherine claims, the soul has attained an inseparable relation to God.

> To such a soul, it is granted never to feel my absence. I go away from others (in feeling only, not in grace) and then return. I do not act thus with those most perfect ones who have attained great perfection and are dead to every selfish impulse. I am always at rest in their souls, both by grace and feeling ... They have shed every earthly affection and sensual selfishness, and have risen above themselves to the height of heaven by the stairway of virtue, having climbed by the three stairs which I symbolized for you in the body of my only-begotten Son.[16]

But, like Gregory of Nyssa, Catherine sees no end to the soul's progress. Even the most perfect can always grow further, except, she says, Jesus Christ himself.

The third woman mystic to be considered in this chapter is another Catherine, born just about a century later than Catherine of Siena. This was Catherine of Genoa (1447–1510). She had much in common with the earlier Catherine, though I think the later one exemplified the basic characteristics of mysticism in a more intense or more extreme form. There was, however, one very important difference between Catherine of Genoa and the two other women already discussed. All three were attracted to the religious life at an early age, but whereas Julian of Norwich and Catherine of Siena were able to fulfil their desire (though we cannot be sure about Julian's early life), Catherine of Genoa was pressured into a marriage deemed desirable by her family, and spent several unhappy years with an uncongenial husband. So she certainly knew at first hand what it is like to live in the supposedly 'real' world. But in 1474, when she was twenty-six, she underwent a kind of conversion experience. She had been persuaded by her elder sister, a nun, to accompany her to the convent and to make her confession.

> And suddenly, as she knelt before the confessor, she received in her heart the wound of the unmeasured love of God, with so clear a vision of her own misery and of her faults, and of the goodness of God, that she almost fell upon the ground. And by these sensations of infinite love, and of the offences that had been done against this most sweet God, she was so deeply drawn by purifying affection away from the poor things of this world that she was almost beside herself, and for this she cried inwardly with ardent love, 'No more world! No more sin!' And at this point, if she had possessed a thousand worlds, she would have thrown them all away ... And she returned home, kindled and greatly wounded with so great a love of God, the which had been shown her inwardly, with the sight of her own wretchedness, that she seemed beside herself and shut herself in a chamber, the most secluded she could find, with burning sighs. This was followed by an interior vision of Christ bearing the cross, which further increased her love and self-abasement. She cried again, 'O Love, no more sins! No more sins!' and her hatred of herself was more than she could endure.[17]

What may strike us most forcibly in this passage is the close and constant correlation that Catherine makes between the love of God and the sense of her own unworthiness. It is not surprising that the writing for which she is most remembered (though experts on her history tell us that probably she did not write down her thoughts herself, but had them recorded by her friends) is a treatise on *Purgation and Purgatory*. Of the three stages on the mystical way, always remembering that these are not successive stages but are intertwined and recurring, Catherine seems to find that purgation is the really important one. But for her, purgation is essentially positive. Purgation from the worldliness of self takes place to the extent that it is replaced by divine love. True purgation opens the door to love of God. I think this point needs to be stressed, and it is supported by Catherine's distancing herself from any doctrine of eternal punishment or of hell as a penalty imposed by a vengeful God on his disobedient creatures. Hell, according to Catherine, is something we impose on ourselves through our sinfulness, the disintegration of our being which is spiritual death. 'Hell is evil will, and since God does not manifest his goodness there, the souls in hell remain in a state of desperately evil will. The evil lies clearly in the perverse will that opposes God.'[18]

Just as Catherine of Siena talked of God as personified Truth and addressed him as Eternal Truth, so Catherine of Genoa talks of him as personified Love or Pure Love. It is unfortunate that the expression 'self-hatred' appears in the passage quoted above, for it conceals the positive intention of what is being said. I do not think myself that it is a bad thing that we should feel a sense of guilt when we have done wrong, and I have no time for modern sentimentalists, especially those with a smattering of psychology, who try to persuade us that we should not have feelings of guilt. But I would agree that there is something pathological in self-hatred and excessive concern with sinfulness. Catherine, we are told, mortified herself with very severe fasts. She is recorded as having abstained from food for more than forty days, except for the consecrated bread of the eucharist, which she received every day. It is also said that she showed no diminution of energy, in spite of her fasting. If Catherine herself had made such claims, I suppose one would have to accept them, since it would have been quite out of character for her to have lied.

But I suspect that these were exaggerations on the part of those who recorded her thoughts and experiences, due no doubt to the excessive admiration which they felt for her. Nevertheless, it can hardly be doubted that she took on herself an overly severe discipline of mortification, and that it tended in a morbid direction.

Perhaps too there is exaggeration in the ways used to express her sense of union with God, and again we have to remember that it is doubtful whether we are hearing Catherine's own words, or words put into her mouth by some fervent admirer. She held that her relation to God was not one of participation but was a transformation of her being into the being of God. This seems to go quite as far as Meister Eckhart, and suggests that the finite soul is somehow transformed into God or identified with God – a dangerous idea which again verges on the pathological. She says, for instance, 'In this transformation the action of God in penetrating the soul is so fierce that it seems to set the body on fire.'[19] Perhaps a lengthy explanation and interpretation could justify even this language, but I think it should be avoided, and I prefer Catherine of Siena's imagery of the little fish swimming in the sea.

But over against some problematic passages, we must set the fact of Catherine's wholehearted involvement in the affairs of the city of Genoa. After some years, her husband too had been converted to a living faith. The two of them worked together in an enormous hospital for the sick and poor of the city. Catherine's ideal became Francis of Assisi. She was what in later times would have been called the matron of this great institution, and her mystical visions of Pure Love were translated into actions of love. It should be noted also that two of the most perceptive students of mysticism, Baron von Hügel and Evelyn Underhill, both write enthusiastically about the high qualities of Catherine of Genoa. But it is important too that in studying the lives and thought of persons who are the recipients of experiences beyond the range of the great majority, we should be cautious. If there is much to admire in the mystics, there are also matters that must be very carefully scrutinized.

Catherine of Genoa died in her sixties, of a disease which seems to have been psychosomatic. Her spirit burned within her with its accustomed ardour while her body was consumed by a raging fever. I cannot help recalling some words of Dryden:

> A fiery soul, which working out its way,
> Fretted the pygmy body to decay.
> Great wits are sure to madness near allied,
> And thin partitions do their bounds divide.[20]

10

Some Spanish Mystics:

Ignatius Loyola, Teresa of Avila, John of the Cross

At this point our attention switches to Spain in the sixteenth century. For most of that century, Spain was probably the major political power in Europe. In 1492 Ferdinand and Isabella, called by Spaniards *los Reyes Católicos*, finally liberated the Iberian peninsula from the Moorish control that had lasted for more than 700 years, and in the same year Columbus, commissioned by these rulers, discovered America. As well as these political events, the following century was a golden age for literature and the other arts.

Mysticism was among the activities which flourished at that time, and we shall consider three of the leading figures: Ignatius Loyola, founder of the Jesuit order; Teresa of Avila, a worthy successor to the women mystics considered in Chapter 9; and John of the Cross, a poet and one of the best-known mystics of any time. But, strange to say, this burst of mystical inspiration provoked within the Church a violent reaction against mysticism. These were the years of the Spanish Inquisition, and all three of the mystics I have mentioned were harassed in varying degrees by the inquisitors or their minions.

Ignatius of Loyola (1491–1556) was born in the north-west of Spain of a noble family, and in his youth was trained as a courtier. He later entered military service in Navarre, a former kingdom which was annexed to Spain only in 1512. Invading French forces laid siege to the city of Pamplona, and Ignatius was involved in its defence. He was severely wounded in the legs and permanently lamed, so was invalided out of the army and sent home to Loyola to recuperate. In the tedious days of his convalescence, he asked for some of the romantic literature popular in those days to be brought to him to help while away the time. This was the kind of writing so wittily satirized about a hundred years later by Cervantes in *Don Quixote*. In his autobiography[1] Ignatius confesses his vanity at this period of his life, when, 'without knowing, he would spend two, three or four hours' in romantic day-dreams in the service of an imaginary lady. However, no romantic novels were available at Loyola, and instead he was given two volumes, one a life of Christ and the other lives of the saints. This reading produced a profound effect. Writing about himself in the third person, he says, 'Our Lord came to his help and allowed other thoughts, born of his new reading, to take the place of the former.' And the new thoughts satisfied him in a way that the former romantic imaginings could never have done:

> He checked his thought, and said to himself, 'How would it be, if I were to do as Francis did and Dominic did?' So he set before his fancy many things that seemed good, and always he set before himself things difficult and painful; and as he fancied them, he seemed to find within himself the ability to discharge them. And always, at the end of his meditations, he returned to say to himself, 'St Dominic did this, I too must do it. St Francis did that, therefore I too must do it.'[2]

He tells us that he found consolation in these thoughts, and even when he turned to other matters, there remained with him joy and contentment. But so far this conversion experience seems to have affected chiefly the imagination. When he had recovered as far as was possible from his wound, he went to the Benedictine monastery of Montserrat, laid up his armour in the chapel there, exchanged his nobleman's clothes for those of a beggar, and then made his way to the small town of Manresa, not far from Montserrat. There he lived for nearly a year in the utmost simplicity and austerity, reading every day the story of Christ's passion, other books, especially *The Imitation of Christ* of Thomas à Kempis, spending many hours in prayer and in works of charity. It was there that he began the writing of his own *Spiritual Exercises*. At Manresa he began to receive visions and illuminations, culminating in one in which 'the eyes of his mind were opened and he received an understanding of many things, spiritual, as well as matters concerning faith and theology'.

In the next few years of his life, he visited various centres of learning, hoping to acquire an education that would enable him to engage in a life of service to God and his fellow human beings. He finally came to the University of Paris in 1528 and stayed there for about seven years. He gathered about him a group of young men with aspirations similar to his own, and in 1534 they met together and decided that they would work together when they had completed their studies. A plan for them all to go to the Holy Land was not feasible, and instead they went to Rome and with the approval of Pope Paul III formed the Society of Jesus, placing themselves at the disposal of the Pope for service in any part of the world. The new order, with Ignatius himself as its Superior, was different from traditional ones. Service took priority over everything else. Even the daily prayer offices were not to be observed corporately in church. Each member would be out in the world on the business of God, and would read the office on his own. Nor would any distinguishing habit be worn. Within a decade,

Jesuit missionaries were to be found in India, Japan, Brazil and Africa. They learned the languages of the countries to which they went, dressed like the natives and, as far as possible, adopted local customs. They also founded schools, believing in the importance of education. The United States benefited greatly from the educational zeal of the Jesuits in the nineteenth century, when they established many fine colleges and universities to meet the needs of the masses of immigrants from Europe.

But, with Ignatius as with some of the other figures we have considered, the question comes up, 'Was he really a mystic?' I think so, and persons much more knowledgeable on the spiritual life than I am support me in this. Evelyn Underhill writes, 'The concrete nature of Ignatius' work, and especially its later developments, has blinded historians to the fact that he was a true mystic; own brother to such great actives as Teresa of Avila and George Fox, actuated by the same vision of reality, passing through the same stages of psychological growth.'[3] Kenneth Kirk writes, 'No one has excelled Ignatius in emphasizing the truth that it is through meditation on the incarnate Lord that the soul is brought nearest to the contemplation of the eternal Godhead.'[4] The question whether Ignatius is a mystic could only arise if we fail to notice that not only did he revise the conception of a religious order and its rules, he also revised some traditional ideas about mysticism; in particular, when he talks of 'contemplation', he means what many other mystics call 'meditation'; or perhaps one should say that he sees them as two stages on the way to union with God, and certainly does not think of meditation as somehow inferior to contemplation.[5] This was not really something new in the history of mysticism, for whenever it strays too far from the world of history, human beings and material things, someone draws it back (see above, John of Damascus, pp. 103–5 and Bonaventure, pp. 134–5). In any case, we must not forget that Ignatius had his mystical visions and illuminations at Manresa, though in fact mystics tend to play down such extraordinary experiences.

The aim of the *Spiritual Exercises* is explained by Ignatius as follows:

> Under the name of spiritual exercises is understood every method of examination of conscience, of meditation, of contemplation, of vocal and mental prayer, and of other spiritual operations, as shall hereafter be declared: for as to go for a walk, and to run, are bodily exercises, so in like manner all methods of preparing and disposing the soul to rid itself of all inordinate affections, and after it has rid itself of them, to seek and to find the divine will in the ordering of one's life with a view to the salvation of one's soul, are called spiritual exercises.[6]

The full course of exercises occupies about thirty days, with several hours of meditation each day, but Ignatius very sensibly made provision for the course to be adapted to the age and condition of the participants. Those engaged in the exercises are conducted through the episodes of Christ's earthly life, from the Annunciation to the Ascension, and are invited at each stage to visualize the scene, place themselves imaginatively in it, listen to the words of Christ and of the other persons involved, and consider what it means for their own lives. What is intended is that they will become one with God in the service of his Kingdom. It has been said that the exercises are a new version of the *Imitation of Christ*, enriched by Ignatius's own experience of following in that way; or again, that it is like a detailed description of the life of the disciple as summarized in the Epistle to the Hebrews:

Therefore, since we are surrounded by so great a cloud of witnesses, let us also lay aside every weight and the sin that clings so closely, and let us run with perseverance the race that is set before us, looking to Jesus the pioneer and perfecter of our faith, who for the sake of the joy that was set before him endured the cross, disregarding its shame, and has taken his seat at the right hand of the throne of God. (Heb. 12.1, 2)

Teresa of Avila (1515–82) is one of the most outstanding women mystics in the history of the Church. We have already noted that, in company with Catherine of Siena, she was declared one of the first two female Doctors of the Church in 1970 (see above, p. 151). Long before that, she had been canonized in 1622.

Teresa was born in Castile, and like some other women mystics had to struggle against the wishes of her family in order to embrace the religious life. In 1535 she entered the Carmelite monastery of the Incarnation at Avila, and was professed two years later. She was stricken by a serious illness which permanently damaged her health. But, like Ignatius, she used the time of illness for serious reading. Her commitment to the life of prayer deepened, she took Augustine as a model, and also began to write down her experiences, which included raptures and visions. She was distressed by what she perceived as the laxity of the Carmelite order, and in 1562 founded a new and smaller convent, where about a dozen sisters devoted themselves to serious contemplation and unceasing prayer. She continued her writing, including an autobiography and a meditation on the *Song of Songs*, but her principal work, *The Interior Castle*, completed in 1577, gives a detailed account of the spiritual pilgrimage as she had experienced it, and we shall turn to that writing in a moment.

Meanwhile, Teresa had been busy trying to reform the Carmelite order, and founded about a dozen new convents in which a stricter rule would be observed. Her work, like that of other reformers, met with opposition and attempts were made to prevent her from travelling around Spain. The hostility of the Inquisition was probably aroused by a fear that anyone claiming direct visions from God was weakening the power of the ecclesiastical authorities. It was during this period that she met a younger priest who was attracted by her teaching and later became a noted saint and mystic, John of the Cross. Teresa died in 1582.

The leading idea in *The Interior Castle* is one which Teresa had learned from Augustine. The latter had looked for God in various places, but it was when he turned inward and explored the depth of his own being that he at last saw the light. This idea is expounded in detail by Teresa. The human person or soul is like a castle. There are outer courts and many rooms, and for the most part people are content to stay in these outer areas. But the work of the spiritual life is to penetrate to the very centre of the castle, and there one finds both one's own true self and God in his triune majesty. 'His Majesty' is a form of words which Teresa likes to apply to God, but it does not imply the homage it often has when used of a remote earthly ruler. With Teresa, 'his Majesty' is almost a term of affection. 'Mental prayer,' she tells us, 'in my opinion is nothing else than an intimate sharing between friends.'[7] Yet, in spite of this intimacy, Teresa recognizes the difference between divine and human, and does not confuse the two, as perhaps some mystics are in danger of doing. Our relation to God is multiform. As well as Friend, he is Father, as well as Companion (especially in tribulation) he is Teacher, he is Bridegroom and Spouse but also Lord of the world, our King. In all these capacities, God is very near.

The interior castle has seven dwelling places, the first three attainable by human effort and ordinary grace, the remaining four by infused or mystical prayer. It is said that on the eve of Trinity Sunday, 1577, the whole plan of Teresa's book was revealed to her in a flash:

> There was a most beautiful crystal globe like a castle in which she saw seven dwelling places, and in the seventh, which was in the centre, the King of Glory dwelt in the greatest splendour. From there, he beautified and illumined all those dwelling places to the outer wall. The inhabitants enjoyed more light, the nearer they were to the centre.[8]

While she was admiring this beauty, the light suddenly disappeared, no doubt as a salutary reminder that in the absence of God, we live in the darkness of sin.

I suppose this sudden vision of the whole theme of her book is an illustration of what mystics call 'contemplation'. A parallel experience would be that of some composers who tell us that in what seems an instantaneous experience, they conceive a whole movement of a sonata or symphony, though then they have the labour (from which the vision has not excused them) of giving form to the movement, stating the themes, developing them, deciding about harmonies, instrumentation and many other problems. So Teresa's vision of life has to be worked out in a step-by-step analysis of the way that must be patiently and even painfully followed by those who would reach the centre of the castle. The chapters of Teresa's book were originally given as lectures to the sisters, and she is very frank in her written version in reporting moments in the lecture when she would tell the sisters that she did not fully understand some point or that she had lost her way in the argument.

The body is the outer wall of the castle, and the way to the interior is prayer. Even to enter the first dwelling place is something valuable, but she warns that pleasures and vanities, with their honours and pretences, are still dominant in the minds of those who have entered, and that 'hardly any of the light coming from the King's royal chamber' reaches these first rooms. Yet she stresses the beauty of a human soul in its pristine condition. Nothing is comparable to it. Our intellects cannot comprehend it, and that is no surprise since it is in the image of God. She then stresses the importance of self-knowledge. The advance of the disciple takes place in the alternation of self-knowledge and knowledge of God. The darkness which mortal sin brings upon the soul is an inducement through fear to seek God, but it also induces humility. So it is good, she says, to enter first into the room where we begin to learn self-knowledge.

In the second dwelling place are those who have made some progress in prayer, and what is chiefly demanded here is perseverance. There are many temptations and distractions, but there is also the hope of moving further into the interior.

Even in the third room, there is no security, and there never is security in this life. Again she emphasizes perseverance. We must not give up. Humility helps, and anticipation of what lies ahead in further dwelling places. If dryness is experienced, that is probably due to lack of humility. We should not complain that we deserve better. 'We are fonder of consolations than we are of the cross.' In this third stage there is advance in prayer and the practical virtues, but still a lingering desire for wealth and material prosperity.

One may remain a long time in these three outer rooms before advancing to the fourth, where supernatural experiences begin. Here one must learn passivity: 'The Lord gives when he desires, as he desires, to whom he desires.' Teresa offers an analogy. Let us suppose that there are two troughs containing water. One is supplied by an elaborate system of pipes and ducts, and is like the spiritual satisfaction that we might achieve by complicated systems of meditation. The other trough is fed directly from an underground spring; that is to say, it is a parable of how God supplies his grace directly to the soul.[9] This mystical claim that God might act directly on an individual and not necessarily through the ecclesiastical channels was one of the ideas that upset the church authorities.

Teresa visualizes the possibility of paranormal experiences involving the body as well as the soul, for instance, a feeling of warmth. She speaks too of a form of recollection in which the self is unified not by its own effort but by God. 'The senses and exterior things seem to be losing their hold, because the soul is recovering what has been lost.' She reminds us that the mind is more than the investigative intellect. God is the agent in these matters. Our business is to be open, to listen, when the soul, instead of engaging in discourse, strives to remain aware and attentive to what God is saying. But we should not seek these experiences; the first thing needed is to serve God without self-interest. She also warns against counterfeits. But she does say, 'Let persons who have not experienced those things understand that truthfully they do happen ... and that the soul understands them in a manner clearer than I can explain.'[10]

In the fifth dwelling place, we come to union with God, and Teresa tells us there is little she can say, for every comparison is inadequate. She has already in the fourth room mentioned a union of the believer's will with the will of God, but now she seems to have an even more intimate union in view. This union is above all earthly joys, a different feeling, like the difference between feeling on the surface of the body and feeling in the marrow of the bones. After the experience, the soul is in doubt whether it really happened or was an illusion. During the union, the soul neither sees nor hears nor understands, but when it returns to itself, 'it can in no way doubt that it was in God and God was in it'.[11] Here one may think of Bernini's famous sculpture, *The Ecstasy of St Teresa*, in which an angel (though resembling more a pagan Cupid) has plunged the spear of love into Teresa, and when it is withdrawn, 'the saint ecstatically sinks back on to a cloud, her eyes nearly shut, her lips parted in a soft moan'. The sculpture illustrates an incident in Teresa's own autobiography in which she was 'utterly consumed by the great love of God'.[12] But Teresa insists that love of God implies love of neighbour: 'Be certain that the more advanced you see you are in love for your neighbour, the more advanced you will be in love for God.'[13] At this point Teresa, while admitting that it is still inadequate, tells us that the sacrament of marriage is the best comparison she can find to explain spiritual union.

But the moment for the spiritual marriage has not yet come. The sixth dwelling place is a kind of pause in the progress towards God. The soul has been wounded by the arrow of love, but the Spouse holds off the marriage to increase the desire. There are new trials, joy is mingled with pain. One may receive locutions, but some of them are illusory. How may they be tested? There are various ways. Is a locution close to scripture? Does it bring quiet to the soul? Does it stay in the memory? Perhaps ambiguity can never be eliminated. There are also moments of rapture, such as the one immortalized by Bernini, or glimpses of heaven (not described), or words of pardon. The soul is in a room with many treasures, and though they cannot all be described, the impression remains. These moments of rapture do not usually last for long. Some of them are forceful to the point of being frightening, and in such a moment the soul may grasp many things instantaneously. These special favours are like jewels given by the Spouse.

When we come to the seventh and last dwelling, is there anything more to be said? Teresa answers this question: 'Since the greatness of God is without limit, it would be foolish to think that no more could be said.'[14] For now the soul is joined to God and the two become one. We are told that there is the greatest difference between all the foregoing visions and this one. In the spiritual marriage, God dwells inseparably in the very centre of the soul. The soul is made one with God and he reveals to it the glory of heaven. Again the recurrent problem about pantheism arises, and Teresa does not dispel it when she says that the union of the soul with God is like a raindrop falling into the sea.

So what point have we reached on this spiritual journey? Teresa mentions five effects of the divine presence in the soul:

1. Forgetfulness of self.
2. Willingness to suffer.
3. Deep joy, even in misfortune.
4. No hostility towards wrongdoers.
5. A detachment that no longer seeks consolations or raptures, but dwells in stability.

Teresa, it seems to me, gives us one of the loftiest and most attractive accounts of the experience of a Christian mystic.

I have already made a brief mention of a young priest who was attracted by Teresa's teaching and who helped in her work of reforming the Carmelite order. This was John of the Cross (1542–91). This is the name or designation by which he is universally known: his original name, Juan de Yepes, being unknown except to those who still want to study his life and teaching. For John turned out to be a mystic and spiritual leader almost as important as Teresa herself. But he is more problematical. Like Teresa, he did not shrink from the practical tasks of the Church, and was, like her, active in reforming the Carmelites. But on the theoretical side, he taught a view of the mystical life which perhaps unduly dwelt on its more negative aspects. Even those who have not read much of John have heard the expression, 'the dark night of the soul', for it has become inseparably associated with him and already conveys a warning that one must not look in his direction for much in the way of consolation. Rowan Williams, the present Archbishop of Canterbury, gives quite a sympathetic exposition of John in his book on spirituality,[15] but W. R. Inge, a former Dean of St Paul's, is quite sharply critical.[16] I suspect that the debate for and against John of the Cross will continue.

First, we note the facts of his life. Brought up in modest circumstances by a widowed mother, John was sent by a patron to the University of Salamanca, where he received a good education and became a member of the Carmelite order. We have already seen that he came under the influence of Teresa and shared in her reforming zeal. Like her, he was suspect in the eyes of the Inquisition, but suffered even more severely. When he died in 1591, virtually a prisoner in a remote monastery, his life had indeed been largely a 'dark night', though that is to use or misuse the expression in a popular sense, and John himself understood the 'dark night' in a spiritual sense, as describing the journey of the soul to God.

The phrase is in fact the opening words of one of his poems: 'En una noche oscura . . .'

En una noche oscura,	One dark night,
con ansias, en amores inflamadas,	Fired with love's urgent longings,
(¡oh dichosa ventura!)	(ah, the sheer grace!)
sali sin ser notada	I went out unseen,
estando ya mi casa sosegada.	My house being now all stilled.[17]

This picture of a lover going forth by night in search of the one whom he loves is the beginning of John's spiritual journey. But John was to discover that no Lover could be more exacting in his demands than the God whom he was seeking.

God is more often associated with light than with darkness, but to claim that God is found in the darkness was not new. We may remember that Gregory of Nyssa in his *Life of Moses* contrasts Moses' first encounter with God in the light of the burning bush with his later summons to meet God in the darkness of the cloud at the giving of the law (see above, p. 44). But in John of the Cross, darkness bulks more largely than light. His writings are partly in the form of poems, very highly esteemed in Spanish literature, and partly in the form of prose commentaries on the poems. His three major writings are *The Ascent of Mount Carmel,* where we meet again the familiar image of the mystic way as the journey upward towards God; *The Dark Night of the Soul,* which describes the stripping away; and *The Spiritual Canticle,* when the pilgrim reaches the end.[18] Within these poems and commentaries, we can distinguish the established pattern of purgation, illumination and union, but these three stages do not correspond except very approximately to the three literary works, and they are not in any case successive but are mingled together throughout the journey.

At the beginning of *The Ascent,* the word 'night' is introduced, and we are given a summary of the journey that lies ahead:

> We can give three reasons for calling the journey toward union with God a 'night'. 1. Individuals at the point of departure must deprive themselves of their appetite for worldly possessions, like a night for all the senses. 2. The road is faith, and this is night for the intellect. 3. The point of arrival is God, and God is also a dark night to the soul in this life.[19]

What we have to do now is to unpack this summary and try to come to some judgement on whether John presents us with a convincing account of the mystical way.

The first stage of the journey – or we may call it the first night – is the night of the senses. God and the created things of the world are not compatible. 'Empty your spirit of all created things.'[20] God and things are not compatible: as one side grows, the other side must diminish. Created things cannot be a ladder to the divine, they are rather a hindrance. If the soul is to grow towards God, it must be stripped of all created things. Revelation is totally divorced from intellect. The conclusion would seem to be that there can be no natural theology, no recognition that the things of this world can be sacraments opening a way to their Creator. This initial clearing of created things from the mind is something achievable by our own efforts. It is an activity of the soul, but only a preparatory one.

Next comes the night of the spirit. Now we are passive, and submit to the purifying work of God. We let go of the intellect, we do not seek visions or consolations. On the contrary, we are bidden to seek 'bitterness in God, rather than sweetness'.[21] Yet we are told that this is not purgation but illumination. Rowan Williams remarks: 'If God is to work in us as he wills, we must become Christ-like; and that is to bear the living death of inward and outward darkness and lack of consolation.'[22] W. R. Inge sees John's teaching differently: 'We are to denude ourselves of everything that makes us citizens of the world – that *nothing* which is natural is capable of entering into relations with God – that all which is human must die, and have its place taken by supernatural infusion.'[23]

There is a difficult problem of interpretation here. Dr Williams sees the night of the spirit as indeed a 'midnight' that has to come before the dawn. Dr Inge ('The Gloomy Dean', he was called) says that 'John carried self-abnegation to a fanatical extreme, and presents the life of holiness in a grim and repellent aspect'.[24] I find myself tending to agree with Dr Inge, but he may be too negative in his assessment.

I would put it this way. If one lives through the night of the senses and then the life of the spirit, discarding now this, now that, what is finally left of the soul to be united to God? A mere shadow? I find it impossible to believe that God gave to his human creatures reason and intellect, but tells them that they must divest themselves of these gifts if they wish to come into union with himself.

Yet John himself did believe that union is achieved only when finally the soul detaches itself from everything finite:

> The excessive light of faith, bestowed on a soul, is darkness for it; a brighter light will eclipse and suppress a dimmer one. The sun so obscures all other lights that they do not seem to be lights at all when it is shining, and instead of affording vision to the eyes, it overwhelms, blinds and deprives them of vision ... Similarly, the light of faith in its abundance suppresses and overwhelms that of the intellect. For the intellect, by its own power, extends only to natural knowledge, though it has the potency to be raised to a supernatural act whenever our Lord wishes.[25]

He finally visualizes the soul and God in erotic terms as the relation of bride and bridegroom, based on the *Song of Songs*. But I do not see how, except by a *tour de force* (perhaps justifiable), this 'happy ending' can be reconciled with all that he has been saying concerning the earlier parts of the soul's journey.

Post-Reformation Mystics:

Jakob Böhme, Blaise Pascal,
George Fox, William Law

At this point, we do not simply begin a new chapter but enter a new era in the history of Christian mysticism. Up until now, we have seen that there was a recognizable tradition of mysticism, originating in patristic times and stretching to the Spanish mystics of the sixteenth century. With variations in imagery and emphases, many of the same characteristics repeated themselves among the mystics whom we have considered. But the Reformation brought into being a new swath of Christian denominations. We can discern in them too forms of spirituality which fall within the general description of mysticism given in Chapter 1, but Protestant spirituality sought to be biblical and to eliminate those elements of mysticism originating from Greek philosophy, especially neo-Platonism. Luther, for instance, severely criticizes the search for allegorical or mystical interpretations (supposedly) underlying the (again I should say supposedly) plain straightforward scriptural text. Attacking a certain Jerome Emser who had written a book praising the 'spiritual' as against the 'literal' interpretation of the Bible on the basis of some words of Paul (2 Cor. 3.6), Luther calls him 'hyperspiritual' and says, 'He builds on Origen, Dionysius and a few others who taught the same thing', and claims that in so doing Emser is preferring human teachings to the clear words of scripture.[1] Just as medieval ecclesiastics were sometimes suspicious of mystics because the latter seemed to attach more importance to their visions than to the precepts of their superiors in the Church, so the Reformers were afraid that some of the more radical Protestants were emphasizing the spirit in ways which threatened the authority of the Bible.

One of the earliest and most influential of these new Protestant mystics was Jakob Böhme (1575–1624). His name is often spelt Boehme. He was born near the German town of Görlitz, received an elementary education, and set up as a shoemaker in the town. About 1600, he had a visionary experience, which he first wrote down in 1612:

> I saw the Being of all beings, the ground and the abyss; also the birth of the Holy Trinity; the origin and first state of the world and of all creatures. I saw in myself the three worlds: the divine or angelic world; the dark world, the original of Nature; and the external world, as a substance spoken forth out of the two spiritual worlds. In my inward man, I saw it well as in a great deep, for I saw right through as into a chaos in which everything lay wrapped, but I could not unfold it. Yet from time to time it opened itself within me like a growing plant. For twelve years I carried it about within me before I could bring it forth in any external form . . . Whatever I could bring into outwardness, that I wrote down. The work is none of mine. I am but the Lord's instrument, whereby he doeth what he will.[2]

This vision in which Böhme claims to see not only the creation of the world but even of God out of an abyss apparently beyond God, may strike the reader as so wildly speculative that it would be a waste of time to go further in this mystic's company. But I ask the reader to be patient. Let me confess that I have had more bother with Böhme than with any other of the mystics discussed in this book, both to disentangle his ideas and then to present them in a form accessible to a modern reader.

He declared that he had not derived his teachings from other people; indeed in the last sentence of the quotation on the preceding page, he seems to be saying that his thoughts were dictated by the Lord. We have already learned, however, that the mystical spirit is generally aroused by a period, perhaps quite a lengthy one, of perplexity and self-questioning. Görlitz, like many other German towns, was buzzing in those days with controversy on religious topics, with orthodox Lutherans, Calvinistic sympathizers, Anabaptists and other adherents of radical sects all pushing their points of view. Böhme was a very serious man, one of whose favourite words was *Ernst*, 'earnestness', and he must have been pondering the conflicting views in the time before the critical moment when he had his vision. He published his account of the vision in a writing called *Aurora* in 1612, but it aroused hostility in the town, and he was forbidden to publish for five years.

Later on, his views became even more fantastic, as he began to incorporate fragments of philosophy, alchemy and even astrology. We shall exclude all that from consideration. But underlying it all is a fairly definite form of mysticism which he himself expounded in language tolerably free from exotic embellishments. This was *The Way to Christ*,[3] a series of nine treatises interspersed with prayers and serving as a guide to the mystic way as Böhme understood it. Even this mainly devotional writing aroused opposition, and an attempt was made to have him banished from Görlitz. He died there in 1624.

In *The Way to Christ* he proposes to tell the reader about

the way he himself has gone. Before there can be prayer, there must be an honest acknowledgement of the bad state into which the soul has fallen. The imagery he uses is that of the prodigal son (Lk. 15.11–32). We human beings have lost the image of God which was granted at the Creation, we have forgotten our baptism into Christ who had regained for us the divine image, and we are like tattered swineherds. If we are to get out of this wretched condition, there is needed a 'powerful resolution' and we are able to make such a resolution because there remains in us a 'spark' that pulls us towards God and that can lead us towards the transformation of our nature. There seem to be at least three points here in which Böhme's teaching is in conflict with Reformation theology:

1 The Reformers stressed human helplessness and believed that salvation comes entirely from God, whereas we have here a claim that there is a human contribution in the form of a powerful resolution.
2 The Reformers, especially Calvin, believed that the human being has sunk into total depravity, whereas Böhme can speak of a spark which still remains in the soul and which can respond to God.
3 The Reformers thought of justification as a forensic happening, a declaring of men and women to be just or righteous even if they were still in sin, whereas Böhme is saying that justification must take place *in* the man or woman through a transformation of his or her nature. It cannot be a transaction independent of the person justified, nor can it be a mere prelude to sanctification, for any genuine justification must be itself a sanctification, or at least the beginning of it.

How then did Böhme and those who thought like him defend their position in relation to the Bible and to traditional

Christian doctrine? The basis of it is the statement in Genesis that God said, 'Let us make man in our image and likeness' (Gen. 1.26). The original human being (not original in a chronological sense but in an archetypal or ideal sense) bears the image and likeness of God. This image was damaged by the fall into sin, but not, so Böhme and others would argue, entirely destroyed. But even if it had been destroyed, it was renewed by Jesus Christ, the Son of God and the Word of God. At this point appeal was made to a verse in John's Gospel: 'The true light, which enlightens everyone, was coming into the world' (Jn 1.9). Every human being has a share in that light, a 'seed' of the light, an expression also used by the English Quakers (see below, p. 190). Such language has a history going away back to the second century, when Justin spoke of the *logos spermatikos*, though I doubt whether Böhme or Fox, both of them 'unlearned' men, knew anything about Justin. The effect of this line of argument is to interiorize the way to Christ and to God. The Word is already present in our minds, in the very way we are constituted.

When we have considered and understood our actual condition – namely, that the real self has in it the seed of the Word or of the Light, but that this has been reduced to a weak spark by our sins – we may embark on the prayer of penitence, which in Böhme corresponds to what the earlier mystics called the purgative way. Earnestness, again a human contribution, is required for this, but it is the Spirit that prays in our hearts and the Word that becomes the life in our flesh. It is the whole life of Christ, from the Annunciation to the Ascension, not just his atoning death, that brings salvation, and this process takes place within the soul, which becomes a temple of the Holy Spirit.

The imagery here becomes dense, and a complication is added through the introduction of *Sophia*, the divine Wisdom, treated as a personalized female hypostasis. The editor and translator of *The Way*, Peter Erb, frankly acknowledges that 'this is one of the most difficult concepts in Böhme's system to grasp',[4] and Böhme himself says that he cannot write of Sophia's coming into the soul, though he describes her as 'the rose of Sharon' (*Song* 2.1). Sometimes Sophia seems to act as a mediator between Christ and the soul, and perhaps this is a reminiscence of the Blessed Virgin Mary reappearing in this Protestant writer. Sophia is said to stand immediately before the door of the (still unawakened) soul and to knock and to warn him or her of danger. She knocks on the centre (*centrum*) of the soul and speaks in the name of Jesus.

I have puzzled over Sophia, and the solution that seems to me most probable is that she is the ideal or archetypal self, formed in the image of God and bearing the seed of the Word. She comes as a bride, and here Böhme reverses the usual mystical imagery, for it is now the soul that is the bridegroom. Sophia restores the soul's true nature. This is a process rather than an instant happening, a process which is both purgation and illumination, in which the soul must overcome all the false trails it has been following, such as pride, lust, envy and whatever else has obscured and diminished the presence of the Word. The more these false desires are removed, the more the soul enters into grace.

There is a conversation between the soul and Sophia.[5] The soul asks her for a pearl which she possesses, but she replies that she must keep it to herself until he is purged of all earthliness. This may be Böhme's way of distancing himself from other mystics of his time who believed that perfection is possible in this life. But though Sophia does not for the time being give him the pearl, she promises to visit him often and to give him her presence.

As the process of reclaiming the true humanity of the soul goes on, its interiority is stressed. The earnest prayer of the soul is: 'Arise in my spirit and in my interiority, and ignite within me the fire of your love, so that my spirit burns in your love; open my interiority to me, so that I may properly know what I am.'⁶ Even heaven and hell are interiorized. If the question is asked, 'Does not the soul go into heaven or hell just as a man goes into a house?' the answer is, 'No, there is no entrance in such a way, for heaven and hell are present everywhere. There is only the changing of the will either into God's love or into wrath.'⁷ The whole account of the Christian life given by Böhme seems to carry the subjectivizing of religion just about as far as possible. The questions that troubled us with some of the earlier mystics come back with new urgency. Does God exist independently of and prior to human souls as their Creator, or is he simply an aspect or phenomenon belonging to the human mind itself? Or is the human soul in its centre simply a spark thrown off by the divine Being? Or are God and the soul a unity in some mysterious way? Whatever answer we give to such questions, it would be hard to stay within the limits of orthodox Christian belief.

I think that we have now moved sufficiently along the way to Christ to have grasped the essentials of Böhme's teaching. Obscure though it may be, it has been quite influential and has been studied by some very distinguished thinkers, including Sir Isaac Newton, William Law, Nicolai Berdyaev and Paul Tillich, and we shall encounter his ideas again in later contexts.

Although in this chapter we are concerned chiefly with mystics or quasi-mystics from the churches of the Reformation, there is an important Roman Catholic thinker who shared a similar type of spirituality, Blaise Pascal (1623–62). Educated at home by his father, he began even in adolescence to make important contributions to mathematics and physics. His significance for a study of mysticism is that this Renaissance scientist did not claim that science is the only path to secure knowledge but believed that alongside science there is another kind of knowledge which is actually more important when we face the ultimate questions about the significance of human life. Near the beginning of this book (see above, p. 4) we took note of Russell's summary dismissal of mysticism as mere emotion, and his claim that there is only one way to knowledge, the way of rational investigation as practised in the sciences. Not only Russell but many scientists and philosophers in modern times have held this view, but Pascal was and remains a brilliant exception, and perhaps we can still learn from him. We may notice too that although he was a Roman Catholic, he belonged to the unorthodox school of Jansenism, associated with a religious house at Port-Royal. The main characteristic of Jansenism lay in the claims that it made for the theology of Augustine, even for a strict doctrine of predestination. But from the point of view of mysticism, what was important in Augustine was his teaching that God is to be sought within, in the depths of the soul, where one disovers the light (see above, p. 17). This is what links Pascal to the other mystics considered in this chapter. There is an inner light by which we learn about the spiritual world, and this has to be set alongside the rational investigations by which we learn about the natural world. In some often-quoted words of Pascal, 'We know the truth not only by reason, but even more by the heart ... The heart has its reasons, which reason does not know.'[8] In support of this point of view, Pascal refers to the fact that the first principles of mathematics and, indeed, of all thinking, need no logical proof but are intuited, already given in the very constitution of the mind.

He sees an analogy between the situation just described and the question of the existence of God, though I do not think he spells out this analogy adequately:

The metaphysical proofs of God are so far removed from ordinary human thinking and so convoluted that they make little impression; and when they do with some people, that happens only for as long as their demonstrative force is seen clearly, but an hour later, these people fear they may have been mistaken.[9]

He is fascinated, as were the existentialists of a later time, by the paradox of the human condition, in which are conjoined finitude and an infinite outreach:

What is man in nature? A nought with respect to the Infinite, an all with respect to the nought, a middle point between the nothing and the all. Man is only a reed, one of the feeblest things in nature, but this is a thinking reed. The greatness of man is great in the very fact that he knows his misery.[10]

A being in such a condition cannot escape answering the ultimate and apparently unanswerable questions about human existence itself. Is there a God? Is the human being annihilated by death? Is there any direction or purpose or meaning in the world? There can be no certainty in such matters. Anything like logical proof is unattainable. There are only the intuitions of the 'heart'. This seems a pretty desperate situation. We might contrast it with the situation described by Pascal's contemporary and rival, René Descartes. For Descartes, every-thing can be doubted, except one's own existence, for at that point doubt does give way to certainty. But for Pascal, doubt is never fully eliminated. Or is it? We shall consider that in a moment.

So the argument has brought us to the point where we must look at Pascal's famous wager argument for the existence of God: 'Let us weigh the gain and the loss in wagering whether God exists. Let us evaluate the two cases; if you win, you win everything, and if you lose, you lose nothing. So don't hesitate, wager that he exists.'[11] There has been and very likely will be much discussion about what this means. I think it would be simplistic to suppose that it is merely a matter of chance, for that would suggest that the existence or non-existence of God does not matter. Pascal thinks that it does matter, that it is in fact a life-and-death matter. If you win the wager, you win eternal life. If you lose, you lose this prize. It reminds me of what Socrates said in his apology about death. His argument was that death is something good. If there is life beyond death and one meets again one's friends, then nothing could be better than that. If death is annihilation, then it is like an undisturbed sleep, and that is a good thing too, though not so good as the other. Socrates does not consider a third possibility, nor shall we – the barbarous notion that there might be eternal punishment.

In his mathematical speculations, Pascal worked on probability theory. Some scholars have attempted to interpret the wager argument in terms of such a theory. According to the *Port-Royal Logic* of 1662, Pascal's theory of probability may be summarized thus: 'To obtain a good or avoid an evil, one must consider not only the good and the evil in themselves, but also the probability of their happening or not happening, and view geometrically the proportion that all these things have together.'[12] I question, however, whether one should attempt to give too precise an account of the logic behind Pascal's argument, for such a procedure would seem to be in contradiction to his assertion that the 'heart' has its reasons which reason cannot know. I believe that the incentive to wager on God depends rather on some non-rational (but not anti-rational) experience of a mystical sort. 'It is the heart that perceives God and not the reason.'[13] The 'heart' is an unsophisticated term used by Pascal to include feeling, conscience, intuition and other experiences which are not to be dismissed as non-cognitive, but in which intellect is combined with emotion, will and even prayer. Or, to express it in another way, alongside the senses which interpret the material world for us under the aegis of reason, there is a spiritual discernment which opens up spiritual realities, including God. So I think that what underlies the wager argument is not a theory of probability but the shattering mystical experience which Pascal had in 1654. In the testimony to this event, which he carried about on his person until his death, he asserts the reality of religious experience over against the speculations of metaphysics, and claims to pass beyond probability to certainty:

> The year of grace, 1654, Monday, 23 November, Feast of St Clement, Pope and Martyr, from about half past six in the evening until about half past midnight. Fire. The God of Abraham, the God of Isaac and the God of Jacob, not the God of the philosophers and the scholars. Certitude, certitude, feeling, joy, peace. The God of Jesus Christ. Your God will be my God. Forgetfulness of the world and of everything, save God.[14]

These are words which try to express an ecstatic experience. Jesus Christ had become for Pascal the centre of a mystical contemplation in which the truths of God and religion were opened to him in a way that he could not doubt. He goes so far as to say, 'Jesus Christ is the goal of everything and the centre to which everything tends. He who knows him knows the reason for everything.'[15] Certainly these are bold words, but not to be dismissed as fideism or enthusiasm. The recipient of such experiences believes them to bear the stamp of truth, and those of us who do not have the experience must at the very least respect the testimony of those who do.

Pascal's mind seems to have been equally at home in science and religion.

We turn now to George Fox (1624–91), founder of the Quakers, an English mystic whose Christian faith was not far from Böhme's but which had nothing corresponding to the speculative or metaphysical ideas which the German thinker advanced. Fox was unlettered, and preferred to stay that way, rejecting the use of any philosophical terms such as 'essence' (see below, p. 191). His *Journal*[16] is a straightforward day-to-day record of his preaching and of various pamphlets which he wrote. It tells the story of his life from his early days until 1676, when he discontinued it. It was published in 1694 and gives a most interesting account of the man himself, the Society of Friends (popularly called the Quakers) which he founded, and of the state of religion in seventeenth-century England, especially in the Cromwell years.

Fox's father was a weaver in a Leicestershire village in the English Midlands. When he was about nineteen, the young man left home in search of spiritual satisfaction. At that time there were many so-called 'seekers' in the country, for religion was very important to the majority of people and there was much restlessness as those who were dissatisfied with the traditional ways searched around for what they thought would be better.

Where did Fox get his ideas? He had had a religious upbringing and was well versed in the Bible, but from an early age he was critical of his religious teachers. They might have been trained at Oxford or Cambridge, but that does not qualify anyone for a genuine Christian ministry. None can be a minister of Christ except in the eternal Spirit, who was before the scriptures were. He claimed that he had got his understanding of Christian faith not from any human teachers, nor even from scripture, but directly by revelations, which he called 'openings'. He did not disparage the scriptures, but believed that the Spirit which had enlightened the authors of scripture is more authoritative than the scriptures themselves, and that this Spirit still speaks directly to chosen persons. The light which Jesus Christ, the true Word, brought into the world is a light that has a seed in everyone (Jn 1.9).

From this basis of belief Fox derived other beliefs which remained with him throughout his life. He believed that people should use few words, and that their 'Yea' and 'Nay' are sufficient without an oath, which is not only unnecessary but a profaning of the name of God. He gave up attendance at churches, which he called 'steeplehouses', for the Church is the company of believers, who are the true temples of the Holy Spirit. He denounced all professional Christian ministry because the ministers received payment and the gospel should be free. He believed in the equality of all human beings, and refused to take his hat off to anyone, even when he was brought into court. He abjured violence and if he was struck by someone, would not retaliate. Likewise he refused to bear arms for either side in the English Civil War between King and Parliament. He also had a sense of unity with the whole creation. At least some of these points have much to commend them. Less acceptable, however, was his conviction of his own rightness, perhaps even his perfection; and correspondingly of the blindness and sinfulness of anyone taking a different view of things. He even stated that until he came on the scene, the history of Christianity from the end of the apostolic age onwards had been one of unrelieved apostasy. Also, many people would find objectionable his somewhat vindictive belief that those who opposed him were marked out for judgement by God, and could be expected to drop dead or suffer some other misfortune before long.

These ideas sprang from what he believed were direct communications (openings) from God or Christ; that is to say, from the Word or Light that was within him. It was to preach this version of the Christian gospel that he embarked on a lifelong nomadic ministry, going from town to town in Britain and later in America and northern Europe. In the course of his preaching, he built up the Society of Friends, said to number about 200,000 at the beginning of the twenty-first century. Though such a small body, they have an integrity that has won them influence and respect. Fox tells us that 'It was Justice Bennett of Derby who first called us Quakers, because we bid them tremble at the word of God, and this was in the year 1650'.[17] So originally it was not the Friends who quaked, but their opponents.

It is impossible not to feel sympathy and even some admiration for Fox as one reads through his lengthy *Journal* (nearly 800 pages in the standard edition) though in a sense it is the same story told over and over again. He comes to a town with two or three companions, they put up at an inn or with a friendly family, he preaches in the streets or the fields, occasionally in the church or steeplehouse after the regular service has ended. A number of people will usually be convinced by his preaching, but it is likely that a larger number will be hostile and will throw stones at him or give him a beating. Sometimes he is haled before the magistrates for causing a disturbance. In face of this, he shows remarkable patience and perseverance, and to some extent one can overlook some of the less desirable traits in his character.

One of his most serious brushes with the civil authority took place at Lancaster in 1652,[18] when he was jailed for six months. It is interesting to read the charges laid against him and his answers, for they throw considerable light on his ideas. There were eight charges:

1 That he did affirm that he had the divinity essentially in him. Answer: For the word 'essentially', it is an expression of their own, [not mine], but that the saints

are the temple of God and that God doth dwell in them, that I witness and the scripture doth witness, and if God doth dwell in them, the divinity dwelleth in them, and the scriptures say the saints shall be made partakers of the divine nature, this I witness.

2 Both baptism and the Lord's Supper are unlawful. Answer: As for the word 'unlawful', it was not spoken by me, but the sprinkling of infants I deny, and there is not scripture that speaketh of a sacrament. But the baptism that is in Christ with one Spirit into one body, that I confess; and the bread that the saints break is the body of Christ and the cup that they drink is the blood of Christ, this I witness.

3 He did dissuade men from the reading of scripture, telling them it was carnal. Answer: For dissuading men from reading the scriptures, it is false, for they were given to be read as they are and not to be made a trade upon. But the letter is carnal and killeth, yet that which gave it forth is spiritual and eternal and giveth life. This I witness.

4 That he was equal with God. Answer: That was not so spoken, but he that sanctifies and they that are sanctified are all of one in the Father and the Son, and that ye are the Sons of God. The Father and the Son are one, and we of his flesh and of his bone; and this the scripture doth witness.

5 That God taught deceit. Answer: That is false, and was never so spoken by me.

6 That the scriptures were anti-Christ. Answer: That is false and was never spoken by me; but they which profess the scriptures' spirit and live not in the life and power of them, as they did who gave them forth, that I witness to be anti-Christ.

7 That he was the judge of the world. Answer: The saints

shall judge the world, the scripture doth witness, whereof I am one, and I witness the scripture fulfilled.

8 That he was as upright as Christ. Answer: Those words were not so spoken by me, but as he is, so are we in this present world, and that the saints are made the righteous of God; that the saints are one in the Father and the Son; that we shall be like him; that all teaching which is given forth by Christ is to bring the saints to perfection, even to the measure, stature and fullness of Christ, this the scripture doth witness, and this I do witness to be fulfilled.

Although the language is different, it is not difficult to recognize in some of these charges ideas which we met in the earlier classical mysticism, and about which I felt constrained to raise questions, as to whether humans and God were being confused, whether God was being assimilated to the inner life of the human soul, whether everything was being too much spiritualized to be compatible with human life in the body, whether such views allow of incarnation or leave any significance to the historical life of Jesus Christ. Perhaps the ideas that we find both in Fox and in earlier mystics can be given an interpretation that does not infringe any major Christian doctrine, but this is not certain and Fox's own replies are, at least some of them, equivocal. One seems especially wide of the mark. By definition, a sacrament includes some visible material substance or action. A meaning may be attached to the notion of spiritual baptism, but where this is entirely distinct from water baptism, it is not the baptism of the New Testament, nor could it possibly be described as a sacrament or quasi-sacrament.

There is no doubt, in my opinion, that George Fox may be justly classified as a mystic. This is plain from the charges that were laid against him, and from the answers which he gave.

In addition, we have seen that he claimed to have visions or 'openings' and that there were silent meetings of the Friends when they waited for the inner Light. It is worth remarking that although Fox was a Protestant and even a radical Protestant, he and his Friends endured the most severe persecutions under the Commonwealth, the period of Protestant ascendancy in English history. He complained, 'Great sufferings we went through in these times of Oliver Protector and the Commonwealth.'[19]

Passing on to somewhat happier times, we come to William Law (1686–1761), a Nonjuring Anglican priest. The Nonjurors were so called because they remained loyal to the Stuart dynasty, and refused to take an oath of loyalty to those sovereigns who came after James II. Law was in 1711 elected to a fellowship in his Cambridge College, but because of his Nonjuring views, he was not allowed to hold a position in either the Church of England or a university, so he had to resign his fellowship in 1716, and he was ordained by a Nonjuring bishop and exercised his ministry outside the established Church. His writings belong to the eighteenth century, but it is convenient to treat him here since his ideas had close affinity to those of both Böhme and Fox.

The book for which he is best known is *A Serious Call to a Devout and Holy Life*, to which is added as a subtitle the words, 'Adapted to the State and Condition of All Orders of Christians'. This was published in 1728. Like George Fox, William Law had been since his youth a very serious or earnest person, determined to devote all his energies to God and to religion. Already as a young man he had written out for himself a strenuous rule of life which he sought to observe:

> To avoid all concerns with the world or the ways of it, except when religion requires. To remember frequently that no condition of this life is for enjoyment, but for trial; that

every power, ability or advantage we have are all so many talents to be accounted for to the Judge of the whole world. To avoid all excess in eating and drinking. To be always fearful of letting time slip away without some fruit. To avoid all idleness. To think humbly of oneself, and with great charity of all others. To think often of the life of Christ, as a pattern for one's own life. To spend some time in giving an account of the day: How have I spent it? What sin have I committed? What temptations have I withstood? Have I performed all my duty?[20]

Stern stuff for a young man, and perhaps unnatural! But this early essay in self-discipline foreshadows the teaching of *A Serious Call*.

The book sets forth an austere ethical version of Christianity, very much along the lines of his own private rule. Though very likely unaware that George Fox had said the same thing, Law claimed that a training at Oxford or Cambridge did not provide what is needed for Christian ministry. Nor is prayer, whether public or private, the chief requisite. The essential is complete and heartfelt devotion to God:

> He therefore is the devout man who lives no longer to his own will, or the way and spirit of the world, but to the sole will of God, who considers God in everything, who serves God in everything, who makes all the parts of his common life parts of piety by doing everything in the name of God and under such rules as are conformable to God's glory.[21]

Let us remember, too, that although I have mentioned Christian ministry, Law was summoning all Christians in whatever condition or vocation to a devout and holy life. He is not writing for the clergy, still less for monks and nuns, but for all Christians. So far, however, we have not found anything in his writing that could be called 'mystical', except that in a general way the serious devotion which Law demands is a precondition of a mystical spirituality.

A Serious Call became a very popular book and was valued by Dr Samuel Johnson, John Keble, John Wesley and many other prominent figures in the eighteenth and nineteenth centuries. This was partly because of its literary qualities. Law gave life to his book by introducing fictitious characters who illustrate the various lifestyles current in his time. For instance, Cognatus personifies the clergy, though we would hope not all of them. He skilfully combines service to God with a healthy respect for Mammon:

> Cognatus is a sober, regular clergyman of good repute in the world, and well esteemed in his parish. All his parishioners say he is an honest man, and very notable at making a bargain. For twenty years he has been a diligent observer of the markets, and has raised a considerable fortune by good management.[22]

As was mentioned above, Law was unable to be appointed to a regular parish of the Church. He seems to have had private means, but he also acted as a private tutor. For some years he was tutor to the Gibbon family (to which the famous historian belonged), and about 1740 the historian's aunt and another lady set up a small semi-monastic community in Law's native village, and engaged Law as chaplain and spiritual director. The members of this community lived very strictly along the lines set out in *A Serious Call*. For instance, they gave nine-tenths of their income to the poor.

But a change was coming over Law. As I mentioned, there was little in his earlier career that could properly be described as mystical. However, in the 1730s he had discovered the writings of Jakob Böhme, and became fascinated, even obsessed, by them. They supplied, so he believed, a metaphysical and theological vision which fitted in with his own deepest convictions. He wrote:

> When I first began to read Böhme, he put me into a perfect sweat. But as I discovered sound truths and glimmerings of a deep ground of sense even in passages not then intelligible to me, I found in myself a strong incentive to dig in these writings, and I followed the impulse till at length I discovered the wonderful treasure that was hidden in this field.[23]

Though Law did not claim himself to be the recipient of private openings or revelations, he made those granted to Böhme his own. He declared, surely in exaggerated terms, that 'the mystery of all things was opened by God in his chosen instrument, Jakob Böhme'.[24] He was particularly impressed by that early vision of Böhme's in which he had claimed to learn more in a quarter of an hour than he could have done in years at a university (see above, p. 179). Since God is potentially in all human beings, there is finally no distinction between what are usually called 'natural theology' and 'revealed theology'. 'All the mysteries of the gospel, however high, are yet true and necessary parts of the one religion of nature, because they are no higher or otherwise than the natural state of man absolutely stands in need of . . . For the fallen, corrupt, mortal state of man absolutely requires . . . that the divine life or the life of God must be quickened again or revived in the soul of man.'[25] Revelation or opening cannot be something merely external, but must take place in the very centre of the human soul. So Law is in agreement with Böhme on the three points on which the latter departed from the Protestant orthodoxy of those days: the human being co-operates with God in the work of redemption; the human being is not totally depraved but retains some spark of affinity with the Creator, however this is to be conceived; there is no merely forensic justification, but a true reconciliation. 'The whole truth is this. Christ given for us is Christ given into us.'[26]

I have said that Law depended on the testimony of Böhme for his openings, but at the end of his life he had his own overwhelming revelation. His companion in the community reported that before he died in 1761, 'He said he had such an opening of the divine life within him that the fire of divine love quite consumed him.'[27]

Eighteenth Century:

Jonathan Edwards, John Woolman

More than once in the earlier chapters of this book I have had to pause in order to justify the inclusion of one or other of the persons whom we have been discussing as mystics. In the opening chapter, I listed ten characteristics that seem to be common to many of those persons who are universally recognized as mystics. Perhaps there is no one who exhibits all ten, perhaps indeed they could not all be present together in a single person. But where someone has been chiefly remembered for something other than his or her contribution to mystical spirituality, but has shown what I call 'strong mystical tendencies', I have thought it permissible and even desirable to include that person. Thus, Augustine is remembered principally as a theologian, Ignatius of Loyola as founder of the Jesuits, George Fox as founder of the Quakers; but each of them was, in different ways, a mystic.

The problem arises again as we come to the eighteenth century. That was not a century in which mysticism flourished. In the Roman Catholic Church, the tradition survived, but in the new Protestant communions, mysticism was generally rejected. The situation was exacerbated by the rise of rationalism, which sometimes took on an anti-religious or anti-Christian character. It is an age which is remembered more for Voltaire than, let us say, for John Woolman.

The question, 'Can this person be fairly presented as a mystic?', arose for me most acutely in the case of Jonathan Edwards (1703–58). Few would deny his outstanding qualities as a theologian and philosopher of religion. He was probably the most important American theologian down to modern times when, I would say, Reinhold Niebuhr emerges as at least an equal. But Edwards has been very unfortunate in the way in which he has been presented in histories of American theology. Everyone who has heard of him at all knows that he preached an infamous 'hell-fire' sermon, 'Sinners in the Hands of an Angry God', that he opposed the Arminian attempt to tone down the excesses of Calvinism, and that he was associated with the mass hysteria which accompanied the evangelical campaign called the Great Awakening. I accepted that picture and thought of him as a quintessential Calvinist until some years ago I was asked to review a volume containing some of his works. I found that there was another side to him, that he did not just stick rigidly to orthodox Calvinism, and that as time went on he became critical of the unstable emotionalism evoked by the Great Awakening. John E. Smith, Professor of Philosophy at Yale University, a person whom I knew and admired, had become, with two associates, the editor of a new edition of the complete works of Edwards, so I began to think there was more to this eighteenth-century figure than I had realized. His editors go so far as to speak of 'the mystical side of Edwards'.[1] A former colleague of mine, the historian Robert Handy, mentions the influence of Edwards' wife, Sarah Pierrepont, 'whose intense mystical piety deepened her husband's interpretation of the spiritual life'.[2] In what follows, I shall first of all bring forward detailed evidences of a genuine mystical tendency in Edwards, and then more briefly I shall try to show that this mystical side signals a modification by Edwards in his understanding of Calvinism.

Jonathan Edwards was born in Connecticut, the son of a Congregationalist minister. Already religiously inclined in boyhood, he was destined for Christian ministry. Motives for entering the ministry are always mixed, and some of Edwards' were not creditable. One was personal ambition: 'If it was plain to all the world of Christians that I was under the infallible guidance of Christ, then I should have power in all the world.'[3]

He was a student at Yale University when he had an experience which set the tone for a mystical spirituality. He was reading in the New Testament, and came on the words, 'Now unto the king eternal, immortal, invisible, the only wise God, be honour and glory for ever and ever. Amen' (1 Tim. 1.17). He writes in his *Personal Narrative*:

> As I read the words, there came into my soul and was, as it were, diffused through it a sense of the glory of the divine Being; a new sense, quite different from anything I experienced before. Never any words of scripture seemed to me as these words did. I thought with myself, how excellent a Being that was; and how happy I should be if I might enjoy that God and be rapt up to that God in heaven, and be as it were swallowed up in him.'[4]

These words certainly have the sound of mysticism about them.

Since directness was the first of the ten characteristics of mysticism set forth in our first chapter, it is significant to find Edwards writing, 'There is such a thing as a spiritual and divine light, immediately imparted to the soul by God, of a different nature from any that is obtained by natural means.'[5] When Edwards first mentions this notion of a direct communication of God with the creature, he seems to be thinking primarily of revelations given to biblical personages; for instance, the revelation to Peter that Jesus is the Christ (Mt. 16.17) But he seems to have had moments of enlightenment which, though one might hesitate to call them revelations, seem rather similar to the 'openings' reported by the Quaker mystics. 'My sense of divine things gradually increased, and became more and more lively, and had more of inward sweetness. The appearance of everything was altered; there seemed to be, as it were, a calm sweet cast or appearance of divine glory in almost everything.'[6]

About this time (1722 or 1723) he drew up a list of resolutions, much as William Law and perhaps many other seriously minded young men at that period did (see above, p. 194). Edwards' list had no fewer than seventy resolutions and is too long to quote in full, and it is very demanding. I shall quote the first resolution, which shows us that even at this point Edwards believed that God's glory coincides with human happiness: 'Resolved, that I shall do whatever I think to be most to God's glory, and to my own good, profit and pleasure.' This sounds very much like the common Calvinist belief that service of God is accompanied and even evidenced by worldly prosperity, but to do justice to Edwards, it should be added that the first resolution included two additional obligations: 'Resolved to do whatever I think to be my duty, and most for the good and advantage of mankind in general. Resolved to do this, whatever difficulties I meet with, how many and how great soever.'[7]

Meanwhile, his spiritual growth was going forward. 'Spent most of my time in thinking of divine things, year after year. And used to spend abundance of my time in walking alone in the woods and solitary places, for meditation, soliloquy, and prayer and converse with God.'[8]

This description seems to have been typical of him during a brief pastorate in New York before he went on to his major period of service in the Congregationalist church at Northampton, Massachusetts. It was there that his evangelical zeal was most in evidence, together with his contribution to the Great Awakening, though there were other preachers just as much or even more involved in that enterprise than was Edwards. It was also at Northampton, in 1737, that he had what seems very much like a mystical vision (he called it a 'view') which he describes as follows:

> Once, as I rid out into the woods for my health, and having lit from my horse in a retired place, as my manner commonly has been, to walk for divine contemplation and prayer, I had a view that for me was extraordinary, of the glory of the Son of God; as mediator between God and man; and his wonderful, great, full, pure and sweet grace and love, and meek and gentle condescension. This grace, that appeared to me so calm and sweet, appeared great above the heavens. The person of Christ appeared ineffably excellent, with an excellency great enough to swallow up all thought and conception.[9]

He adds the information that this experience lasted 'as near as I can judge, for about an hour'.

One further point on Edwards' expanding spirituality at that time may be worth mentioning. We have seen that some mystics distinguished meditation from contemplation, the former proceeding discursively from one point to another through a narrative or description, while the latter fixes on a single thought which nevertheless carries a great weight of significance. There is something of this in Edwards. He tells us, 'Sometimes only mentioning a single word causes my heart to burn within me; or only seeing the name of Christ, or the name of some attribute of God.' He gives as an example the phrase, 'Infinite upon Infinite! Infinite upon Infinite!' which he would repeat to himself in his times of quiet.

Perhaps this phenomenon from American Protestantism is a parallel to the Jesus Prayer in Eastern Orthodoxy.

However that may be, there is still the difficult question of how Edwards reconciled these mystical tendencies in his soul with his Calvinistic theology. The mystical element seemed to be pulling him in the same direction as the three post-Reformation mystics whom we considered in the preceding chapter. We remember that they collided with Protestant orthodoxy in several ways (see above, pp. 181). How did Edwards overcome the differences beween his spirituality and his theology; or, to put the same point in a different way, between his experience and his dogma? Or did he overcome them?

I mentioned three points where the mystics found themselves in conflict with mainline Protestant theology. The first two concerned the human condition. The theologians of the Reformation declared that human beings are helpless to save themselves, and are justified by the work of Christ in which they have no part; and beyond this the theologians, especially Calvin, believed that human beings are in a state of total depravity, which he neatly summed up in the phrase, 'Everything proceeding from the corrupt nature of man, damnable.'[10] These two points can be considered together. Certainly, Edwards took a very serious view of sin, but so did the three mystics we considered. Yet the mystics did not accept *total* depravity. They allowed some 'spark', however weak and however ill-defined, in the human soul, which still directs humans to God and is still capable of responding to God and of working *with* God in salvation. They would agree that without God, the human race is powerless to resist sin, but they would also claim that without the human response, God's grace cannot produce anything worthy to be called salvation. It is not enough for Christ to be born; he must be born *in* us. Now, I think, Edwards was at least on his way to accepting this. He does recognize that even among pagans there is a 'natural religion', admittedly dark and confused, but nevertheless furnishing some ideas of morality and even of God. I think, however, that the overwhelming evidence that Edwards did not accept the dogma of total depravity is to be found not so much in his texts as in his evangelical activity. Though he came to doubt the value of the more emotional and transient victories of the Great Awakening, the very act of preaching the Kingdom of God presupposes that those to whom the preaching is addressed have the possibility of making an intelligent response.

There remains the difficulty arising from conflict about how we think of God. Does the idea of a sovereign God who has already predestined some human beings to salvation and others to damnation and apparently leaves no freedom of decision to them – does not that idea demolish the whole mystical view of an ascent to God and an ultimate union or communion with God? I do believe that Edwards would have rejected and would have continued to reject some of the more speculative views of God held by some mystics. Whether or not he had Böhme in mind, Edwards, in a couple of brilliant sentences, demolishes Böhme's idea that God himself was born from an aboriginal abyss (see above, p. 179). Edwards says,

> If any man thinks he can think well enough how there should be nothing, I'll engage that what he means by 'nothing' is as much something as anything that ever [he] thought of in his life; and I believe that if he knew what nothing was, it would be intuitively evident to him that it could not be. So that we see it is necessary that some Being should eternally be.[11]

But Böhme has not been entirely eliminated, and later his ideas reappear in Berdyaev.

But, returning to Edwards, it could be said that he is engaging in a problem which faces every theologian, Calvinist or of any description. This is the problem of how to recognize a divine providence and yet not surrender a belief in what is always a limited human freedom. To believe in God is not merely to believe that he created the world in the beginning, but that he 'programmed' the world so that it moves in accordance with certain laws towards an end which he has set for it. He exercises a general government of the world, yet it seems to me that Edwards does not think of this government as so rigid and particularized that human beings are reduced to being mere puppets. One might appeal here to one of the less attractive elements in Edwards' thought, his emphasis on the 'wrath' of God. If the salvation or damnation, indeed every action of each human individual, has already been decided from all eternity; if, as the *Westminster Confession of Faith* expressed it, 'God from all eternity did, by the most wise and holy counsel of his own will, freely and unchangeably ordain whatsoever comes to pass',[12] then it would be quite absurd to imagine that God would be angry when his own decree worked itself out in the history of the world. It cannot be denied that Edwards did affirm the wrath of God and even the quite un-Christian idea of eternal punishment, but this was surely inconsistent in one who also dwelt much on the mercy and sweetness of God. It is, however, understandable in one whose own experience was leading him beyond constricting dogmas to a view like that of William Law, who denied that there is any anger in God, and that what some have called divine anger is simply the working out of sin in those human beings who try to live in opposition to the laws, both natural and moral, of this world. At his best, Edwards perceives that God's glory, which he took to be the goal of the world process, could not possibly be served by anything like eternal punishment, for the glory of a loving God must include the perfecting of his creatures. Edwards does not quote the celebrated words of Irenaeus, but I think he would gladly have identified with them: 'The glory of God is a living man; and the life of man consists in beholding God.'[13]

Perhaps if Edwards had lived longer, some of the inconsistencies in his thought might have been resolved, but in 1749 he fell out with his congregation in Northampton. He took up another pastorate in Stockbridge, Massachusetts, where he ministered to a native American congregation. In 1757 he was appointed to be president of New Jersey College (now Princeton University) but died the following year at the age of fifty-four.

We pass now to another American, John Woolman (1720–72), a younger contemporary of Edwards, but one in the Quaker rather than the Calvinist tradition. He inherited the spirituality of George Fox, but in the century that separated these two men, Quaker mysticism had undergone a kind of purification, especially of any elements that might be called superstitious. Whereas Fox believed that on some occasions he could foretell future events, Woolman tried to dissuade people from believing that he himself had any such powers; and whereas Fox tended to rejoice when any of his opponents met with misfortune and claimed that it was a judgement of God on the said opponent, there is nothing of that in Woolman. In the chapel of Boston University, there are shown in stained glass a group of four mystics: John of Damascus, Bernard of Clairvaux, Teresa of Avila and John Woolman.[14] The first three are world-famous and have all been recognized as saints and are duly honoured as such in the Church's calendar. In comparison, Woolman is a little-known figure in Christian history, but if Quakers ever get around to canonizing any of the Friends, Woolman would surely be among the first to be so honoured.

John Woolman was born in New Jersey into a family of

Quakers who had settled there in the preceding century. The boy grew up with an early tendency towards religion. He tells us that after school he preferred to study the Bible rather than play with the other boys,[15] which provokes me to say what I said also about William Law's precocious religiosity: 'How unnatural!' Woolman wrote about himself as he was in his teens:

> [I] was early convinced in my mind that true religion consisted in an inward life, wherein the heart doth love and reverence God the Creator, and learn to exercise true justice and goodness, not only toward all men but also toward the brute creatures; that as the mind was moved on an inward principle to love God as an invisible incomprehensible Being, on the same principle it was moved to love him in all his manifestations in the visible world.[16]

In this statement, it is clear that Woolman's mysticism was of the kind which sees God in the world as well as in the inward spiritual life. Especially interesting is the expression of his concern for the 'brute creatures'. Apparently this was something he had learned from his father, and in those days such concern was quite rare. Of course, he was equally or even more conscious of the claims of his fellow human beings, and one would certainly need to call Woolman a 'social mystic', an expression which we first met when we were discussing Catherine of Siena (see above, p. 151). Indeed, Woolman has been credited with being one of the very first champions of the 'social gospel' which was later to become a powerful influence in American Christianity. We shall see, however, that Woolman's essentially gentle nature led him to champion social causes by personal persuasion of those who could be influential in promoting them, rather than by political means or by verbal abuse of his opponents.

Although his formal education did not go beyond the elementary stage, Woolman appears to have been an avid reader and to have had access to books, so that he was self-taught beyond what he had learned at school. Much of his reading was of Quaker literature, including writings by George Fox and William Penn, but he also read or at least knew something about the writings of Thomas à Kempis, John Locke, Jakob Böhme and William Law.

When he was about twenty, he felt moved to speak at a Friends' meeting. It seems that he said more than he had intended, and was distressed and embarrassed. For about the next six weeks, he remained silent, but then felt once again that he was presented with an 'opening', and this time spoke effectively. The experience was valuable to him and taught him to wait in silence, sometimes for weeks together, until he felt 'the pure spirit that moves inwardly on the heart' before venturing to speak. But he gained a reputation for speaking sensibly and wisely, and eventually became a minister among the Quakers. Unlike most Christian churches and denominations, the Friends have no professional ministry, and anyone suitably qualified and approved may exercise the ministerial function. Also, their ministry is not organized on a parochial basis, but follows the pattern set by George Fox. We have seen that his ministry was itinerant. He would go from town to town, seemingly at haphazard, but probably believing that his journeys were in response to divine promptings.

In the meantime, Woolman had to earn a living, for a Quaker minister must not accept any pecuniary reward for his services. So Woolman became attached to a small business in New Jersey and kept the books and dealt with any legal or commercial matters that required attention. It was in the course of such duties that he was quite suddenly confronted with a moral problem which was designed to become his major preoccupation for the rest of his career. His employer had a negro slave whom he wished to sell, the buyer was himself a Friend, and Woolman was required to draw up the bill of sale. At that time, slavery was an accepted institution in the colonies of America and the Caribbean. Hundreds of thousands of Africans had been shipped to these colonies, and they were bought and sold in markets much as cattle and sheep are bought and sold. Now that he was all at once involved personally in such a transaction, Woolman had to confront the institution of slavery in a new way. He realized that the buying and selling of fellow human beings, of owning them and having almost absolute power over their lives, made a mockery of the faith which he believed and which he taught and proclaimed as a minister. 'I said before my employer and the purchaser that I believed slave-keeping to be a practice inconsistent with the Christian religion.'[17] Out of a sense of duty to his employer, Woolman did what was required, but it sadly troubled his conscience and he attributed his action to a moment of weakness. So when another Quaker approached him soon afterwards to arrange the conveyance of a slave to him, Woolman excused himself, and there began his campaign against slavery, more than a century before the American Civil War. But I should probably not have used the word 'campaign' in the last sentence. Woolman, confident in the justice and rationality of his cause, advanced it quietly by reasonable persuasion.

His first itinerant ministry, undertaken in company with an older Friend, took place in eastern New Jersey. Most of the speaking was done by his companion, and Woolman, chastened no doubt by his early experience, was often silent through the meetings and spoke only with care, that '[he] might speak only what Truth opened'.[18] On this journey, which lasted two weeks, he had time to reflect on his future. Though he was doing well in business, he felt he must be free of the restrictions it placed on him. Wealth seemed to have little attraction for him. He saw clearly that the more wealth one accumulates, the stronger becomes the desire for still more. So he took up the trade of being a tailor, and from that he earned a modest income and was able to apply himself to ministry.

His first journey on ministry was confined to New Jersey. It was followed by others, which lasted longer and took him further afield. One such journey took him into the southern colonies including Virginia and North Carolina. In these areas, he became much more aware of the institution of slavery than he had been in New Jersey. In his home area, the European settlers worked hard to cultivate their lands, but further south the hard agricultural work was done by slaves. What he saw increased Woolman's desire to bring an end to what he regarded as an indefensible blot on American society. In the opposite direction, he undertook an itinerary that took him into New England. This was in 1747. Jonathan Edwards was still at Northampton at that time, but there is no report that Woolman ever met him. It is unlikely that they would have found much about which they could agree, not only because of Edwards' Calvinism but even more because he was a slave-owner, though not on a large scale.

On his journeys, Woolman made a point of visiting Friends who owned slaves and of trying to persuade them by friendly argument that the practice was at variance with their Christian convictions. It seems that quite a number of Quakers, even in the north, were slave-owners. George Fox had not condemned the institution, though when he visited Barbados, he pleaded for a humane treatment of slaves. In 1754 Woolman published the first part of his *Considerations on the Keeping of Negroes*. His quiet methods were remarkably successful. Many Quakers were turned away from keeping slaves, and, as in those days Quakers were numerically much stronger in proportion to the general population than they are now, their example spread to other religious communities. Unfortunately, however, it was not enough to prevent the bitter events of the nineteenth century.

In regard to another moral problem, whether it is ever right to use violence or to engage in warfare, the Quakers did have a view which they had inherited from Fox, and according to which violence is not to be opposed by violence. Woolman led the opinion of the Friends on this matter also, because the rivalry between British and French colonizers erupted into war in the 1750s.[19] He upheld the Quaker tradition of refusing to take up arms, but was obviously not quite so sure of the morality of withholding taxes levied for the war effort.[20] Perhaps he recognized that such a practice runs the risk of so undermining government that society falls into the worst condition of all, anarchy. It is also significant that it was less easy to persuade the Friends to be pacifists than to give up slavery.

No doubt the people who suffered most in these wars were not the French and British but the native Americans ('Indians') who were drawn in on both sides. Woolman entertained towards the native Americans the same friendly spirit that had led him to seek the amelioration of the blacks, and he made at least one journey, unarmed, deep into Indian territory. However, he was less successful in persuading his fellow settlers to be friends with the Indians, as subsequent history showed.

Woolman was above all a very humble, self-effacing person (in this respect, something of a contrast to Fox) and so, although he mentions 'openings', he does not say much about any special visions which he may have received, or what interpretations he put upon them. Nevertheless, there are two such visions mentioned in his *Journal*, showing the mystic element in his nature.

The first of the two visions took place when he was lodging

at the house of a Friend. He had gone to bed, and woke up from his sleep (perhaps his way of saying, 'This was *not* a dream'). He writes:

> It was yet dark, and no appearance of day or moonshine, and as I opened my eyes I saw a light in my chamber, at the apparent distance of five feet, about nine inches in diameter, of a clear easy brightness, and near its centre the most radiant. As I lay still looking upon it without any surprise, words were spoken to my inward ear, which filled my whole inward man. They were not the effect of thought, nor any conclusion in relation to the appearance, but as the language of the Holy One spoken in my mind. The words were, 'Certain evidence of divine Truth'. They were again repeated exactly in the same manner, and then the light disappeared.[21]

He does not offer any interpretation of this vision, but it seems to have been a subjective experience of certitude, comparable to what Kierkegaard says about the subjectivity of truth. The description of the experience also recalls strongly the similar experiences of Augustine and Pascal (see above, pp. 17, 188).

The second vision occurred in 1770, when Woolman had a serious illness. He tells us:

> I was brought so near the gates of death I forgot my name. Being then desirous to know who I was, I saw a mass of matter of a dull gloomy colour and was informed that this mass was human beings in as great misery as they could be, and live, and that I was mixed with them, and that henceforth I might not consider myself as a distinct or separate being. In this state I remained several hours. I then heard a soft melodious voice, the words were 'John

Woolman is dead.' I soon remembered that I was once John Woolman, and greatly wondered what that heavenly voice could mean . . . Then the mystery was opened, and I perceived that it meant no more than the death of my own will.[22]

It was in fact a typical mystical experience, in which the boundaries between self and not-self (God, world, other people) disappear, and the recipient becomes part of a larger whole.

By about 1770, Woolman was strongly drawn to make a visit to England, a kind of pilgrimage in which he would go back to his roots, both ethnic and spiritual. He sailed for London in 1772, journeyed in stages to the north of the country, visiting Friends' meeting-houses on the way. He came eventually to the city of York, but by this time was ill and worn out. He died there in a Friend's house before the end of the year, and was buried in the city. Woolman is among the most attractive of the mystics, both for his personality and for the way in which he brought his mysticism to bear on the problems of the world of his time. He also showed that the essential spirit of mysticism can play a part in the modern post-Enlightenment world.

13

Nineteenth Century:

John Keble, Søren Kierkegaard, Charles de Foucauld

Towards the end of the eighteenth century, a change was taking place in the intellectual fashions of the time. The formal classicism and somewhat narrow rationalism that had been predominant for several decades was beginning to give way to what is generally called Romanticism. It is virtually impossible to give any brief definition of Romanticism. Negatively, it was a reaction against the Enlightenment. Affirmatively, importance was being attached to aspects of experience that had been ignored or underestimated in the Age of Reason, but there was much variation in the choice of those aspects. In a general way, it could be said that the personal began to be stressed over against the impersonal, feeling and willing as over against ratiocination, and there was a tendency to glorify the past as a time supposed to be simpler and more authentically human than the modern age. On the other hand, science continued to expand, and that expansion continued dramatically all through the nineteenth and twentieth centuries.

In the limited area which is our concern, we have seen that mysticism did not attract very many adherents in the eighteenth century, but there was something of a revival in the nineteenth, though in new forms. Sometimes it took the form of a Nature-mysticism. Some poets believed that the objectifying matter-of-fact value-free approach of the scientists was a demeaning of Nature, depriving it of its aesthetic qualities, which had been dismissed as merely emotional reactions with no cognitive content or any basis in the 'real' (understood as 'material') world. Recognition of the aesthetic properties of Nature passes easily into a religious or mystical sense of a reality beyond the physical but communicating itself through the physical.

For the English-speaking world, a defining moment was the publication in 1798 of the *Lyrical Ballads* of Wordsworth and Coleridge. It was in the same year that Wordsworth had written his famous *Lines Composed a Few Miles above Tintern Abbey*, lines in which he traces the development from a youthful sympathy with nature to a more mature mystical sense of a divine Presence:

> For I have learned
> To look on nature, not as in the hour
> Of thoughtless youth; but hearing oftentimes
> The still, sad music of humanity,
> Nor harsh nor grating, though of ample power
> To chasten and subdue. And I have felt
> A Presence that disturbs me with the joy
> Of elevated thoughts; a sense sublime
> Of something far more deeply interfused,
> Whose dwelling is the light of setting suns,
> And the round ocean and the living air,
> And the blue sky, and in the mind of man:
> A motion and a Spirit that impels
> All thinking things, all objects of all thought,
> And rolls through all things.

This is not 'sheer Romanticism', when that expression is used as a term of abuse to designate something that is regarded as mere emotion without thought. It differs from much of the mysticism we have met in earlier chapters chiefly in the fact that this Nature-mysticism is outward looking. God is found not so much within the depths of the human soul (as in Augustine, Teresa and John of the Cross, to name three examples) but in the natural world. Perhaps I am making too much of this difference, for Wordsworth does speak of the 'still sad music of humanity' and of what goes on 'in the mind of man', while Augustine and the others at least did not deny that something of God can be known from Nature. But certainly there is a shift of emphasis away from inward experience to experience of surrounding Nature, from an 'inner light' to a light that shines in everything, if we are able to see it.

If it is a mistake to dismiss Wordsworth's lines as 'sheer Romanticism', it is no less a mistake to designate them as the 'higher pantheism'. He is not saying that the ocean, the sky and so on are divine or a part of God but, in true mystical fashion, he is looking for a deeper reality in or behind or beyond these physical phenomena, and apparently finding that deeper reality, not so much perhaps in any particular natural phenomenon as in the way that all together they constitute a unity so harmonious that it strikes us with awe. This is what permits him to speak of a Presence in Nature.

The mystical feeling for Nature continued in the decades following Wordsworth. The lines of Tennyson are equally well known:

> Flower in the crannied wall,
> I pluck you out of the crannies,
> I hold you here, root and all, in my hand,

Little flower – but *if* I could understand
What you are, and all, and all in all,
I should know what God and man is.

Here the thought is perhaps as metaphysical (Hegelian) as it is theological.

The first nineteenth-century figure whom we shall consider is John Keble (1792–1866), best known along with Newman and Pusey as one of the founding fathers of the Oxford Movement which brought about a spiritual renewal of the Church of England in an age dominated by science, technology, industry and power politics. The Church of England is noted for its moderation in all things, even in its Christianity, and, as an archetypal Anglican, Keble could be described as a moderate mystic, well suited to the age in which he lived. He exhibits several of the characteristics of Romanticism, as we listed them above. He had respect for the past; himself a poet, he was responsive to the writings of Wordsworth and others like him; he prized human relationships, and treated people with gentleness and courtesy; he knew the importance of feeling and willing, but that did not make him any less intellectual (he was in fact described by Newman as the most brilliant man in Oxford in his day).[1]

The son of a clergyman, he was educated at the University of Oxford, where his intellectual gifts earned him in 1811 a prestigious Fellowship at Oriel College. He was already writing poetry.

In 1833 Keble emerged into the public arena. The occasion was a sermon which he preached in the university church of Oxford at the opening of the assizes or annual session of the lawcourts for the county of Oxfordshire. The title of the sermon was provocative – 'National Apostasy'. Probably most people in Britain at that time thought of the Church of England as little more than a department of the state, and Parliament had in fact recently abolished a number of Irish bishoprics for political and economic reasons, and without proper regard for the pastoral care of the people affected. Keble had a high spiritual view of the Church, a mystical view in which the Church is more than a human institution, for it is an institution of God existing to promote holiness in the nation. It derives its authority not from Parliament or the state, but from Christ through the apostles and their successors. This high view of the Church, demanding that it be seen in its full depth as divinely founded, underlay a book which Keble had already published six years earlier. This was *The Christian Year*, a work which by the time of his death nearly forty years after it was written, had passed through ninety-five editions and sold 265,000 copies. The subtitle of the book was 'Thoughts in Verse for the Sundays and Holy Days throughout the Year'. It was based on *The Book of Common Prayer*, and consisted of poems on the themes prescribed for each Sunday and festival in the Prayer Book, as well as for the times of day and the sacraments of the Church. This book of Keble's expresses his spirituality, and had a tremendous influence. Many of the poems are still sung as hymns in the churches. In some ways, it invites a comparison with the spirituality of Ignatius Loyola. Just as Ignatius had composed a series of meditations on the events of Christ's career as recorded in the Gospels, so Keble offers a scheme of meditations based likewise on the life of Christ, but as this is called to mind in the yearly cycle of worship that begins every Advent.

I do not feel myself qualified to pass any judgement on Keble's standing as a poet. The general view is that he was good, but not quite in the first class. This is perhaps shown by the fact that none of his compositions has found a place in *The New Oxford Book of English Verse*. He tells us that 'poetry, in general, is the expression of an overflowing mind'.[2] It follows that, for a deeply religious person, as Keble was, poetry and mysticism are not far from one another, for the mind of the mystic too goes out beyond the surface phenomena of experience to explore deeper meanings. If Keble's mysticism is less obvious than that of some of the others we have considered, so that I called him a 'moderate' mystic, this was not because I thought of him as lacking in sensitivity but because his mysticism expressed itself in so many directions that it may seem to lack the depth and passion of someone who concentrates attention on a single direction; for instance, Teresa battling towards the very centre of the interior castle, or John of the Cross, a fellow poet stripping away all superfluities.

Perhaps I should rather have described Keble as an 'all-round' mystic. He was, like Wordsworth, a nature-mystic:

> There is a book who runs may read,[3]
>   Which heavenly truth imparts,
> And all the lore its scholars need,
>   Pure eyes and Christian hearts.
>
> The works of God, above, below,
>   Within us and around,
> Are pages in that book, to show
>   How God himself is found.

He then goes on to express the religious or mystical significance that he finds in the natural world. The open sky, for instance, does not speak to him of some abstract idea such as infinity or nothingness or being (see above, pp. 15–16), but of love:

> The glorious sky, embracing all,
>   Is like the Maker's love,
> Wherewith encompassed, great and small
>   In peace and order move.

He may even have had in mind the prayer of an earlier Anglican poet-priest, George Herbert:

> Teach me, my God and King,
> In all things thee to see.

But even in this reading of the book of Nature, he is not forgetful of the inner light that also speaks of God. In the verses already quoted, he uses the words, 'within us and around', and later in the same poem comes the stanza:

> Two worlds are ours: 'tis only sin
>   Forbids us to descry
> The mystic heaven and earth within,
>   Plain as the sea and sky.

Neither did Keble think it necessary to go into a monastery in order to cultivate that mind in which we can see God in everything and act accordingly.

> We need not bid, for cloistered cell,
>   Our neighbour and our work farewell,
> Nor strive to wind ourselves too high
>   For sinful men beneath the sky:
>
> The trivial round, the common task,
>   Would furnish all we ought to ask;
> Room to deny ourselves; a road
>   To bring us daily nearer God.[4]

Keble found another outlet for the overflowing of his mystical spirit in the interpretation of scripture. In his time, as indeed even today, many people insisted on a strictly literal reading of the biblical text. This was true not only among those who would later be called 'fundamentalists' and who took the whole biblical history, even the most improbable miracles, as descriptions of what actually happened, but also of the increasing number of those who studied the text in a more scientific manner, and who would write an entire commentary on a book of the Bible without a word on its spiritual significance but with their attention fully occupied in ascertaining the precise original text or the nuances of meaning in the vocabulary. I do not say that the latter tasks are unimportant, but they have value mainly as a prelude to the study of the meaning. Even in ancient times, many early Christian writers sought allegorical or spiritual meanings behind the surface text. The two great Alexandrian theologians, Clement and Origen, are notable examples. Their methods were in Keble's time being attacked by literalists of one kind or another, and they were called 'mystical', where the word was used as a term of abuse, meaning, as Keble understood, victims of a 'dreamy, soaring indistinct fancy'.[5] He vigorously defends these ancient writers in one of the tracts put out by the Oxford Movement (though we should remember that these 'tracts' were not just flimsy pamphlets; in the present instance, Keble's tract was a book of 200 pages, in which he dealt pretty thoroughly with the problem). He points out that Origen, for instance, approaches the text with a certain reverence. The meaning cannot be simply read off from the words like a piece of information. To penetrate to the inner layers of meaning needs meditation, contemplation, prayer. This is the principle of reserve, characteristic of the Oxford Movement. There can be no glib or easy talk of spiritual realities. They have to be safeguarded, even sometimes by silence.

If there is a word which best describes Keble's mysticism, it is, I think, the word 'sacramental'. For him, the whole creation was a sacramental world. The material creation is not to be despised, for matter too belongs to God and owes its existence to God: it can be a vehicle for God's presence. In this matter, we can see Keble in the spiritual line of John of Damascus, who defended the icons against their detractors. It is not surprising that another of Keble's writings[6] had as its theme 'eucharistic adoration'. In the traditional mass, there were moments of elevation when the consecrated elements were held up for veneration by the people. These were fleeting moments in the liturgical drama, and outside of the actual celebration the consecrated host was reserved in an aumbry or tabernacle before which people could engage in prayer and contemplation. These practices had fallen into disuse in the Church of England after the Reformation, but it is to the credit of the Oxford Movement that they were revived in the nineteenth century and are valued by many Anglicans as perhaps the nearest they can come to a mystical experience of God in Christ.

It is not surprising either that Keble chose the word 'adoration' for this recognition of the 'real presence' of Christ in the eucharist, for adoration, as I pointed out in the first chapter of this book (see above, p. 34), is the highest reach of prayer, when the soul, as it were, sinks into God and God envelops the soul. As the Anglican Prayer Book so well expresses it, our prayer in the eucharist is that 'we may evermore dwell in him and he in us'. This is a true mystical union. It avoids two dangers that are not always clearly avoided by mystics. One danger is that of supposing that the soul somehow becomes God or part of God or equal with God, the other that of supposing that the individual is totally absorbed into God, and ceases to exist as a person. Catherine of Siena avoided the same dangers in her quaint metaphor that the soul is like a fish and God is like the sea. Keble, I have said, was a moderate mystic, steering clear of the extremes of some mystics, but for that very reason he can be commended to those who, like him, have to live with the trivial round and the common task.

Keble left his academic post at Oriel College in 1836 to take up work as vicar of the rural parish of Hursley, near Winchester. There he laboured until his death in 1866. Unlike those mystics who found the Church too constricting in its doctrines and practices, Keble was a loyal priest of the Church which indeed is described in one of the prayers of the Anglican eucharist as 'the mystical Body of thy Son, which is the company of all faithful people'.

Roughly contemporary with Keble was the Danish thinker, Søren Kierkegaard (1813–55). At first glance, he seems to have very little in common with Keble. The latter had strong catholic leanings, while Kierkegaard, though not uncritical of Luther, was unmistakably Protestant. Keble found fulfilment in the Church, but Kierkegaard was decidedly an individualist who declined ordination and believed that each human person must define his or her own relation to God. Both of them thought that the state churches in which they grew up had become so secularized that their spiritual nature had been forgotten. But whereas Keble sought to revivify the Church of England, Kierkegaard seems to have despaired of the Danish Church. Both of them were reacting against the rationalistic objectifying thought of the eighteenth century, and both of them looked for a remedy in a more mystical interpretation of religion, though they sought it in divergent ways.

But let us begin from what they shared. We have noted Keble's sense of reserve in speaking of God and the spiritual life. This was a moderate expression of that apophaticism which we noted as a characteristic of mysticism in general (see above, p. 14). David Law, in a thorough and penetrating study which he entitled *Kierkegaard as Negative Theologian*,[7] draws attention to the important place which apophaticism has in his writings. There are indeed passages in Kierkegaard (we shall consider some of them) where his apophaticism (though he does not use that word) is carried to such lengths that God and even Jesus Christ appear to have been placed beyond human speech and thought. Even if God is beyond speech and thought, there might still be an experience which yielded a silent, inexpressible apprehension of God. Perhaps one could find an analogy in some forms of communion between one human being and another. Perhaps adoration comes into the category. I am doubtful, however, if Kierkegaard ever gives us cause to believe that there is such an experience of God. But we are still only at the beginning of trying to understand him.

I think we can say first of all that he does make a good case for believing that the powers of reason are limited. In the Age of Enlightenment, the reach of reason was unrestricted. According to natural theology, one could prove the existence of God, and often his beneficence as well. Certainly, the later Enlightenment turned against natural theology, and Kant is usually credited with having exposed fallacies in the traditional arguments for the existence of God. Kierkegaard too claims that reason cannot reach God. Reason searches for God and has even a passion to engage in this search, but 'comes repeatedly into collision with the Unknown, which does indeed exist, but is unknown and in so far does not exist'.[8] This sentence is not clear, but it does suggest that reason shatters against the Unknown, and God is the Unknown, for God is not a matter of fact that could be an object for rational investigation but by definition a transcendent reality. Must then God remain unknown, and if so, what would it mean to believe in God or to use the word at all?

Here we return for a moment to Kant. For him, God was 'off limits', so to speak, as far as pure reason is concerned. But God is reinstated as a postulate of moral experience. For Kant, to be human implies that one accepts the demands of the moral law, and that law is an ultimate. To make sense of it, we must, in his view, postulate the reality of God. Kierkegaard too appeals to moral experience, but he couches his appeal in a negative form. It is not the summons to righteousness or to transcendence that leads the mind to God, but the consciousness of sin: 'Only through the consciousness of sin is there entry into Christianity, and the wish to enter it by any other way is the crime of *lèse majesté*.'[9] It may have been Kierkegaard's melancholy outlook on life, inherited from a gloomy father, that led him to choose the negative concept of sin rather than the affirmative one of moral obligation, but he comes out at much the same point as Kant: namely, that although pure reason, even if spurred by passion, cannot find the way to God, there are other aspects of our complex human nature which can find that way. The sense of sin is also the beginning of dissatisfaction with one's present condition and of the quest for something better. Furthermore, Kierkegaard in another writing connects sin with *Angst*, that deep-seated sense of insecurity and finitude which carries an intuition of our ontological status as contingent beings who owe their existence to the self-subsistent Being of God. Kierkegaard would doubtless disapprove of this attempt to express his underlying thought in a more metaphysical language, but I think that some such interpretation does throw light on the Danish thinker's obscure reflections.

Up to this point I think we can follow Kierkegaard's line of thought. Although we began from the negative phenomenon of his apophaticism, we have seen that he allowed for a knowledge of God that springs not from abstract reasoning but from the total human experience of existing as a finite being in a world where each person who is not content just to drift along aimlessly has to decide about his/her life and either live that life through faith in God or else accept that it is finally meaningless. I can accept Kierkegaard's point that we cannot know, and that faith demands a leap beyond what we can prove. Faith demands that there must be a way of knowing God other than the rational methods that we use in establishing matters of fact in the world. It is, I should say, part of the human condition that the most important questions of life do not admit of answers that are certain, and that our minds can never be free from the possibility that we are mistaken. It is, I think, a mark of maturity to acknowledge the fallibility of faith and the possibility that what one takes to be a revelation of God may be mistaken.

But while I acknowledge that there is a realism in Kierkegaard's admission of the vulnerability of faith, I wonder if his love of paradox does not lead him into some very questionable positions.

First, I can understand and even applaud his willingness to give up searching for a conclusive proof of God's existence, for, as Pascal had seen 200 years earlier, no proof could be really conclusive and is more likely to stir up doubts over its validity than to bring peace of mind. But when Kierkegaard goes further and tells us that even probabilities, one way or the other, should not enter into our thinking about God, I demur. It does seem to me that any alleged revelation is strengthened if it can be shown to have the support of rational reflection, though it is not founded on reason or reason alone.

Second, there is a problem too in Kierkegaard's understanding of the person of Jesus Christ. Christ, in Christian belief, is the revelation of God, even God incarnate. In Christ, the transcendent God has become, insofar as is possible, a historical figure in the world. But Kierkegaard tells us that Christ has come into the world *incognito*. But if Christ too is unknown, how can one speak of revelation? We are told that historical information about Jesus is irrelevant. But if we had no such information, Jesus Christ would be only an empty name. According to Kierkegaard, 'If the contemporary generation had left behind it nothing but these words, "We have believed that in such and such a year God has appeared among us in the humble figure of a servant, that he lived and taught in our community, and finally died", it would be more than enough.'[10] In my view, it would certainly not be enough. It tells us virtually nothing about the kind of human life that Jesus lived. Here Kierkegaard seems to be going from paradox into sheer incoherence. We would need to know more about Jesus if we were ever to accept him as the revelation of God. Kierkegaard himself seems to have recognized this, for he acknowledged that 'God did not assume the form of a servant to make a mockery of men; hence it cannot be his intention to pass through the world in such manner that no single human being becomes aware of his presence'.[11]

Finally, I think one has to ask whether Kierkegaard had really reached what I called the 'mature' stage of giving up the passion for certainty and acknowledging the vulnerability of faith. For he writes:

> Here is a definition of truth: the objective uncertainty held fast in the appropriation of the most passionate inwardness, is the truth, the highest truth there is for one who exists. There where the way swings off (and where that is cannot be said objectively, for that precisely is the subjectivity) objective knowledge is put in suspension. Objectively then he has only the infinite passion of his inwardness. And truth precisely is this venture, to choose the objectively uncertain with the passion of the infinite.[12]

This is far from clear, but perhaps Kierkegaard is saying about truth something like what Gregory of Nyssa said about perfection: it is not so much a goal as the passionate pursuit of that goal. Also, I think it can be said in Kierkegaard's defence that in stressing the servant role of Christ in the incarnation, he is touching on the revolution in the understanding of God brought about by Christianity: from arbitrary emperor to the servant of his creation.[13]

Kierkegaard was subject to ridicule and vilification in his lifetime. He died in 1855 while still in his early forties, an apparent failure. It would not be until the twentieth century that philosophers and theologians began to take serious notice of this deep but obscure thinker.

In the later part of the nineteenth century, a notable and much admired mystic calls for attention: Charles de Foucauld (1858–1916). A Frenchman, he lived on into the twentieth century, but he died during World War One, which marks the real end of the nineteenth century. He was born of an aristocratic family, was enrolled in the military academy of St Cyr and, on being commissioned, was posted to Algeria, which in those days, together with other North African and Saharan territories, was under French rule. De Foucauld fell in love with North Africa and carried out an exploration of some little-known areas of Morocco. This earned him recognition from the French Geographical Society, but about this time in his life his thoughts began to turn to religion.

Although his family was staunchly Catholic (one member in a previous generation had been assassinated by revolutionaries in 1792), de Foucauld had drifted away from the Church, but he now came back, and sought instruction from a famous confessor of those days, the Abbé Huvelin. He took up his newly awakened faith with enthusiasm, and in 1890 became a Trappist monk. Some of his meditations from this period are worth quoting, because they show us the form which his spirituality was taking. Here are examples.

How can anyone be pitied who is doing the will of the Lord? Is there anything sweeter on earth, than to do the will of him whom one loves? And if it gives one some trouble to carry it out, the sweetness is all the greater.[14]

To worship is to see oneself at your feet, as a cypher, as nothing, as dust that is only fit to be under your feet, but as dust that thinks, that loves, as a dust that admires and loves passionately, that dissolves in love and adoration before you.[15]

The two examples quoted set the tone – a passionate love towards God which rises to adoration, the highest reach of worshipful prayer; this is an intimate love, but it is marked by a humility before God (expressed in terms which verge on the extravagant) indicating that de Foucauld was not in danger of letting his intimate love for God efface the difference between creature and Creator, which we have seen to be a danger for some mystics. We must notice too his understanding that to love God is to do God's will, even when the doing is very difficult. The support for this serious commitment to worship and obedience came from 'long hours' of daily prayer. These are described in two further passages from his *Meditations*, which I now quote.

Our minds must be firmly fixed on God, and our eyes always turned toward him, either by using ejaculatory prayer or simply by turning our thoughts toward him. The hours given up entirely to prayer will give us the strength, with God's grace, to keep ourselves in his presence through the rest of the day and give up all our time to what is called 'perpetual prayer'.[16]

The 'better part' [an allusion to Mary's choosing the better part as compared with Martha, Lk. 10.42] is the contemplative life, the life that is completely detached from material things, and is concerned only with the contemplation of our Lord. In this life the spirit is immersed in the thought of God, contemplates him, listens to him, speaks to him increasingly in a constant sense of his presence; and a prayer, which though it may vary at different hours of the day, never ceases.[17]

From the two passages just quoted, I think that de Foucauld did not trouble to make sharp distinctions between meditation, contemplation and what he calls 'perpetual prayer'. This last seems to be close to what some other writers call 'habitual recollection', the maintenance of a state of mind in which the soul is attuned to God and aware of his presence, even when one is engaged in the most mundane activities. We are reminded again of George Herbert, 'nothing can be so mean', and of John Keble, 'the trivial round, the common task', or of Brother Laurence, constantly aware of God as he did the washing up in the monastery kitchen amid the rattle of dishes.

Another link between de Foucauld and Keble is that both of them stress eucharistic adoration. De Foucauld tells us of his happiness in the presence of the sacramental Host, whether veiled in the tabernacle or exposed in a monstrance. According to Mark Gibbard, he would spend as much as seven hours in contemplative prayer before the sacrament, and sometimes even longer. Some of us might think that this was excessive. How was this time spent? What was going through his mind? Certainly, his mind was not blank, there were meditations on the events of the Gospels and concentrated moments of attention to the whole Christ, marked by those ejaculatory prayers of which he tells us. The time of prayer may seem excessive, but as Mark Gibbard says, 'The genuineness of his contemplative prayer was proved by his ceaseless love which flowed from it, to all his neighbours, even the most abject.'[18] Like some of the other mystics we have discussed, however important the altar and the tabernacle were for him, de Foucauld was always available and was ready to leave them to serve any who needed him.

Charles de Foucauld found that in spite of the austerity of the Trappist life, it was not sufficiently demanding. In 1897, a sympathetic Superior released him from the Order and advised him to work out his own ministry. At this time he spent two years in Nazareth, which he sometimes speaks of as if it were a very long retreat or series of retreats. His ministry at this time consisted in being a kind of odd-job man at the disposal of a convent of the Poor Clares. He lived in a garden shed built against the wall of the convent, available to do the shopping, weed the garden, repair the buildings or the furniture, and spending what time he could either in his shed or in the convent chapel. It was here that he decided on the shape of his future ministry. Ordained to the priesthood in 1901, he eventually settled in Tamanrasset, a village deep in his beloved Sahara. It was situated 400 kilometres from the nearest European settlement, and de Foucauld's aim was to serve the most forsaken people on earth. These were the Tuaregs, a Berber people leading a frugal existence. De Foucauld learned their language, composed a dictionary and grammar, and translated some of their poems into French. That gave to the whole people a new dignity and identity. In the meantime, he continued to go among them wherever he was required. In 1916, he was shot and killed, supposedly by accident when he was caught in crossfire during a skirmish between tribesmen and a French patrol.

Charles de Foucauld did not make any converts and failed to attract any colleagues to assist him in his work. But after his death there were founded orders of Little Brothers and Little Sisters to continue his way of life, combining contemplative prayer with everyday work in the community, wearing ordinary clothes and living as members of the people among whom they lived. It is indeed a mystical way, grounded in prayer, but a way in which words and other outward manifestations are at a minimum, and care for the neighbour is paramount. These disciples work not only in the Sahara but wherever there is a forsaken flock.

14

Twentieth Century:

Henri Bergson, Rudolf Otto, Pierre Teilhard de Chardin, Jacques Maritain, Thomas Merton

Although the twentieth century was a time of the most terrible warfare and destruction that the world had ever seen, it produced quite a number of outstanding mystics. There were perhaps two major reasons for this. One is the fact that efforts were being made on both sides to narrow the gap that had sprung up since the eighteenth century between the natural sciences and theology. Quite a number of prominent scientists defended the compatibility of scientific theories with religious beliefs, several of them giving notable courses of Gifford Lectures on natural theology, while theologians on their side were taking a greater interest in the sciences. Of course, there were still sceptical scientists who found no place for religion, and fundamentalist theologians who, in spite of all evidences to the contrary, clung to pre-scientific ideas, claiming them to be divine revelations. On the whole, however, the kind of antipathy that had marked the end of the nineteenth century, especially in the years following the publication of the theory of evolution, had given way to a desire for reconciliation. A second factor that had a powerful influence in the twentieth century was the new openness which the various religions began to show towards one another. At first this was confined to individual theologians, but after the Second Vatican Council it was adopted as official policy, not only in the Roman Catholic Church but generally among the churches and denominations of Christendom. In virtually all the religions of the world the phenomenon of mysticism has appeared at some time in their history, and mysticism now gained a new importance as a common ground among the religions, not only, let us say, among Christians, Jews and Muslims, but between these so-called 'Abrahamic' religions and the religions of the East. We had even reached a stage when a Christian mystic might find himself more at home in discussion with a Buddhist mystic than he would be with a fellow Christian of fundamentalist tendencies!

We begin by considering the thought of Henri Bergson (1859–1941). Born in France, he illustrates both of the influences noted above. He was a distinguished scientist and philosopher, his special interest being biology, and, in particular, the phenomenon of evolution; and he was by religion a Jew, but one with such an intimate knowledge of Christianity and Christian mysticism that he could not be omitted from this book, even though we are explicitly concerned with Christian expressions of mysticism. He acknowledged that his reading of mainly Christian mystics found an echo in his own mind.

Early in his career, Bergson became dissatisfied with the mechanistic materialism that had been popular in the nineteenth century and had been used in the interpretation of evolution. His first important writing, *Time and Free Will*,[1] had as its subtitle 'An Essay on the Immediate Data of Consciousness', and already hints at a development in the direction of mysticism. He criticizes the way in which the sciences have understood time: namely, as a succession of discrete moments, like the still pictures on a cinematographic film which, when passed rapidly before the eyes, give the illusion of motion. This is undoubtedly useful for many purposes, but it misses the reality, which is a continuous process going on without breaks. That is how we perceive events in immediate consciousness, before they are subjected to intellectual analysis. Our very language breaks up experience into a series of successive moments, but we are in touch with the reality when we intuit experience as taking place in a continuous duration. But if language itself breaks up experience, then experience becomes strictly inexpressible; so, Bergson suggests, we should remain silent, as nature does.

However, he did not himself remain silent, and from 1900 onward, when he had become a professor at the prestigious Collège de France, he built up a wide-ranging philosophy in which he draws out the consequences of his reflections on time and duration. Important in this philosophy was his distinction between intellect and intuition. Intellect is analytic, and breaks up our experience into a succession of fragments, as already indicated. Intuition, on the other hand, is direct experience of the world and participates in the ceaseless flow of events. He is not intending to devalue science, through which we can manage and control the phenomena of Nature, but he insists that it is intuition that puts us in touch with reality. One of the main points in his major work, *Creative Evolution*, is that two ways of knowing are present throughout the world of living creatures: intelligence and instinct. Intelligence has reached its highest point in human experience; instinct has advanced furthest in the insect world.

Intelligence and instinct are two ways of relating to the world. They have developed in different ways from a common origin, but have never quite separated. 'They haunt each other continually; everywhere we find them mingled; it is the proportion that differs. There is no intelligence in which some traces of instinct are not to be discovered, more especially no instinct that is not surrounded with a fringe of intelligence.'[2]

But how could such forms of consciousness have evolved in a universe where, on the unconscious material level, the law of entropy holds, and energy systems run down? Evolution on the contrary is creative and brings forth the new. Already in one of his earlier books, *Matter and Memory* (1896), Bergson believed that he had established that mental life is not simply an epiphenomenon of the material organism. The living, evolving world demands new and more complex categories than those which explain events on the purely material level. Although I do not think that he uses the term 'transcendence', he seems to visualize something of the sort not only in the human species but in the universe as a whole.[3] This is the idea underlying his famous doctrine of an *élan vital*, an 'impulse to life' pervading the world. This impulse is immanent in the world, but of course God too is immanent in the world as well as transcendent of it. The impulse to life is not God, but it is a universal forward-looking drive, a transcending power, which does suggest a theistic interpretation of reality. I believe that Bergson's positing of some such impulse is needed when we consider that evolution has been constantly rising to higher levels of being, though admittedly with many setbacks.

We can now understand the attraction which mysticism had for Bergson, and which he discusses in one of his last books, *The Two Sources of Morality and Religion* (1932). Static morality (the morality of customs and rules) and static religion (the religion of dogmas and rituals) have been devised by intelligence and are conceptualized in fixed forms. But there are also open morality and open religion which strive to go beyond the static forms. The true mystic is not content with contemplation, but seeks to translate his vision into action. (Here we see Bergson's Jewish background asserting itself, for this is the influence of the prophets of Israel; see above, p. 38.)

True mystics simply open their souls to the oncoming wave. Sure of themselves, because they feel within them something better than themselves, they prove to be great men of action, to the surprise of those for whom mysticism is nothing but visions and raptures and ecstasies. That which they have allowed to flow into them is a stream flowing down and seeking through them to reach their fellow men.[4]

For forty or more years, I have maintained myself that Christians should not seek to convert Jews.[5] The two religions were originally one, and should certainly not be opposed to one another. Actually Bergson was strongly attracted by Catholicism, and saw it as the completion of Judaism. But already at that time Nazi anti-Semitism had declared itself in Germany and was imported into France by the Vichy regime. Bergson decided to remain Jewish and to share the sufferings of his people, and surely every Christian would and certainly should applaud that decision (but see below, p. 251).

Rudolf Otto (1879–1937), who spent most of his life teaching in German universities, was described by one of my own teachers, Charles Arthur Campbell, Professor of Logic in the University of Glasgow, as 'by a wide margin the most illuminating religious thinker of modern times', and although that is a sweeping claim to make, I find myself largely in agreement with it. Likewise, with Campbell's further claim that acquaintance with Otto is 'among the most rewarding experiences that anyone with a concern for religious understanding is likely to enjoy in a lifetime'.[6]

Otto in his treatment applied to his subject the phenomenological approach, later refined and systematized by Husserl. In this approach, when applied to religion, what is important is the careful description from various angles of the religious phenomena revealed to the consciousness of the investigator, leaving aside speculative arguments about the origin and validity of the phenomena. Otto's principal writing is known in its English translation as *The Idea of the Holy*, but the German title of the book, first published in 1917, is simply *Das Heilige*, 'The Holy', and this simpler title is preferable, for the holy is more than an idea, if that word is understood as an intellectual concept. The holy is an experience, certainly containing an idea, but an idea which is, so to speak, immersed in feeling. The holy is an experience of the whole person, in which feeling and understanding are inextricably intertwined, and in which the recipient of the feeling participates in the object of his feeling and cannot be a mere spectator. Or, to express the matter in another way, the feeling for the holy cannot be dismissed as non-cognitive because it is not a sense perception and not an intellectual concept. It is a form of awareness which, as we shall see, can be to some extent conceptualized but which conveys suggestions of a depth lying beyond that of everyday experience of the world.

One could argue that the holy is the very heart of religion. It is more fundamental and certainly more primordial from a chronological point of view even than God. Primitive religions do not have highly developed understandings of God or even of the gods, but are aware of a vaguely described background to earthly events and experiences often denoted by the word *mana*. This word comes from the Pacific region, and was used by the English anthropologist Robert Marett and was then universalized to apply to similar religious phenomena found throughout the world. Marett quotes the English missionary, Bishop R. H. Codrington, for a definition of *mana* as 'a force altogether different from physical power, which acts in all kinds of ways for good and evil'.[7] Marett's views were known to and approved by Otto. The development or evolution of religion was understood as the gradual transformation of a feeling of awe before the mystery of existence to belief in gods and eventually in one God, and along with this went a development in the understanding of the holy in moral terms, as the God who demands righteousness, or even a God of love. One advantage in seeing the holy rather than deity as the centre of religion is that it allows for a unifying phenomenon common to all religions, and especially allows for dialogue between the religions of the West, including Islam, and those of the further East where in some cases there is no recognition of a God in the personal or quasi-personal terms common in the West, and the concretion of the holy is visualized rather in terms of an impersonal or suprapersonal Absolute. I do not myself believe that these two different ways of thinking are finally irreconcilable.

As early as 1911, Otto had been deeply impressed by the importance of the holy through an incident which befell him on visiting a synagogue in Morocco. A choir sang in Hebrew the words which Isaiah had heard in his prophetic-mystical experience in the Temple at Jerusalem, probably in the year 742 BCE:

> Holy, holy, holy Lord God of hosts,
> Heaven and earth are full of your glory!

Otto's comment on this experience shows how deeply it affected him and helps to explain why he chose the holy as the key-word for an understanding of religion:

> In whatever language these words are spoken, the most sublime words that human lips have ever uttered, they always seize one in the deepest ground of the soul, arousing and stirring with a mighty shudder the mystery of the other-worldly that sleeps therein.[8]

The process by which the holy was gradually acquiring a moral significance did not, in Otto's view, mean that the original shudder of awe before the ungraspable mystery of divine Being was eliminated. His well-known analysis – and let us remember that this was no cold logical analysis but the elucidation of the total experience – is expressed in three Latin words: *Mysterium tremendum fascinans.* The holy includes not only the connotations of righteousness, purity and love, which belong to it in the higher religions, but still confronts one with the original and deeper content arising from the encounter with the spiritual reality beyond the boundaries of the earthly. This fundamental element in the holy was called by Otto the numinous, a word derived from Latin, expressing but not explaining or defining the character of divinity. Let us briefly examine the three Latin terms used by Otto.

Mysterium. The meaning of the word 'mystery' was one of the very first points raised at the beginning of this book (see above, p. 1), so here we can be very brief. A mystery is not simply unintelligible, but rather is something possessing such depth of meaning that we are drawn more and more into the exploration of it and may come to believe that there can be no end to our exploration. This was a point clearly made by Gregory of Nyssa, who held that if God is infinite, then there can be no final or complete knowledge of God. This helps us to understand also why the mystics tend to alternate between light and darkness when they talk about knowing God. To have the knowledge of God is like living in the light. But if every advance in the knowledge of God opens up new areas still to be entered, these areas are still dark. However, though dark, they are not forbidding: we are invited to go into them. Gregory illustrated the point by reminding us that although Moses is first drawn into converse with God by the light which shone from the bush on Mount Horeb, he is later, on the same mountain, summoned to meet God in the cloud where he is to receive the law. In the life of faith, one has got to go into this darkness, which is potentially a greater light. Here we may think of the experience of John of the Cross, the 'dark night of the soul', or even of Jesus's own experience of forsakenness on Calvary.

Tremendum. This is the first of the two adjectives by which Otto qualifies the mystery. We tremble before it. Perhaps in the earliest phases of human religiosity, trembling was the dominant response to an experience of the numinous. The finite confronted by the Infinite could scarcely refrain from trembling. This is what the Bible calls the 'fear of the Lord'. But we are told that 'the fear of the LORD is the beginning of wisdom' (Prov. 9.10). It is not merely negative: we can learn from it, just as fear of physical injury can be a healthy and useful emotion. The fear of the Lord is perhaps better expressed by the word 'awe'. Awe is the realization of one's littleness and apparent insignificance in the face of that which is truly great. In Pascal's metaphor, the human being is like a weak broken reed in the universe. But he or she is a *thinking* reed, if one can make sense of such an oxymoron. It is in such a moment of awe that one understands *realistically* one's ontological status, the strange contradiction of a thinking reed. The mystics are surely right in putting humility and penitence at the beginning of the spiritual pilgrimage, but they are already looking towards the goal of closeness to God.

Otto has been criticized, for instance, by the Scottish philosopher of religion, John Oman, for overstressing the *tremendum*, but I do not think this is just. Otto certainly goes too far when he speaks of God as 'totally other' from man. The Infinite and the finite, the Creator and the creature, are certainly on opposite sides of a fundamental gulf, but if the difference were total, there could be no question of any communion. Perhaps Otto was right to emphasize the divide between the two, for in the modern world, human beings have since the time of Nietzsche come to regard themselves as the lords of the universe, who have no need of any God or any obligation to a God. Even some of the mystics, as we have seen, speak as if their relation to God were so intimate that it puts them on a level with God. Whether one is thinking of atheistic humanists or of over-enthusiastic believers in the spiritual marriage, Otto's stress on the *tremendum* is a justifiable corrective.

Fascinans. But the real reply to the critics of Otto is that they have failed to pay attention to the other characteristic which he ascribes to the mystery–fascination. The mystery of holy being draws us to itself and into itself. But surely that can only happen if there is some deep affinity between the infinite Being and the finite being. I do not think it could happen if God were 'wholly other' or if there were an 'infinite qualitative difference' (as Kierkegaard expressed it) between him and the creature. God is both transcendent and immanent, and through his immanence in all creation, he is, as we have heard many of the mystics testify, to be found in the depths of the human soul as well as in the surrounding world. Only, as we have also learned from the mystics, it is necessary that all the obscuring dust and rust and corrosion that sin has deposited on the soul is cleared away, so that the image of God can again appear. And this is where, in a distinctively Christian mysticism, we learn the place of Jesus Christ as the Mediator, the God-man as we call him, the person in whom the essence of the incomprehensible Deity is communicated to us; translated, so to speak, into a form accessible to our minds. For although we are but weak reeds, we are thinking reeds, able or rather enabled to perceive the supernatural light and to respond to it.

Although he was a staunch Protestant, Otto had an appreciation for the sacraments, and believed that the eucharist affords a special channel for the experience of the holy. He writes: 'Christ's eucharist does indeed include what is called a "real presence"; it is not divine materials that are present, but, by virtue of the blessing words of Christ, what is present is the most numinous *fact* in the world's history, the fact of Golgotha.'[9]

In addition to the phenomenological description of the experience of the holy which we have just been considering, Otto went on to more speculative thoughts about what we may call the epistemology of religion. There is a burning question here which keeps coming up and cannot be avoided in any discussion of mystical experience. Is such experience purely subjective; is God or holy Being a projection of the human mind, or does mystical experience really provide access to a divine Being, who transcends both the human and the natural? I am not sure that any secure answer to this question could be given, unless in some way the human mind can itself transcend beyond its natural reach. But let us hear what Otto has to say in the matter.

Otto believes that feeling does have a cognitive character, and is intuitively aware of some properties of our environment other than the properties that can be read off by the senses. A feeling of fear, for instance, is an implicit or preconceptual awareness that a particular environment is threatening. Similarly, a feeling of joy is a tacit recognition that a particular environment is supportive. These are natural feelings, but he claims that the feeling for the numinous, the *sensus numinis*, as he calls it, is a unique feeling. It belongs to what Otto calls the 'faculty of divination' and describes as 'a faculty, of whatever sort it may be, of *genuinely* cognizing and recognizing the holy in its appearance'.[10] Using Kantian or quasi-Kantian language, Otto makes the claim that the holy is an *a priori* category of the mind, arising 'from the deepest foundation of cognitive apprehension that the soul possesses'.[11] Whether or not one accepts Otto's explanation of the matter, he seems here to be on the right track towards refuting the view that religious feelings are no more than subjective emotions.

The path from science to mysticism which we met in the work of Bergson was taken up later in the twentieth century by another French thinker, Pierre Teilhard de Chardin (1881–1955). He was a priest in the Society of Jesus and became also a world expert in palaeontology and the theory of biological evolution. The Jesuit Order, as well as being a religious organization, is also a great educational enterprise, with schools and colleges all over the world. Members of the Order teach a wide range of secular subjects in these colleges, and this explains why Teilhard, though a devout Jesuit, was at the same time a leading palaeontologist; that is to say, an expert on ancient or prehistoric forms of life, and on the evolutionary trends which they exhibited. He spent many years in China, and was involved in the investigations concerning 'Peking man', an early hominid figure estimated to have lived about 350,000 years ago. Because some of his views were not acceptable to the ecclesiastical authorities, he was forbidden to publish his writings during his lifetime, and prevented from lecturing at the Collège de France. But when his writings were published after his death, they were, as Bergson's had been, very widely received, not only in catholic circles but in the scientific community as a whole. It need hardly be added that he was also subject to severe criticism from diehards on both the religious and scientific sides, and it is a great pity that he did not have the opportunity of considering and answering his critics during his lifetime. His reception was so enthusiastic that in 1962 the Vatican issued a warning against the uncritical acceptance of his teaching. But that is a long way from a condemnation, and we ought to be critical of any teaching, including that of high ecclesiastics, before we accept it.

Teilhard's principal work, *The Phenomenon of Man*,[12] was

published in France in 1955 and the English translation in 1959. At that time I was teaching theology in the University of Glasgow, and I remember that the book excited quite a lot of interest in the Science Faculty, and I was invited to discuss it with some members of that faculty. Fortunately, I had taken at one time a course in zoology at the University, so I had some understanding of what the issues were.

The book begins from the scientific point of view, and attempts to see the phenomenon not only of the living world but of the entire cosmos, and of the human race in particular, in the context of an evolutionary understanding. Teilhard's approach, like Otto's, is phenomenological in the sense that he is seeking to describe what anyone can *see* when we look at the phenomena and appearances, leaving aside attempts at interpretation or speculation. What we see is a process, the process of evolution, and although there appear to be elements of chance in that process, dead-ends and tentative gropings, there is, generally speaking, a direction from what we call the lower to the higher. Life keeps advancing and developing through various stages, from the merely alive through sentience to consciousness and then to personal existence, exemplified on this planet by the human race. Teilhard thinks that it is quite likely that similar developments may have taken place elsewhere in the universe, and he also thinks that we are not at the end of the process but still in midstream. He notes two characteristics of the evolutionary process: there is an enhancement of consciousness and a corresponding increase of complexity as one surveys the scene from the relatively (but by no means quite!) simple structure of a single-celled protozoon to the overwhelming complexity in unity of a human body. Evolution appears to be going somewhere, it is not a blind happening. Is this a new version of Bergson's *élan vital*? Up to a point, yes, but we shall see that Teilhard also points to differences between his views and Bergson's.

There are critical moments in the great sweep of evolution as it has manifested itself on earth. The first was the appearance of life, when molecules of sufficient complexity had been built up; the second was the appearance of reflective thought in humans beings, 'hominization' in Teilhard's language, a new phase in which the process has become conscious of itself and can begin to have a part in its further development. This is the point at which Teilhard goes a step beyond Bergson, for now evolution is understood as not just something that is happening to the human race but an enterprise in which we have to participate. Evolution is not just something that, so to speak, pushes us from behind, it is now something that draws us from the future.[13] Teilhard does not speak of an *élan vital*, but of God, a spiritual reality of such unimaginable greatness and power that our minds are unable to grasp him. Even the word 'mind' seems totally inadequate when speaking of God, though there must be some affinity, some analogy between God and finite minds, for in evolution things do not 'come out of the blue', so to speak, but are the unfolding of potentialities that were already there concealed in the earlier phases. The opening chapters of Genesis are certainly not a guide to the origins of the universe as modern science reveals it, but there must have been some inspiration in those ancient writers, who told first of the creation of the physical universe and of living creatures, and then of the breathing by God of his own breath or spirit into the creature who was destined to be the bearer of mind on earth, namely, the human being. It is a tremendous vision that Teilhard sets before us, described in a generous tribute by the eminent scientist and thinker, Sir Julian Huxley, as 'a threefold synthesis, of the material and physical world with the world of mind and spirit; of the past with the future; and of variety with unity'.[14]

Can we extrapolate and say anything about the future towards which evolution is tending? It is at this point that

Teilhard introduces the distinctively Christian aspect of his teaching. The goal of evolution he calls the 'omega-point' and he claims that the end is already reflected back into the process in the person of Jesus Christ. He is the fulfilment of our human nature. Teilhard is saying very much what that earlier scientist Pascal was saying: 'Jesus Christ is the goal of everything and the centre to which everything tends', but Teilhard is saying this in the light of scientific knowledge that was not available in Pascal's time.

So far I have been dwelling mainly on the scientific side of Teilhard's thought, but to appreciate his contribution to mysticism, we have also to consider his spiritual writing. We have already seen how some modern mystics, such as Keble and de Foucauld in the nineteenth century, went out of their way to stress that one need not embrace the monastic life to find God and live in communion with him. We can find him in the everydayness of ordinary life, nothing can be so mean that it cannot speak to us of God. Whereas many of the early mystics despised matter, seeing in it merely a source of temptation, Teilhard praises matter because out of its potentialities all the riches of the evolutionary process have flowed:

> I bless you, matter, and you I acclaim; not as the moralizing preachers depict you, debased, disfigured, a mass of brute forces and brute appetites; but as you reveal yourself to me today, in your totality and in your true nature. I acclaim you as the inexhaustible potentiality for existence and transformation, I acclaim you as the universal power which brings together and unites. I acclaim you as the melodious fountain of water from which spring the souls of men and women. I acclaim you as the divine *milieu*, charged with creative power, as the ocean stirred by the Spirit, as the clay moulded and infused by the incarnate Word.[15]

Or we may think of his 'Mass on the World', when during a journey in China he found himself on a Sunday without bread and wine for the celebration of the eucharist, and offered in his spirit the round earth itself as the Host to be transformed into the Body of Christ who 'is the image of the invisible God, the firstborn of all creation ... He himself is before all things, and in him all things hold together' (Col. 1.15, 17).[16]

Or we may wonder if there could be any more eloquent expression of mystical adoration than these words of Teilhard:

> To adore – that means, to lose oneself in the unfathomable, to plunge into the inexhaustible, to find peace in the incorruptible, to be absorbed in the immeasurable, to offer oneself to the fire and the transparency, to annihilate oneself as one becomes more deliberately conscious of oneself, and to give of one's deepest to that whose depth has no end.[17]

It is exposure to the Absolute in adoration that helps to draw human beings out of their own pettiness, stretching them to a fuller stature in which they will be fit to live in communion with God and in true community with one another. Some aspects of Teilhard's philosophy are controversial, but it can hardly be denied that he presents us with a vision of the physical universe that is sacramental and compatible with Christian faith in its mystical form.

Passing on to our fourth representative of twentieth-century mysticism, we come to another Frenchman, Jacques Maritain (1882–1973). In his youth, politics had been his chief interest and he declared himself a socialist, but once again we find the influence of Bergson at work in drawing Maritain away from the shallow agnostic humanism fashionable in

France at that time to a religious and Christian understanding of the human being as a spiritual being. Also, we should not underestimate the influence of his Russian and mystically inclined wife, Raïssa, whom he had met when they were students in Paris. They both felt depressed by the materialism they encountered at the university, and it was the lectures of Bergson which led them towards a more spiritual understanding of themselves. They married in 1904, and were both baptized in 1906, becoming devout Catholics. Their household, which included Raïssa's sister, seems to have lived like a tiny religious order. We may remember that something similar took place in the career of William Law (see above, p. 196). Maritain, when duly qualified, became a Professor of Philosophy.

As a college teacher, he was exempt from military service in World War One, but found himself much in demand among young soldiers seeking advice. One of these, who was killed on service, unexpectedly bequeathed a considerable fortune to Maritain, who at this time switched his political allegiance from socialism to the right-wing movement *Action française*. This switch was allegedly due to the influence of his spiritual director, and would be followed a few years later by a switch back to the political left. The switching was due not to political indecision, but to Maritain's belief that the spiritual has primacy over the political, so the latter can never have an absolute claim. To give a concrete example: in the Spanish Civil War, an issue on which people in France and Britain were sharply divided at that time, both sides were guilty of atrocities against their opponents, and a Christian could not support either side consistently.

Maritain's first book, published in 1913, was on the Bergsonian philosophy, but like many another young scholar seeking to establish his intellectual independence from his teacher, Maritain took up a very critical stance towards Bergson, though he later expressed regret about this. When Bergson died in 1941, Raïssa (she and Jacques were in the United States at this time) wrote in her journal, 'Bergson died yesterday, January 5. Great pain for us. I think of all that we owe him, and that many others do as well. We heard in a letter from France that he had been baptized and did not want to declare it publicly out of consideration for the Jews, subject to persecution in recent years. Our master, lost and found.'[18] Perhaps that was a sufficient, if belated tribute.

However, we must return to the earlier part of Maritain's career. Even before he wrote his book on Bergson, he had become interested in Thomism, the thought of Thomas Aquinas (1225–74). Thomism is both a philosophy and a theology. It fell into neglect at the end of the Middle Ages, then was revived and was highly influential at the time of the Council of Trent. Then it fell again into neglect, but in 1879 Pope Leo XIII in the bull *Aeterni Patris* called for a renewed study of Thomas. Jacques Maritain became probably the most distinguished representative of the neo-Thomism, as it was called, which came into being in the early decades of the twentieth century, though there were many other theologians and philosophers, notably Etienne Gilson, who responded to the papal summons. Thomism has continued to flourish since Maritain's time, though now in the form called transcendental Thomism, which inspired much of the thinking of Vatican II. Because of its persistence through more than seven centuries and its capacity for renewal after intervals of being left on the shelf, Thomism has with some justice earned the title of *philosophia perennis*, the perennial philosophy.

The fruits of Maritain's study became apparent with the publication in 1932 of his *magnum opus*, known in English as *The Degrees of Knowledge*.[19] In the French original, the main title is *Distinguer pour unir*. According to Professor Ralph McInery, the dominant theme of the book is that 'things hang together' and he claims that 'No one has better expressed the fusion of the intellectual and the spiritual, the natural and the supernatural, the conceptual and the mystical, than Maritain did in *The Degrees*'.[20]

The book falls into two parts. The first of these is entitled 'The Degrees of Rational Knowledge' and consists of a detailed examination of the sciences and of a broader philosophy of Nature, based on the sciences. Here Maritain follows Thomas in two important matters. He acknowledges a wide area of knowledge in which reason must be our guide, and where it cannot be set aside or short-circuited by premature appeals to instinct or intuition or revelation or anything of that sort; and he also follows Thomas in declaring himself a realist – our knowledge is a knowledge of the real world, not just of ideas or language or any other interposed medium. His argument is frequently punctuated by references to Sir Arthur Eddington, the Cambridge astronomer, physicist and mathematician whose Gifford Lectures, *The Nature of the Physical World* (1928) fairly represented the generally received scientific understanding of Nature at that time.

But the human mind is not satisfied with knowledge of Nature alone, though that is as far as reason can reach. The goal of human life lies in God and likewise the goal of human knowledge, so that we are drawn beyond the bounds of the natural to what Maritain calls the 'supernatural' or the 'suprarational', and if someone objects to these words, perhaps we could simply say the 'spiritual'. The human mind, in other words, cannot rest in a positivism, though it does recognize that there is a point where, in Kierkegaard's words, reason 'makes a collision' (see above, p. 225). Even more today than in Eddington's time, natural science in its furthest reaches tends to pass over into some kind of metaphysical philosophy. For instance, the 'string theory' of the ultimate constitution of matter has been around for several years, but since it seems to be beyond the possibility of any empirical verification, it is no longer science, though it invokes the support of reason and of mathematics. If a thinker erects a metaphysic, even a theistic metaphysic, on the grounds of his understanding of the natural world, this falls short of that knowledge of God demanded by our condition as beings directed to a spiritual end.

So Maritain writes, 'Metaphysics naturally engenders in the soul a certain velleity it is unable to satisfy, a confused and indeterminate desire for a higher knowledge that is only genuinely attained in mystical experience, in the contemplation of the saints.'[21] But he insists that this does not conflict with his belief that within its own sphere metaphysics does not demand the supervention of mysticism, and he criticizes both Bergson and Teilhard for what he thought was their premature invocation of the mystical.

Perhaps next in importance among Maritain's writings is the book, *Integral Humanism*, first published in 1936. There have been many theologians who have so exalted God that they have felt it proper to demean the human race, by dwelling on the themes of sin and corruption, and suggesting that these have entirely obliterated that image of God in which the human being was created. This anti-human tendency has led in modern times to the idea that humanism is a kind of rival to traditional religion. It is alleged to safeguard human freedom and development over against the rule of a tyrannous God. Maritain did not, of course, agree with such a position. In atheistic humanism, human beings have sought to usurp the place of God; but the result, as was seen in the totalitarian states, both Communist and Fascist, is 'man's inhumanity to man' (Burns). A genuine humanism is one which recognizes that the goal of humanity is a spiritual one. Its 'governing principle is the fact that man has been called to a supernatural end; that is the end of his endeavours with reference to which action must be assessed as good or bad'.[22] So once again we see that Maritain will not allow himself to be tied to any political ideology which offends against the Christian interpretation of what it means to be human. We see also that in going on from metaphysics to mysticism he is still following in the way of Thomas Aquinas. When Thomas, who died at the early age of forty-nine, discontinued his work on the *Summa Theologia*, he had himself a mystical experience, apparently a form of contemplation in which he was able to grasp in a unitary vision the faith which he had spent so much time and labour in spelling out, question by question, article by article, and he said that all the work he had done was as straw in the light of his mystical vision.

Maritain differed from Thomas in living to the venerable age of ninety-one, by which time he had become a revered figure in the worlds both of learning and religion – Ambassador of France to the Vatican, 1945–48, Professor of Moral Theology at Princeton University, finally taking vows in the order of the Little Brothers of Jesus, founded in honour of another modern mystic, Charles de Foucauld (see above, p. 232).

We come now to the last of the mystics with whom we have been trying to converse in this book, the American Trappist monk Thomas Merton (1915–68). We have seen that mysticism has had a long history, and Merton reminds us that it is still with us. I am particularly interested in Merton because he and I were close contemporaries and formally our lives had a similar pattern, though they were very different in content. He was born in 1915, I was born in 1919, so we both belong to that generation which came into being during or immediately after World War One. Both of us at an early age felt a call to Christian ministry and were eventually ordained to the priesthood. Both of us had to cope with World War Two which broke out just as we were reaching maturity. From then on, our paths diverged. He remained celibate and indeed became a Cistercian monk in the strict observance of the Trappists, though unlike most monks, he became known to a wide public through his writings. I married and exercised a ministry in secular society as army chaplain, parish priest and then for most of my working life as theological teacher and writer. An obvious difference is that Merton was lost to this generation because of his early death at the age of fifty-three, while I am still surviving at almost eighty-five. At least, I can pay my tribute to him and reinforce his witness that faith and prayer have still their significance in our disordered world of the twenty-first century.

Merton wrote an autobiography which is in the main a spiritual journal. He called the book *The Seven Storey Mountain*[23] and it was first published in 1948. One hardly expects an autobiography to be written when the author is still only thirty-three! However, it does bring us to the point where Merton had found his vocation as a Trappist monk. His life story was recapitulated and continued on to his death by Michael Mott, who entitled his biography *The Seven Mountains of Thomas Merton*.[24] These titles are rather confusing. Merton's own autobiography suggests by its title that it might, like the works of some earlier mystics, trace stages in his spiritual development, but there is no attempt to divide his career into stages. The story is told as a continous narrative, a long-drawn-out conversion or purgation, like Dante's Mountain of Purgatory, a great mountain rising out of the sea into the sunshine and with a garden on the summit. Mott's book sees the seven mountains in a different way. Merton himself had talked of 'high places' in his life and in fact he had always lived near some mountain or hill, and he mentions twelve such high places at the very end of his autobiography. Mott has chosen seven out of the twelve, and one of them is not a geographical mountain but the Mountain of Purgatory, associated with Merton's life as a Trappist monk. In the study of Merton which follows, I shall follow in the main the order of these two books, with illustrations when required from other writings of Merton.

Merton was something of a cosmopolitan. His father was British, his mother American, he was himself born in France and eventually became a United States citizen at the age of thirty-six. His father was a painter and spent much time painting in France. Neither of Merton's parents was particularly religious, and Merton himself seems to have begun with a kind of romantic attachment to Christianity. He enjoyed going into the French churches, and was impressed by the wholesome piety of the country people whom he met.

Both his parents died while he was quite young. He received most of his schooling and university education in England, at an independent school in Oakham, and at the University of Cambridge. During these years, his interest in religion was developed mainly through reading. He was greatly impressed by the writings of the eighteenth-century mystic William Blake (1757–1827) and was also strongly affected by his reading of Dante. He himself had genuine literary ability and wrote a great many pieces – novels, essays, poems – during his university years and later.

But he was becoming increasingly dissatisfied with the twentieth-century way of life. As with Maritain before him, he found it shallow, sensual anything but spiritual. He himself slipped into this mode of existence, and in despising the society around him, he was honest enough to despise his own lifestyle. Perhaps his mastery of the English language was never better revealed than when he was heaping invective on the societies and institutions in which he moved. I cannot resist the temptation to quote a couple of instances.

First, on Cambridge:

Some people might live there for three years, or even a life-time, so protected that they never scent the sweet stench of corruption that is all around them—the keen thin scent of decay that pervades everything and accuses with a ter-rible accusation the superficial youthfulness, the abounding undergraduate noise that fills these ancient buildings. But for me, with my blind appetites, it was impossible that I should not rush in and take a huge bite of this rotten fruit.[25]

On New York City, where he had gone after Cambridge to do further study at Columbia University, he was even more devastating:

On Judgement Day, the citizens of that fat metropolis with its mighty buildings and its veins bursting with dollars and its brains overreaching themselves with new optimistic philosophies of culture and progress, will be surprised, astounded when they find out who it was [men and women of the religious communities] that was keeping the brim-stone and thunderbolts of God's anger from wiping them long since from the face of the earth.[26]

Having myself taught for many years at Oxford rather than Cambridge, I am doubtless biased, but even so I would say that Merton has gone over the top in his assault on Cam-bridge; and having lived for eight years in New York, I have to confess that I enjoyed that city and found it to be like most other big cities, a mixture of the good and the bad.

But now Merton had reached a very difficult stage in his ascent of the mountain. His attraction to the Christian faith and his need for spiritual satisfaction continued to be strong, but so did the attractions of worldly society, including drink-ing, sexual adventures and other indulgences. Like Socrates, he began to hear an inner voice. It said to him, 'Go to mass! Go to mass!'[27] He did in fact go to Corpus Christi Church in upper Manhattan, and was impressed by the sense of worship there. Incidentally, that was the first Roman Catholic parish that ever invited me, an Anglican priest, to preach, and the invitation was to give the sermon at High Mass on the Feast of Corpus Christi, 1970. Almost as noteworthy was the invitation to bring my wife with me to lunch in the clergy house after the mass, the first time a woman had been entertained there!

Merton continued to dither and from time to time lapsed into ways from which he was trying to get away, but again the voice came to him in peremptory tones: 'What are you waiting for? You know what you ought to do. Why don't you do it?'[28] He put up a struggle, but soon was walking along to Corpus Christi Church in search of Father Ford. We must pass over the details of further lapses and false starts, but he was baptized into the Catholic Church in late 1938, and soon afterwards began to have the desire to become a monk and beyond that to be ordained a priest. These things all happened – he entered the Trappist Monastery of Gethsemani (*sic*), Kentucky, in 1941, became a novice in the following year and was ordained priest in 1949.

One might have supposed that now his spiritual aspirations had been fulfilled and he could live in quiet contentment. But that was not the case. He was destined to spend twenty-seven years at Gethsemani, but when the first euphoria had passed, he had much trouble. Even about his baptism, he wrote: 'I was about to set foot on the shore at the foot of the high seven-circled Mountain of Purgatory, steeper and more arduous than I was able to imagine, and I was not at all aware of the climbing I was about to have to do.'[29]

What then were his problems? The first was simply his own eminence, gained through his writings. He was a 'celebrity', as they say, but part of the monkish vocation is to bury oneself in anonymity. Merton was conscious of this tension and thought of giving up writing. But on the other hand that writing was a gift from God, and surely it was right to use it to promote faith and prayer, especially for those living outside monastery walls amid all the distractions and temptations of the world. This was also a problem for the monastery. There was a measure of resentment at the distinction of Merton, but on the other hand he attracted recruits, and the monastery, from being quite small, grew to having 150 monks, to say nothing of the money that came in from visitors and from the royalties on Merton's books. Another part of the monastic discipline was stability, the obligation on the monk to live in the monastery and not to be a gad-about. But Merton found this irksome, and it led to friction between him and the abbot, Dom James Fox. The situation was partly resolved when Merton got permission to live alone as a hermit in an isolated cottage within the monastery grounds. More serious problems arose from the recrudescence of some of the vices of his pre-Christian days. He was still liable on occasion to drink more and so to talk more than was good for one who had taken a vow of silence. There was also in the background an 'affair' with a woman, known only as 'S'. How far this went is not clear, but it did create scandal, though I do not think there was a real danger that Merton would run off with his lady friend. At any rate, his life had become confused, and in 1966 he decided that the time had come to clear matters up. His real love was for God, and indeed his last book extols the mystical relation to God. Entitled *Contemplative Prayer*,[30] it visualizes such prayer as living in the constant awareness, almost as if you saw him, though at the same time acknowledging that God is beyond our comprehension or imagination.

But however his life might have developed, we do not know, for it came to a sudden end. After protracted negotiations with

Dom James, Merton obtained permission to travel to Asia in order to attend an interfaith conference on the religious life. This was to take place in Bangkok in December, 1968, and Merton flew to that city (travelling first class, I regret to say). On the second day of the conference, he gave a lecture in the forenoon, and after lunch went to have a rest in his room. He did not reappear, and his friends became alarmed. They found him lying dead in contact with a faulty fan which had delivered a lethal electric shock. He had a simple belief in the providence of God, and I sometimes wonder how he would have understood this apparently pointless end to his own life. Perhaps he would have said, as a true mystic must, that God's ways are beyond us.

15

Concluding Remarks

We have now completed our journey through the writings of some of the most eminent Christian mystics, but before we leave them, it may be useful to take a few minutes to cast our mind back over the way we have come. Near the beginning of the book, I warned the reader that I cannot claim to be a mystic myself, but I did confess to being sympathetic towards them – even an admirer. But my aim was to let them be heard for themselves in their own words. So far as possible, we have been trying to live in their company and to enter into their experiences.

In order to write the book, I had to spend many hours during the past two years or so in reading or rereading the mystical texts and in thinking about what they tell us. The result has been to increase my admiration for the authors of these texts, and I hope that readers of the book will also have had their sympathies aroused or strengthened. But I have tried, where it seemed appropriate, to be critical as well as sympathetic, and so at the end of the book I am still in the position of the observer, looking in from the fringes, rather than one of the company. Let me try to explain this more clearly, for some of my readers may find themselves in a similar position.

First, I think we should bear in mind the very wide range of lifestyles that are possible for mystics. I have, of course, interpreted the concept of mysticism in a very broad way, and some students of the subject might wish to narrow the application of the concept much more than I have done. I mentioned in the opening chapter ten characteristics of the mystical way, but I doubt if any of my examples exhibited all ten of them. All of the men and women about whom we have been thinking believed in God and were seeking a closer relation to God, and these are matters where I would feel myself in agreement with the mystics, for I think that they are matters that are common to all Christians, though they are taken more seriously by the mystics than by most of us. The majority of those we have considered believed that they must 'leave the world', to use the common expression; that is to say, to go into a monastery or even to live as a solitary hermit and to spend as much time as possible in prayer and contemplation. Only a very small number of human beings can do that, and they can do it only because many others are out there in the world, working in fields or factories, teaching the young, keeping house for the family, tending the sick, ministering in parishes, doing innumerable other jobs that are necessary if human life is to go on. So if mysticism demands withdrawal from the everyday life of the world, for most of us this is not an option.

The danger is that the few who are able to enter the 'religious life' in the narrow sense of life in a monastery or a hermitage may come to think of themselves as a kind of spiritual élite, mature Christians or 'gnostics' as they were sometimes called in the early centuries (see above, p. 69). I suppose in a general way the Church always includes persons who are deeply committed and a wide circle of others who are moderately committed or merely nominal in their allegiance, but too much should not be made of these differences or there would be the danger of self-righteousness and complacency. It ought to be possible to be a Christian in any situation of life.

Fortunately, however, it is usually the case that as soon as one begins to ask critical questions about mysticism, one discovers that genuine mystics are already aware of the dangers and are taking measures to prevent them from taking hold. This, I think, has been very clear in what may be called 'modern' mysticism, say from the eighteenth century onward. The automatic identification of mysticism with the religious life has been loosened. John Woolman, for instance, earned his living as a tailor for much of his life; John Keble was a tutor and then a parish priest, and specifically tells us not to ask for 'cloistered cell' and not to despise 'the trivial round, the common task'; Bergson and Teilhard were active in down-to-earth scientific studies, and found these not only compatible with mystical contemplation but contributory to it; Charles de Foucauld was indeed for a time in a religious order, but found his ultimate vocation in simply being available to his neighbours; Merton was a writer, and although he sometimes felt that his writing was a distraction from the spiritual life, surely that was outweighed by the benefits which he brought to those who found inspiration in his writings. Even in earlier times, the great mystics insisted that although prayer was at the centre of their vocation, it was sometimes necessary to forgo prayer in order to take up some practical service. Catherine of Siena and Ignatius Loyola are illustrations of this. So our first criticism of mysticism turns out to be not very telling.

Second, doesn't a mystic claim very special experiences, such as visions and supernatural voices, experiences of light which is not just ordinary light, and sometimes a special sense of a divine Providence which directs him or her in highly particularized ways, perhaps saving the mystic from danger or fulfilling a desire? Certainly there is a long history of such events. In the Christian tradition, that history goes back all the way to Paul, who had a vision of light and heard the voice of Christ on his way to Damascus. Visions of light are so common among mystics that we can hardly doubt that they are experienced, though whether they come from God or arise from unconscious processes in the mystic's own mind or whether both of these factors are involved is not easy to decide, and those of us who have not had any visions of the sort may feel that we have to reserve judgement. Locutions – that is to say, hearing a voice which is taken to be the voice of God or of Christ or of an angel (messenger), speaking in Hebrew or Greek or Latin or English or whatever earthly language it might be – are perhaps slightly easier to explain, as I suggested in the case of Moses (see above, pp. 40–1). In such cases, I am inclined to think, the mystic has an intense experience of the holy, a contact with the divine, probably in itself wordless, but as he or she reflects upon it, it is put into words which embody the recipient's interpretation of what has taken place. Even modern mystics report both visions and locutions. Our most up-to-date exemplar of the mystical way, Thomas Merton, mentions two or three occasions on which an inner voice spoke to him and requested him to act in a certain way (see above, p. 258); and Merton also, though I did not mention it in the chapter which includes a treatment of him, tells of attending a mass in Cuba where, at the consecration, 'there formed in my mind an awareness, an understanding, a realization of what had just taken place on the altar . . . but what a thing it was, this awareness: it was a light that was so bright that it had no relation to any visible light and so profound and so intimate that it seemed like a neutralization of every lesser experience'.[1] Merton was a very sophisticated person, and we must respect his testimony, even if we cannot be sure what underlay his experience.

On the whole, mystics tend to play down the importance of such experiences as visions and locutions. They regard them as special favours, but are also conscious that such experiences may not be authentic awarenesses of God. Like Catherine of Siena, they may recommend a pragmatic test: if the experience issues in works of love, it is genuine, but if not, it may just be a fancy or even a product of pride.

I have not said anything about the sense of a personal Providence, which I mentioned above. It is here, I think, that the danger of pride is most subtle. I feel sure, for instance, that George Fox was a man of simple faith and probably free of personal pride. But when he writes as if all his actions were done at the bidding of God and even that his opponents were struck down by God because of their opposition to George Fox, he was surely deceiving himself into believing that he had a much more important place in the divine scheme of things than was really the case.

Third, I come to what, for me, is the chief criticism of mysticism, though it applies to some mystics – perhaps most mystics, but not to all. What I mean is their denigration of reason. It is one thing to say that the reach of reason is limited and that when we speak of God or of the spiritual life, we are relying not only or primarily on rational speculation or metaphysics, but on non-rational experiences, such as the sense of the holy, or the sense of the sublime, or revelations or openings or showings or whatever they may be called: experiences which are not primarily rational but have nevertheless some cognitive content. Such experiences, I believe, need to be subjected to rational scrutiny, and need whatever support they can get from reason. From a rational point of view, we must be able to judge the experiences to be veridical rather than illusory, though reason will never take us beyond probability. But it is another thing to be anti-rational, to hold that faith and reason have nothing in common, and this is a view held by some mystics, even great mystics like John of the Cross (see above, pp. 176–7). I can go along with Maritain, himself following Aquinas, when he tells me that metaphysics reaches a point where it can go no further and finds completion in the mystical vision. But that moment, as Maritain insists, must not be invoked prematurely (see above, p. 253).

So I still find myself unable fully to identify with the mystics, while at the same time giving thanks for the rich treasury of spiritual experience which they have opened to us. Again at this point Merton, the most up to date in our company of mystics, has something to say to us. His belief in God is founded chiefly on religious experience, but alongside it he recommends the proof of God's reality given by the medieval scholar, Duns Scotus.[2] Mysticism has much to teach us, but it must not be separated from reason.

To sum up, the mystic at his or her best is the person who takes with the utmost seriousness the commands, 'You shall love the Lord your God with all your heart, and with all your soul, and with all your mind, and with all your strength', and 'You shall love your neighbour as yourself' (Mk 12.30–31); and whose constant prayer is 'that we may evermore dwell in him and he in us'. These commands and this prayer surely represent the goal of all Christians, whatever path they find leading to it.

Notes

Chapter 1: What is Mysticism?

1 Gabriel Marcel, *The Mystery of Being*, Chicago, Regnery (Gateway Books), 1960, I, p. 262.
2 Walter Burkert, *Ancient Mystery Cults*, Cambridge, MA, Harvard University Press, 1987, p. 51.
3 Bertrand Russell, *Mysticism and Logic*, London, Longmans Green, 1918, p. 12.
4 W. T. Stace, *Mysticism and Philosophy*, London, Macmillan, 1960, p. 18.
5 John Macquarrie, *The Mediators*, London, SCM Press, 1995.
6 William James, *Varieties of Religious Experience*, London, Longmans Green, 1952, p. 371.
7 S. Kierkegaard, *The Concept of Dread*, Princeton, NJ, Princeton University Press, 1957.
8 Eric Blakeborough, *No Quick Fix*, Basingstoke, Marshall Pickering, 1986, p. 112.
9 W. James, *op. cit.*, p. 377.
10 The relation between mind and body is too obscure for any snap judgement about visions, locutions, stigmata, etc.
11 Paul Tillich, *Systematic Theology* (three volumes in one edition), Chicago, University of Chicago Press, 1967, I, p. 239.
12 Clement of Alexandria, *The Miscellanies*, V, 11.
13 Gregory of Nyssa, *Vie de Moïse*, Paris, Cerf (Sources chrétiennes), 1968, p. 315.
14 Augustine, *Confessions*, Edinburgh, T. & T. Clark, 1876, VII, 10.
15 Augustine, *op. cit.*, VII, 18.
16 John Macquarrie, *Stubborn Theological Questions*, London, SCM Press, 2003, p. 133.

17 Evelyn Underhill, *Mysticism*, London, Methuen, 1911.

18 F. H. Bradley, *Appearance and Reality*, Oxford, Oxford University Press, 1893, pp. 396–7.

19 Paul Tillich, *op. cit.*, I, p. 186.

20 Parmenides in G. S. Kirk and J. E. Raven, *The Presocratic Philosophers*, Cambridge, Cambridge University Press, 1957, p. 279.

21 M. Heidegger, *Existence and Being*, Chicago, Regnery, 1949, p. 336.

22 John Macquarrie, *Heidegger and Christianity*, London, SCM Press, 1994, p. 59.

23 Iris Murdoch, *The Sovereignty of Good*, London, Routledge & Kegan Paul, 1970, p. 101.

24 Iris Murdoch, *op. cit.*, p. 99.

25 John Macquarrie, 'Adoration' under the entry 'Prayer', in *A Dictionary of Christian Spirituality*, ed. G. S. Wakefield, London, SCM Press, 1983, pp. 307–308.

Chapter 2: Biblical Roots of Christian Mysticism:
Old Testament, Moses

1 Usually, the syllables 'moses' would appear as a suffix after the name of an Egyptian God, for instance, Rameses means 'son of Ra'. So it has been supposed that the biblical Moses may originally have had a fuller name, but that when he began to serve the God of Israel, the part of his name referring to an Egyptian deity was dropped.

2 F. Brown, S. R. Driver and C. A. Briggs, eds, *A Hebrew and English Lexicon of the Old Testament*, Oxford, Oxford University Press, 1907, p. 611.

3 After the giving of the Ten Commandments, the narrative breaks off and there is inserted the series of laws called 'The Book of the Covenant' (Ex. 20.22–23.19). Various sources are combined in the text of Exodus, and the reader who wishes to study these matters in detail is referred to any up-to-date and reliable commentary.

4 J. H. Newman, 'A Letter to the Duke of Norfolk', in *Newman the Theologian*, ed. Ian Ker, London, Collins, 1990, p. 233.

Notes

Chapter 3: Biblical Roots of Christian Mysticism: New Testament, Paul

1 Probably the designation 'prophet' would be the one that would come most naturally to his contemporaries when Jesus began his ministry. Edward Schillbeeckx, in his book *Jesus: An Experiment in Christology* (London, Collins, 1979), claims that already in the concept of 'prophet' there were connotations that could be developed into a full-scale christology.

2 A. Deissmann, *Paul: A Study in Social and Religious History*, London, Hodder & Stoughton, second edition, 1926.

3 I first encountered this explanation of the outward event associated with Paul's conversion, in a BBC television programme on Paul.

4 It is a mistake to think that Paul ignores or regards of no importance the events in the life of the historical Jesus. See Chapter 3, 'The Testimony of Paul', in John Macquarrie, *Jesus Christ in Modern Thought*, London, SCM Press, 1990, pp. 448–68.

Chapter 4: Greek Input, Platonism: Clement of Alexandria, Origen

1 Plato, *Republic*, 509 (D. L. Davies and J. D. Vaughan translation, London, Macmillan, 1935).

2 Plato, *Symposium*, 210–12 (Benjamin Jowett translation, New York, Random House, 1937).

3 Walter Burkert, *Greek Religion*, Cambridge, MA, Harvard University Press, 1985, p. 323.

4 Justin Martyr, *First Apology*, xlvi, Edinburgh, T. & T. Clark, 1867.

5 Justin, *Dialogue with Trypho a Jew*, cxxvii, Edinburgh, T. & T. Clark, 1867.

6 The writings of Clement were published in English translation by T. & T. Clark, two volumes, 1867 and 1869. The quotations will be found in I, pp. 17, 49; and II, p. 140.

7 Origen, *Commentary on the Song of Songs*, London, SPCK, 1979, p. 217.

8 *Ibid.*, p. 225.

9 Anders Nygren, *Agape and Eros*, London, SPCK, 1957, pp. 368–92.

10 Origen, *Contra Celsum*, trans. H. Chadwick, Cambridge, Cambridge University Press, 1965, vii, 46.

11 From a sermon on Luke 16, quoted by Hans Urs von Balthasar in his Preface to the SPCK volume mentioned in n. 7.

Chapter 5: Greek Input, Neo-Platonism: Gregory of Nyssa, Augustine of Hippo, Dionysius the Areopagite

1 A. H. Armstrong, *The Architecture of the Intelligible Universe in the Philosophy of Plotinus*, Cambridge, Cambridge University Press, 1940, p. 26.

2 Plotinus, *Enneads*, VI, 6, 13. This and the following references to the *Enneads* are to the Loeb Classical Library edition, translated by A. H. Armstrong, Cambridge, MA, Harvard University Press, 1966–88.

3 See John Macquarrie, *Principles of Christian Theology*, London, SCM Press, revised edition, 1977, p. 188.

4 Plotinus, *op. cit.*, IV, 8, 6.

5 Plotinus, *op. cit.*, IV, 9, 1.

6 The words, 'flight of the alone to the Alone' (*phyge monou pros Monon*) are the last words of the whole work, VI, 9. We should note also that Plotinus explicitly relates union to the One with union to other finite beings. 'If the soul in me is a unity, why need that in the universe be otherwise? And if that too is one Soul, and yours and mine belong to it, then yours and mine must also be one', VI, 9, 1.

7 Plotinus, *op. cit.*, V, 2, 1.

8 The Greek text of Gregory's *Life of Moses*, together with a French translation, is available in *La Vie de Moïse*, ed. and trans. Jean Daniélou, Paris, Cerf (Sources chrétiennes), 1968; and there is an English translation in *Gregory of Nyssa*, London, SPCK, Classics of Western Spirituality, ed. and trans. A. J. Malherbe and E. Ferguson, 1978. References below are to the pages of the English translation.

9 *Life*, p. 57.

10 *Ibid.*, p. 63.

11 *Ibid.*, p. 93.
12 *Ibid.*, pp. 94–5.
13 *Ibid.*, p. 116.
14 *Ibid.*, p. 31.
15 Plotinus, *op. cit.*, VI, 7, 32.
16 Peter Brown, *Augustine of Hippo*, London, Faber & Faber, 1967, p. 426.
17 Augustine, *Confessions*, Edinburgh, T. & T. Clark, 1876, I, 1, 1. Further quotations from the *Confessions* refer to this volume.
18 Kenneth E. Kirk, *The Vision of God*, London, Longmans Green, 1932, p. 327.
19 Augustine, *op. cit.*, VII, 9, 14.
20 Augustine, *op. cit.*, X, 43, 69.
21 Paul Tillich, *A History of Christian Thought*, New York, Harper & Row, 1968, p. 92.
22 C. E. Rolt in his introduction to Dionysius the Areopagite, *The Divine Names*, London, SPCK, 1940, p. 4.
23 *Ibid.*, p. 54.
24 *Ibid.*, p. 195.
25 *Ibid.*, p. 106.

Chapter 6: The Dark Ages: Maximus Confessor, John of Damascus, John Scotus Eriugena

1 John Macquarrie, *Jesus Christ in Modern Thought*, London, SCM Press, 1990, pp. 166–7.
2 Jaroslav Pelikan in his introduction to Maximus Confessor, *Selected Writings*, London, SPCK, 1985, p. 6.
3 *Ibid.*, p. 36.
4 *Ibid.*, p. 211.
5 *Ibid.*, p. 165.
6 John of Damascus, *In Defence of the Holy Icons*, trans. D. Anderson, Crestwood, NY, St Vladimir's Seminary Press, 1980, pp. 23–4.
7 *Ibid.*
8 Quoted by Bishop Kallistos Ware, *The Orthodox Church*, London, Penguin Books, p. 41.
9 *Ibid.*, p. 39.

10 W. R. Inge, *Christian Mysticism*, London, Methuen, 1899, p. 133, n. 3.

11 Eriugena, *De Divisione Naturae*, 621A. Eriugena's principal work is *De Divisione Naturae*. It is known also by its Greek title, *Periphyseon*. The critical edition, with English translation, is by I. P. Sheldon Williams, and is published by the Dublin Institute for Advanced Studies, 1968 onward. Unhappily the editor died after publishing Books I and II, but leaving Book III in an advanced state of preparation. The work was continued and completed by Professor John J. O'Meara. The sections of the work are numbered according to the system of J. P. Migne's *Patrologia Latina*, which contains the collected works of Eriugena in Volume CXXII. There are critical editions of two other works, *Homélie sur le prologue de Jean* (1969) and *Commentaire sur l'évangile de Jean* (1972). These are edited by M. Edouard Jeauneau, and published by Cerf, Paris, in the series Sources chrétiennes.

12 *De Divisione Naturae*, 621B.

13 *Ibid.*, 677C.

14 *Ibid.*, 621B.

15 *Homélie sur le prologue de Jean* (see n. 11 above), pp. 200ff.

Chapter 7: The Early Middle Ages: Symeon the New Theologian, Bernard of Clairvaux, Richard of St Victor

1 Symeon the New Theologian, *The Discourses, etc.*, London, SPCK, 1980, p. 2.

2 *Ibid.*, pp. 245–6.

3 *Ibid.*, p. 14.

4 *Ibid.*, pp. 57, 109, 83, 195 (*sic*).

5 Etienne Gilson, *The Mystical Theology of St Bernard*, Kalamazoo, MI, Cistercian Publications, 1990.

6 Bernard of Clairvaux, *The Steps of Humility and Pride*, Kalamazoo, MI, Cistercian Publications, 1973.

7 *Ibid.* Definitions: humility, p. 30; pride, p. 42.

8 Bernard, *On the Song of Songs*, four volumes, Kalamazoo, MI, Cistercian Publications, 1971–80. The stages of the three kisses are summarized in I, Sermon 3. The quotation is from sermon 7, pp. 38–9.

Notes

9 Both treatises are published in the volume, Richard of St Victor, *The Twelve Patriarchs, etc.*, London, SPCK, 1979.

10 Richard of St Victor, *The Mystical Ark*, Chapter V, in the volume mentioned in n. 9 above, pp. 316–17.

Chapter 8: The High Middle Ages: Bonaventure, Meister Eckhart

1 Bonaventure, *The Journey of the Soul into God, etc.*, London, SPCK, 1978.

2 *Ibid.*, pp. 55–6.

3 The theme of the *pathos* of God is developed by Abraham Joshua Heschel in his book, *The Prophets*, New York, Harper & Row, 1962.

4 Bonaventure, *op. cit.*, p. 98.

5 M. Heidegger, *Nietzsche*, New York, Harper & Row, 1982, IV, p. 193.

6 Bonaventure, *op. cit.*, p. 88.

7 *Ibid.*, p. 115.

8 *Ibid.*, p. 116. The phrase, 'a pulse in the eternal Mind', is from Rupert Brooke's poem, 'The Soldier', in *The New Oxford Book of English Verse*, ed. Helen Gardner, Oxford, Oxford University Press, 1972, p. 863.

9 Meister Eckhart, *The Essential Sermons, Commentaries, Treatises and Defence*, London, SPCK, 1981, pp. 77–8.

10 *Ibid.*, p. 72.

11 *Ibid.*, p. 198.

12 *Ibid.*, p. 27.

13 *Ibid.*, p. 288.

14 R. B. Blakney, *Meister Eckhart: A New Translation*, New York, Harper Torchbooks, 1957, p. 238.

15 Eckhart, *op. cit.*, p. 187.

16 *Ibid.*

17 *Ibid.*, p. 50.

18 Blakney, *op. cit.*, p. 204.

10 *Ibid.*, p. 110.

Chapter 9: Women Mystics: Julian of Norwich, Catherine of Siena, Catherine of Genoa

1 Grace Jantzen, *Julian of Norwich: Mystic and Theologian*, London, SPCK, 1987, p. 53.
2 Julian of Norwich, *Showings*, London, SPCK, 1978.
3 There is a good example of a squint in St Mary's (Anglican) Cathedral, Limerick.
4 Julian, *op. cit.*, pp. 143, 211.
5 *Ibid.*, pp. 153, 225.
6 *Ibid.*, pp. 130, 183.
7 *Ibid.*, p. 295.
8 *Ibid.*, pp. 296–7.
9 Quoted by Suzanne Noffke, OP, in her introduction to Catherine of Siena, *The Dialogue*, London, SPCK, 1980, p. 13.
10 *Ibid.*, p. 25.
11 *Ibid.*, p. 29.
12 *Ibid.*, p. 57.
13 *Ibid.*, p. 54.
14 *Ibid.*, pp. 63, 72.
15 *Ibid.*, p. 140.
16 *Ibid.*, p. 145.
17 Translated and quoted by Evelyn Underhill from *Vita e Dottrina di Santa Caterina di Genova*, by Ettore Vernazza, a younger contemporary and friend of Catherine, in Evelyn Underhill, *Mysticism*, London, Methuen, 1911.
18 Catherine of Genoa, *Purgation and Purgatory, etc.*, London, SPCK, 1979, p. 74.
19 *Ibid.*, p. 81.
20 Dryden, 'Absalom and Achitophel', lines 156–7, 163–4, in *Dryden's Political Works*, ed. J. Sargeaunt, Oxford, Oxford University Press, 1910.

Chapter 10: Some Spanish Mystics: Ignatius Loyola, Teresa of Avila, John of the Cross

1 Ignatius Loyola, *Autobiography*, New York, Harper Torchbooks, 1970.

Notes

2 *Ibid.*, p. 23.

3 Evelyn Underhill, *Mysticism*, London, Methuen, 1991, p. 468.

4 Kenneth E. Kirk, *The Vision of God*, London, Longmans Green, 1932, p. 401.

5 Ignatius, *Spiritual Exercises*, London, Robert Scott, 1919, p. 4. Karl Rahner is worth quoting here: 'True spiritual exercises, as they are envisioned by Ignatius, are not a series of pious meditations that a person with good will can make anywhere and any time . . . Rather, real spiritual exercises are the serious attempt, following a certain plan, to make a definite decision or choice at a decisive point in one's life' (*Spiritual Exercises*, London, Sheed & Ward, 1967, p. 8).

6 *Ibid.*, pp. 4, 7, etc. Ignatius sometimes talks of meditation *and* contemplation as if they were distinct, sometimes of meditation *or* contemplation as if they were the same. The distinction which some mystics make between meditation and contemplation (see above, pp. 31–2) should not therefore be rigidly applied to the usage found in Ignatius.

7 Teresa of Avila, *The Interior Castle*, London, SPCK, 1979, p. 33. Teresa introduces the expression 'His Majesty' on the very first page of the prologue.

8 *Ibid.*, p. 20.

9 *Ibid.*, p. 74.

10 *Ibid.*, p. 75.

11 *Ibid.*, p. 89.

12 Robert Wallace, *The World of Bernini*, New York, Time-Life Books, 1970, p. 144. He quotes from Teresa's *Autobiography* her own account of the incident illustrated in the sculpture: 'I saw an angel close by me, on my left side, in bodily form. This I am not accustomed to see, except very rarely. He was not large, but small of stature, and very beautiful. I saw in his hand a long spear of gold, and at the iron's point there appeared to be a little fire. He appeared to me to be thrusting it at times into my heart, and to pierce my very entrails; when he drew it out, he seemed to draw them out also, and to leave me all on fire with a great love for God. The pain was so great that it made me moan, and yet so surpassing was the sweetness of this excessive pain that I could not wish to

be rid of it. The soul is satisfied now with nothing less than God.'

13 Teresa, *op. cit.*, p. 100.

14 *Ibid.*, p. 172.

15 Rowan D. Williams, *The Wound of Knowledge*, London, Darton, Longman & Todd, 1990, pp. 162–83.

16 W. R. Inge, *Christian Mysticism*, pp. 223–30.

17 John of the Cross, *Collected Works*, p. 50 and elsewhere, almost like a refrain.

18 *The Collected Works* of John of the Cross, translated into English by K. Kavenaugh and O. Rodriguez, were published in 1964, rev. 1991, by the Institute of Carmelite Studies, Washington, DC.

19 John of the Cross, *The Ascent to Mount Carmel*, in *Works*, p. 120.

20 *Ibid.*, pp. 121 ff.

21 John of the Cross, *The Dark Night of the Soul*, in *Works*, p. 387.

22 R. Williams, *op. cit.*, p. 171.

23 W. R. Inge, *op. cit.*, pp. 228–9.

24 *Ibid.*, p. 223.

25 John of the Cross, *Ascent*, in *Works*, p. 157.

Chapter 11: Post-Reformation Mystics: Jakob Böhme, Blaise Pascal, George Fox, William Law

1 Martin Luther, *Basic Theological Writings*, ed. T. F. Lull, Minneapolis, Fortress Press, 1989, p. 74.

2 Jakob Böhme, *Aurora*, as translated in W. R. Inge, *op. cit.*, p. 277, n. 1.

3 Jakob Böhme, *The Way to Christ*, New York, Paulist Press, 1978.

4 Peter Erb, in his introduction to *The Way to Christ*, p. 9.

5 Böhme, *op. cit.*, pp. 56 ff.

6 Böhme, *op. cit.*, p. 86.

7 Böhme, *op. cit.*, p. 182.

8 Quotations from Blaise Pascal are from his *Pensées*, text as established by Louis Lafuma, Paris, Garnier-Flammarion, 1973. The references in the following notes are to the pages of this edition. I have made my own translations. The best English translation of the complete *Pensées* is by Alban Krailsheimer,

London, Penguin Books, 1966. This quotation is from pp. 90, 92.

9 *Ibid.*, p. 136.
10 *Ibid.*, p. 140.
11 *Ibid.*, pp. 127–8.
12 Quoted in the article 'Decision Theory' in the *Cambridge Philosophical Dictionary*, Cambridge, Cambridge University Press, 1999.
13 *Ibid.*, p. 93.
14 *Ibid.*, p. 247.
15 *Ibid.*, p. 48.
16 George Fox, *The Journal*, edition revised by John L. Nickalls, Philadelphia, Religious Society of Friends, 1997.
17 *Ibid.*, p. 58.
18 *Ibid.*, pp. 134–5.
19 *Ibid.*, p. 353.
20 William Law, 'Rules for my Future Conduct', in the introduction to *A Serious Call to a Devout and Holy Life*, London, SPCK, 1978, pp. 12–13.
21 *Ibid.*, p. 47
22 *Ibid.*, p. 179.
23 *Ibid.*, pp. 24–5.
24 *Ibid.*, p. 418.
25 *Ibid.*, p. 453.
26 *Ibid.*, p. 435.
27 *Ibid.*, p. 31.

Chapter 12: Eighteenth Century: Jonathan Edwards, John Woolman

1 Jonathan Edwards, *A Reader*, ed. John E. Smith *et al.*, New Haven, Yale University Press, 1995, p. xii.
2 Robert Handy, 'Some Patterns in American Protestantism', in *The Study of Spirituality*, ed. Cheslyn Jones, *et al.*, London, SPCK, 1986, p. 475.
3 Edwards, *op. cit.*, p. xv.
4 *Ibid.*, p. 284.
5 *Ibid.*, p. 107.

6   *Ibid.*, p. 285.

7   *Ibid.*, p. 274.

8   *Ibid.*, p. 286.

9   *Ibid.*, p. 293.

10 J. Calvin, *Institutes of the Christian Religion*, II, 3.

11 Edwards, *op. cit.*, p. 9.

12 *Westminster Confession of Faith*, III, 1.

13 Irenaeus, *Against Heresies*, IV, 20.

14 See David Sox, *John Woolman: Quintessential Quaker*, York, Sessions Book Trust, and Richmond, IN, Friends United Press, 1999, p. 1.

15 John Woolman, *The Journal*, New York, Citadel Press, 1961, p. 1.

16 *Ibid.*, p. 8.

17 *Ibid.*, p. 15.

18 *Ibid.*, p. 17.

19 *Ibid.*, p. 33.

20 *Ibid.*, pp. 74 ff.

21 *Ibid.*, pp. 48–9.

22 *Ibid.*, p. 214.

Chapter 13: Nineteenth Century: John Keble, Søren Kierkegaard, Charles de Foucauld

1   Geoffrey Faber, *Oxford Apostles*, London, Faber & Faber, 1933, pp. 86–7.

2   John Keble, *On the Mysticism Attributed to the Early Fathers of the Church* (Tract 89), London, Rivington, 1841, p. 144. Keble's words may possibly be derived from Wordsworth's remark, 'Poetry is the spontaneous overflow of powerful feelings', Preface to *Lyrical Ballads*, second edition, 1802.

3   John Keble, *The Christian Year*, London, Church Literature Association, 1983, Septuagesima Sunday, pp. 42–43.

4   *Ibid.*, Morning, pp. 3–5.

5   Keble, *op. cit.*, p. 6.

6   Keble, *On Eucharistical Adoration*, in Eugene R. Fairweather (ed.), *The Oxford Movement*, New York, Oxford University Press, 1964, pp. 377–83.

7 David Law, *Kierkegaard as Negative Theologian*, Oxford, Oxford University Press, 1993.

8 S. Kierkegaard, *Philosophical Fragments*, Princeton, NJ, Princeton University Press, 1936, p. 35.

9 S. Kierkegaard, *Training in Christianity*, Princeton, NJ, Princeton University Press, p. 71.

10 S. Kierkegaard, *Philosophical Fragments*, p. 87.

11 *Ibid.*, p. 44.

12 S. Kierkegaard, *Concluding Unscientific Postscript*, Oxford, Oxford University Press, 1945, p. 182.

13 John Macquarrie, *The Humility of God*, London, SCM Press, 1978.

14 Charles de Foucauld, *Meditations of a Hermit; Spiritual Writings*, London, Burns, Oates & Washbourne, 1930, p. 3.

15 *Ibid.*, p. 5.

16 *Ibid.*, p. 19.

17 *Ibid.*, p. 21.

18 See Mark Gibbard, SSJE, 'Charles de Foucault', in *The Study of Spirituality*, pp. 419–23.

Chapter 14: Twentieth Century: Henri Bergson, Rudolf Otto, Pierre Teilhard de Chardin, Jacques Maritain, Thomas Merton

1 Henri Bergson, *Time and Free Will*, New York, Harper Torchbooks, 1960.

2 Bergson, *Creative Evolution*, London, Macmillan, 1928, p. 143.

3 Bergson, *op. cit.*, p. 27 ff.

4 Bergson, *The Two Sources of Morality and Religion*, London, Macmillan, 1935, p. 81.

5 John Macquarrie, *Principles of Christian Theology*, pp. 445–6.

6 C. A. Campbell, *On Selfhood and Godhood*, London, Allen & Unwin, 1957, pp. 327, 331.

7 R. R. Marett, *The Threshold of Religion*, London, Methuen, 1909, p. 104.

8 Quoted in Stephen C. Barton (ed.), *Holiness Past and Present*, Edinburgh, T. & T. Clark, 2003, p. 46. See also Rudolf Otto, *The Idea of the Holy*, Oxford, Oxford University Press, 1923, p. 63.

9 Otto, *Religious Essays*, Oxford, Oxford University Press, 1931, p. 50.

10 Otto, *The Idea of the Holy*, p. 148.

11 *Ibid.*, p. 117.

12 P. Teilhard de Chardin, *The Phenomenon of Man*, London, Collins, 1959.

13 Teilhard, *The Future of Man*, New York, Harper Torchbooks, 1964, p. 290.

14 In his introduction to *The Phenomenon of Man*, p. 11.

15 Teilhard, *Hymn of the Universe*, London, Collins, Fontana Books, 1970, pp. 64–5.

16 *Ibid.*, pp. 13–35.

17 Teilhard, *Le Milieu Divin*, London, Collins, Fontana Books, 1960, pp. 127–8.

18 Raïssa's words, as reported by Ralph McInerny, *The Very Rich Hours of Jacques Maritain*, Notre Dame, IN, University of Notre Dame Press, 2003, p. 151. There seems to be a conflict between what Raïssa writes about Bergson's having been privately baptized, and my earlier mention that he had opted to stand in solidarity with the Jews (see p. 238), as is claimed in the article on Bergson by Albert Thibaudet jointly with Otto Allen Bird in the *Encyclopaedia Britannica*. I have not been able to discover which of the versions is factually correct. To my way of thinking, the question is not important, and both versions acknowledge Bergson's feeling for the Jewish people.

19 Jacques Maritain, *Distinguish to Unite* or *The Degrees of Knowledge* (this is the reading of the title page of the English edition), London, Geoffrey Bles, 1959.

20 *Ibid.*, p. 119.

21 *Ibid.*, p. 284.

22 McInerny, *op. cit.*, p. 113.

23 Thomas Merton, *The Seven Storey Mountain*, New York, Harcourt Brace, 1948.

24 Michael Mott, *The Seven Mountains of Thomas Merton*, London, Sheldon Press, 1986.

25 Merton, *op. cit.*, p. 118.

26 *Ibid.*, pp. 347–8.

27 *Ibid.*, p. 206.

28 *Ibid.*, p. 215.
29 *Ibid.*, p. 221.
30 Thomas Merton, *Contemplative Prayer*, London, Darton, Long-
    man & Todd, 1973. This last reference to Merton, ending on the
    theme of God's transcendence of our thought, is another illus-
    tration of a point that has arisen several times in this chapter –
    the convergence of science and mysticism. We have noted how
    empirical science tends to merge into metaphysics and even into
    the mystical, and the other side of this is the reserve or even
    apophaticism which characterize great scientists and mystics
    alike. Consider the following from Albert Einstein: 'We are in
    the position of a little child entering a huge library filled with
    books in many different languages. The child knows someone
    must have written these books. It does not know how. The child
    dimly suspects a mysterious order in the arrangement of the
    books but doesn't know what it is. That, it seems to me, is the
    attitude of even the most intelligent human being toward God.
    We see a universe marvellously arranged and obeying certain
    laws, but only dimly understand these laws. Our limited minds
    cannot grasp the mysterious force that moves the constellations.'
    (From a 1929 interview given to the *Saturday Evening Post*.)

Chapter 15: Concluding Remarks

 1 Thomas Merton, *The Seven Storey Mountain*, New York, Har-
    court Brace, 1948, p. 284.
 2 *Ibid.*, p. 94.

Index

Abelard, Pierre 118
Abraham 40, 56, 188, 235
Adoration 34, 223, 230, 249
Aesthetic experience 105–6, 216
Ambrose 86
Ammonius 70, 76
Amos 38
Anaxagoras 62
Angst 10
Aquinas *see* Thomas Aquinas
Aristotle 76, 100, 137
Augustine of Hippo 16–18, 85–9,
 98, 102, 104, 116, 126, 167,
 168, 185, 217
Awe 241–2
Ayer, Alfred J. 58

Baptism 61, 192–3
Benedict 98, 119
Being 110–1, 131–2
Berdyaev, Nicolas 184
Bergson, Henri 235–8, 245, 249,
 250–1, 263
Bernard of Clairvaux 118–23, 156
Bernini, Gian Lorenzo 73, 172
Blake, William 256
Blakeborough, Eric 12
Böhme, Jakob 179–84, 196–8, 209
Bonaventure 128–35, 166

Bosanquet, Bernard 21
Bradley, Francis H. 21
Breakthrough 140–1
Brooke, Rupert 134
Brown, Peter 85–6
Buddha, Buddhism 7, 15, 140,
 235
Bultmann, Rudolf 135
Burkert, Walter 4, 66
Burns, Robert 253

Caffarini, Tommaso 151–2
Calvin, Jean 71, 181, 200, 204, 206
Catherine of Genoa 157–61
Catherine of Siena 23, 24, 150–7,
 159, 167
Cervantes, Miguel de 163
Christ *see* Jesus Christ
Clement of Alexandria 14, 68–70,
 73, 94, 222
Codrington, Christopher 239
Coleridge, Samuel Taylor 216
Columba 97
Columbus, Christopher 162
Confucius 7
Conscience 45, 89, 187,
Contemplation 31–14, 165, 168–9,
Conversion 16–8, 53–5, 86, 157–9,
 257–8

Index

Cousins, Ewert 128, 135
Cromwell, Oliver 194

Dante, Alighieri 127, 128, 255, 256
Darkness 84, 93, 174–7, 241–2
Deification 69, 94, 102, 111, 117, 139, 173
Deissmann, Adolf 51–2, 112
Descartes, Renā 186
Dionysius the Areopagite 89–96, 100–1, 107, 111, 178
Dominic 31, 163
Drugs 12–13
Dryden, John 161
Duns Scotus, John 106, 266

Eckhart, Meister 9, 15, 21, 135–43, 156, 160
Ecstasy *see* under Mysticism
Eddington, Arthur Stanley 252
Edwards, Jonathan 200–7, 211
Emser, Jerome 178
Erb, Peter 183
Eriugena, John Scotus 106–12
Erotic imagery 72–3, 121–3, 126, 174–5, 177
Eucharist 61, 223, 243–4
Ezekiel 38, 111

Farrer, Austin 25
Foucauld, Charles de 229–33, 254
Fox, George 189–94, 195, 199, 207, 209, 211, 212
Fox, James 259–60
Francis of Assisi 128–9, 160
Freud, Sigmund 47

Gamaliel 53
Gibbard, Mark 231
Gibbon, Edward 196

Gilson, Etienne 119, 251
Gnostics 69–70, 73
God *passim*
   beyond God 21, 110, 140–1,
   and darkness 10, 84, 93, 174–6, 175–7, 241–2
   and the Good 33–4, 64–5
   as light 10, 17, 40, 54–5, 115–6, 116–7, 177, 213, 264
   and the One 78–9
   as mystery 241
   and personality 21–2, 91–2, 140–1
   union with 22, 139–41, 170–3,
Greek elements in mysticism 3–4, 60–1, 62–8, 75–81
Gregory I, the Great 98
Gregory XI 151
Gregory of Nazianzus 114
Gregory of Nyssa 15, 81–5, 95, 157, 228, 241

Handy, Robert 200,
Hegel, G. W. F., Hegelianism 3, 21, 47, 218
Heidegger, Martin 27–8, 132
Heraclitus 68, 110, 132
Herbert, George 221, 231
Holy Spirit 26–7, 116–7, 138
Hosea 38
Hügel, Friedrich von 160
Huxley, Aldous 12
Huxley, Julian 247

Iamblichus 88
Icons 103–5
Ignatius Loyola 135, 162–7, 219
Images, Mystical
   Bridge 154–5, 156–7
   Castle 168–73

Index

Journey 129–34
Marriage 60, 72–3
Mountain 83, 125, 175, 255–6, 258
Sky 15–6, 220
Incarnation 58–60, 87–88, 95–6, 103–5, 134–5
Indwelling 59–60, 153–4
Ineffability *see* Apophaticism
Inge, William Ralph 107, 174, 176
Inner light 15 185, 194 221
Interiority 126, 183–4
Isaac 40, 56, 188
Isaiah 38, 240
Islam *see* Muhammad, Islam

Jacob 8, 40, 56, 124, 188
James, William 9–10, 12–13, 138
Jeremiah 38
Jesus Christ *passim*
  as historical figure 59, 135 165, 219
  humanity of 155–6, 165
  as Logos 66–8, 100–1
  as Person of Trinity 59–60
  spiritualized 105, 134–5
  suffering of 59, 148–9
John XXII 137
John of the Cross 173–7, 217, 220, 242, 265
John of Damascus 102–6, 165
John the Evangelist 111, 115
Johnson, Samuel 196
Julian the Apostate 88
Julian of Norwich 145–50
Justin Martyr 67–8, 182

Kant, Immanuel 225–6, 244
Keble, John 214–24, 231, 263
Kemp, Margery 150

Kempis, Thomas à, *see* Thomas à Kempis
Kierkegaard, Soren 10, 56, 224–9, 252
Kirk, Kenneth 87, 165
Knox, John 52, 60
Koran 19, 77

Law, David 224
Law, William 184, 194–8, 250
Lawrence, Brother 231
Leo XIII 102, 251
Light 17, 40, 54–5, 115–6, 117, 177, 190, 263–4
Locke, John 209
Locutions 8, 55, 63, 258, 264
Logos, logoi 66–8, 69, 71, 100–1, 139–40
Love 73–4, 101, 118–9, 121–3, 149–50, 155, 158–9, 178, 220. 230
Luther, Martin 152, 178, 224

Maimonides 41
Marcel, Gabriel 2
Marett, Robert R. 239
Maritain, Jacques 249–54
Matter 78, 80, 88, 101, 103–5, 248
Maximus Confessor 100–2, 107, 111
Mediators 7
Meditation 31, 134–5, 166–7
Merton, Thomas 254–60, 263, 264, 266
Metaphysics 252–3, 266
Micah 38
Monasticism 101, 146–7, 164–5, 166–7, 221, 229–32, 258–9
Moses 36–47, 52, 53, 54, 55–7, 81–5
Mott, Stephen 255

Muhammad, Islam 6, 7, 97, 103,
Murdoch, Iris 33–4
Mystery, Mystery-cults 1–4, 61,
　241–4
Mysticism *passim*
　and apophaticism 14–6, 222,
　　224–5
　and cognition 9–11
　criticisms of 4–6 22–3, 262–6
　and directness 7–9, 201–2
　and ecstasy 11–3, 65–66, 151–2,
　　237–8, 253
　and holism 27–9
　and individualism 22–4
　and passivity 24–7
　and prayer 29–34
　and science 4–6, 187–8, 235–8,
　　246–9, 252–3,
　and self-knowledge 16–19,
　　153–4, 168–73
　and symbolism *see* also Images,
　　Mystical 14–15, 93–4

Nature, Nature-mysticism 107–8,
　109–10, 216–8, 220
Nero 52
Newman, John Henry 45, 218
Newton, Isaac 184
Nicetas 116
Niebuhr, Reinhold 38, 200
Nietzsche, Friedrich 19
Nothing 15–6, 140–1, 179, 205
Nygren, Anders 73–4

Oman 242
Openings 189–90, 194, 197–8,
　208–9
Origen 70–4, 75, 95, 136–7, 178,
　222
Otto, Rudolf 238–245

Pantheism 21, 77, 109, 138, 173, 217
Parmenides 26
Pascal, Blaise 184–9, 227, 242, 248
Paul 20–1, 48–61, 89–90, 103, 112,
　263
Paul III 164
Paul VI 151,
Pelikan, Jaroslav 101
Penn, William 209
Pennington, Basil 120
Philo of Alexandria 41, 66–7, 69,
　110
Plato, Platonism 63–6, 69, 70–1,
　74, 76, 94
Plotinus, Neo-Platonism 66, 75–81,
　85–6, 87–8
Porphyry 76, 88
Prayer 26–7, 29–34, 129–30, 230–1
Probability 186–8, 226–7,
Proclus 88
Prophecy 37–8, 48–51
Purgation, Purgatory 94, 182
Pusey, Edward Bouverie 218

Rahner, Hugo 140
Rahner, Karl 274 n. 5 to ch. 10
Reason *see* also Probability 4–6,
　176–7, 224–7, 252–3, 266
Reductionism 2–3
Reservation 222–3, 231–2
Reserve 221–2
Revelations *see* Openings, Showings,
　Visions
Richard of St Victor 123–7, 129,
　132, 133
Rolt, C. E. 91
Russell, Bertrand 4–6, 9

Sacramentalism 105, 176, 193, 221–3
Samuel 8

Index

Scripture, Interpretation of 67, 68,
    72–3, 221–2
Seeing God *see also* Visions 7–8,
    83–5, 146–9
Showings 146–9
Slavery 209–10, 211
Smith, John E. 200
Socrates 63, 65, 68 187
Song of Songs 46, 72–3, 121–3,
    126, 133–4, 149, 167, 177'
Sophia 182–3
Spark (of divinity) 18, 77, 89, 126,
    137–41, 181, 182, 184, 198, 204
Stace, W. T. Stace 6–7
Stephen 2–3, 54
Stoicism 66, 69
Suzuki, Daisetz 6
Symbolism *see* Mysticism
Symeon the New Theologian 114–8

Teilhard de Chardin, Pierre
    245–50, 263
Ten Commandments 45
Tennyson, Alfred 217
Teresa of Avila 65, 167–73, 217, 220

Tertullian 141
Thinking *see also* Contemplation,
    Meditation 24–7
Thomas à Kempis 164
Thomas Aquinas, Thomism 102,
    110, 128, 135, 252
Threefold path 68–9, 119–20, 175
Tillich, Paul 14, 21, 25, 90–1, 131,
Tropological sense 125
Truth 120, 153, 185, 188, 210, 228

Underhill, Evelyn 21, 160, 165

Visions 59, 164, 148–9, 167, 203,
    213–4, 263–4
Voltaire 199

Wager argument 186–7
Ware, Kallistos 106
Wesley, John 96
Whitehead, Alfred North
Williams, Rowan 174, 176
Woolman, John 207–214
Word *see* Logos
Wordsworth, William 216–7

Two Worlds Are Ours

Remembering Hazel